Keynote

PROFICIENT
Student's Book
AND Workbook

SPLIT **A** EDITION

NGL.Cengage.com/Keynote

PASSWORD keynoteStdt#

Paul Dummett
Helen Stephenson
Lewis Lansford

Contents Split A

UNIT	TED TALK	GRAMMAR	VOCABULARY
1 Creativity 8–17	**Do schools kill creativity?** Ken Robinson AUTHENTIC LISTENING SKILL Rhythm and stress CRITICAL THINKING The speaker's aims PRESENTATION SKILL Using humour	Definite and indefinite time Language focus: Expressions with statistics	Creativity collocations
2 Hopes and fears 18–27	**Why I live in mortal dread of public speaking** Megan Washington AUTHENTIC LISTENING SKILL Listening to songs CRITICAL THINKING Winning your audience over PRESENTATION SKILL Being authentic	Future forms Language focus: Expressions of certainty	Hopes and fears

REVIEW 1 (UNITS 1 AND 2) | **Pixar** 28

UNIT	TED TALK	GRAMMAR	VOCABULARY
3 Perception 30–39	**The 4 ways sound affects us** Julian Treasure AUTHENTIC LISTENING SKILL Understanding fast speech CRITICAL THINKING Achieving aims PRESENTATION SKILL Giving shape to your talk	Stative and dynamic verbs Language focus: Emphatic structures	Feelings and emotions
4 Human interaction 40–49	**Your body language shapes who you are** Amy Cuddy AUTHENTIC LISTENING SKILL Linking: assimilation and reduction CRITICAL THINKING Avoiding misinterpretation PRESENTATION SKILL Structuring a talk	Past forms Language focus: Inversion with adverbial phrases	Body language

REVIEW 2 (UNITS 3 AND 4) | **Blindekuh** 50

UNIT	TED TALK	GRAMMAR	VOCABULARY
5 Economic resources 52–61	**The magic washing machine** Hans Rosling AUTHENTIC LISTENING SKILL Prediction CRITICAL THINKING Reading between the lines PRESENTATION SKILL Presenting statistics	Passive forms Language focus: Nominalization in passive sentences	Economics
6 Practical design 62–71	**Magical houses, made of bamboo** Elora Hardy AUTHENTIC LISTENING SKILL Word boundaries CRITICAL THINKING Testing arguments PRESENTATION SKILL Persuasive techniques	Causatives Language focus: Expressions with *go* and *get*	Describing objects: collocations

REVIEW 3 (UNITS 5 AND 6) | **Broad Sustainable Building** 72

Grammar summaries 74 | Communication activities 89 and 94

PRONUNCIATION	READING	LISTENING	SPEAKING	WRITING
Emphasis and de-emphasis	What I talk about when I talk about running Sing while you work	A company choir	Creativity survey Learning from experience Describing likes and talents	A progress report Writing skill: Nominalization
Consonant clusters	Outside the comfort zone Being prepared	Travel advice	Attitudes towards the future Comfort zone Giving advice (Giving and justifying advice)	An account of an incident Writing skill: Future in the past
Stress in contrasts	Multi-sensory marketing Not what they seem	The reality of the situation	Impressions and judgements Creating attractive spaces Describing beliefs and facts	A response to a proposal Writing skill: Describing different perspectives
Appropriate intonation	Business and life lessons Getting things wrong	Saying the right thing	Being hyperconnected Can I have my money back? Everyday conversations (Everyday expressions)	A formal letter or email Writing skill: Checking for errors
Silent letters	Land – a fairer system Fact or hearsay?	Discussing facts and beliefs	Headline news Economic prospects Expressing belief and disbelief	A newspaper report Writing skill: Passive reporting verbs
Word stress	Object of desire Tricky questions	An interview	Hired help Classic objects Interview questions	Posting advice Writing skill: Reported speech

Audioscripts   90 | TED Talk transcripts   95

Contents Split B

UNIT	TED TALK	GRAMMAR	VOCABULARY
7 Same but different	**The danger of a single story** Chimamanda Ngozi Adichie **AUTHENTIC LISTENING SKILL** Weak forms **CRITICAL THINKING** Objectivity and subjectivity **PRESENTATION SKILL** Using stories and anecdotes	Comparative forms Language focus: Expressing preferences	Idioms related to choice
8 Food and sustainability	**How I fell in love with a fish** Dan Barber **AUTHENTIC LISTENING SKILL** Word recognition **CRITICAL THINKING** Supporting evidence **PRESENTATION SKILL** Varying the pace	Modal verbs Language focus: Expressions with modal verbs	Synonyms: -able and -ible

REVIEW 4 (UNITS 7 AND 8) | **WD-40 Company**

UNIT	TED TALK	GRAMMAR	VOCABULARY
9 Internet sensation	**Why videos go viral** Kevin Allocca **AUTHENTIC LISTENING SKILL** Dealing with accents: British and American **CRITICAL THINKING** Making assumptions **PRESENTATION SKILL** Being clear and to the point	Gradability Language focus: Collocations with intensifying adverbs	New Internet words
10 The meaning of success	**A kinder, gentler philosophy of success** Alain de Botton **AUTHENTIC LISTENING SKILL** Hedging **CRITICAL THINKING** The message you take away **PRESENTATION SKILL** Remembering what you want to say	Verb and adjective patterns Language focus: Patterns using adjective + that	Success and failure

REVIEW 5 (UNITS 9 AND 10) | **Kickstarter**

UNIT	TED TALK	GRAMMAR	VOCABULARY
11 Learning and memory	**Build a school in the cloud** Sugata Mitra **AUTHENTIC LISTENING SKILL** Understanding mid-sentence changes **CRITICAL THINKING** Bold statements **PRESENTATION SKILL** Body movement and gesture	Conditionals Language focus: Conditional conjunctions	Learning and memory
12 Invention or innovation	**Creative problem-solving in the face of extreme limits** Navi Radjou **AUTHENTIC LISTENING SKILL** Discourse markers **CRITICAL THINKING** Summarizing an argument **PRESENTATION SKILL** Giving examples	Adverbs and word order Language focus: Adverbials	Phrasal verbs: innovation

REVIEW 6 (UNITS 11 AND 12) | **OneLeap**

Grammar summaries | Communication activities

PRONUNCIATION	READING	LISTENING	SPEAKING	WRITING
Linking in discourse markers	The paradox of choice Reading habits	Different viewpoints	Different approaches Criteria for choosing Constructing arguments (Using discourse markers)	Describing and interpreting data Writing skill: Describing graphs
Assimilation and elision	Can business be sustainable? Today's foodies	Talking about food	Discussing the news Encouraging good practice Attitude to food (Describing customs and convention)	An online guide Writing skill: Participles
Stress in opinion giving	The medium is the message Your online identity	Is it ethical?	Life without the Internet Creating a sharing website Giving and explaining opinions	An online professional profile Writing skill: Compound nouns: adjective + noun and noun + noun collocations
Prepositions as weak forms Elision	Success across generations Age no barrier	Looking for a job	Self-help advice Generation Z Talking about success	A formal report Writing skill: Phrases in report writing
Linking vowel sounds	The memory palace Thrown in at the deep end	Starting a new job	The great education debate Memory tips In at the deep end (Describing capabilities)	A formal letter Writing skill: Preposition + participle
Word endings	The innovation that never was Life hacks	Getting good results	Granting patents Pitching a new invention Handy tips (Giving advice)	A review of a product Writing skill: Reporting verbs

Audioscripts | TED Talk transcripts

Featured TED Talks in Split Editions A and B

Unit 1
Do schools kill creativity?
Ken Robinson

Unit 2
Why I live in mortal dread of public speaking
Megan Washington

Unit 3
The 4 ways sound affects us
Julian Treasure

Unit 4
Your body language shapes who you are
Amy Cuddy

Unit 5
The magic washing machine
Hans Rosling

Unit 6
Magical houses, made of bamboo
Elora Hardy

Unit 7
The danger of a single story
Chimamanda Ngozi Adichie

Unit 8
How I fell in love with a fish
Dan Barber

Unit 9
Why videos go viral
Kevin Allocca

Unit 10
A kinder, gentler philosophy of success
Alain de Botton

Unit 11
Build a school in the cloud
Sugata Mitra

Unit 12
Creative problem-solving in the face of extreme limits
Navi Radjou

1 Creativity

Street painter, Florence, Italy

TEDTALKS

SIR KEN ROBINSON is an English educationalist, writer and former Professor of Arts Education at Warwick University (UK). In 1998 he led an inquiry for a British government advisory committee into the significance of creativity in the educational system and the economy. He was knighted for his achievements in this area in 2003. He believes passionately in the innate talents of each individual and that the current western education system is not structured in a way that makes the most of these talents.

Ken Robinson's idea worth spreading is that we radically need to rethink the way education works so that we can foster rather than stifle creativity.

BACKGROUND

1 You are going to watch an edited version of a TED Talk by Sir Ken Robinson called *Do schools kill creativity?* Read the text about the speaker and the talk. Then work in pairs and discuss the questions.

   1 What has been Ken Robinson's focus in education?
   2 What do you think the phrase 'stifle creativity' means?
   3 What do you think is meant by 'creativity' in education? What subjects or activities at your school were not creative, in your opinion?

KEY WORDS

2 Read the sentences (1–6). The words in bold are used in the TED Talk. First guess the meaning of the words. Then match the words with their definitions (a–f).

   1 In the past, **ADHD** in children was not really a recognized condition. Now children are given help with it.
   2 The Minister of Education's **contention** is that history lessons should focus on the country's own history.
   3 Fewer university students study **humanities** than sciences.
   4 Society tends to **stigmatize** those who fail in education and business.
   5 His advice was **benign**, but it made me feel more stressed.
   6 In the Nativity story, three kings come with gifts of gold, **frankincense** and myrrh for the new baby.

   a a claim or argument
   b academic subjects concerned with human culture, e.g. philosophy, history, languages
   c kind, intending to do good or be helpful
   d an aromatic resin from a tree used in perfumes
   e an abbreviation for Attention Deficit Hyperactivity Disorder
   f to label or mark something out as bad or disgraceful

AUTHENTIC LISTENING SKILLS Rhythm and stress

English is a stress-timed language. Rather than giving each word and syllable equal stress and length, the rhythm of English varies and speakers tend to stress the most important (content) words. (For multi-syllable words, only certain syllables are stressed, not the whole word.) The less important words are not stressed and are crowded into a shorter space.

When listening to fast native speech you won't hear every word. But you will hear the content words (or the stressed syllables in them) and from these you will be able to construct the meaning of the sentence. For example:

You <u>won't</u> <u>hear</u> <u>every</u> <u>word</u>. But you <u>will</u> <u>hear</u> the <u>content</u> words or the <u>stressed</u> <u>syll</u>ables in them.

3a 🎧 **1** Look at the Authentic listening skills box. Look at the extract from Ken Robinson's talk. Listen and underline the words and syllables that are stressed.

'What these things have in common, you see, is that kids will take a chance. If they don't know, they'll have a go. Am I right? They're not frightened of being wrong.'

3b Work in pairs. Practise saying the extract in Exercise 3a with the same stress.

3c 🎧 **2** Listen to the next part of the talk. Complete the extract with the content words.

I ¹ _____ mean to ² _____ that being
³ _____ is the ⁴ _____ thing as being
⁵ _____ . What we ⁶ _____ know is,
if you're ⁷ _____ ⁸ _____ to be
⁹ _____ , you'll ¹⁰ _____ come up with
anything ¹¹ _____ .

1.1 Do schools kill creativity?

TEDTALKS 🏠 Watch at home

1 ▶ **1.1** Watch the first part (0.00–5.25) of the edited version of the TED Talk. Complete the sentences using one word per space.

1 Ken Robinson believes creativity in education is as important as _____ .
2 The little girl never paid attention, but in this _____ she did.
3 The little boy in the play didn't say 'I bring you Frankincense.' He said 'Frank _____ this.'
4 Children are not _____ of being wrong.
5 Both companies and education systems _____ mistakes.
6 We grow out of _____ as we are educated and get older.
7 We don't think of Shakespeare being a _____ , but he was in someone's _____ class.
8 His son didn't want to move to Los Angeles away from his _____ . Ken Robinson and his wife were quite _____ about it.

2 Work in pairs. Ken Robinson mixes serious points with jokes and anecdotes. Which points (1–8) in Exercise 1 are serious points (S) and which are jokes / anecdotes (J / A)?

3 ▶ **1.1** Watch the second part (5.25–7.31) of the talk. Answer the questions.

1 According to Ken Robinson, what is the same about education systems around the world?
2 Which subjects are a) at the top and b) at the bottom?
3 What does Ken Robinson think about this hierarchy or order of subjects?
4 According to Ken Robinson, what does the aim of university education seem to be?
5 Where do university professors live, according to Ken Robinson? What do you think he means by this?

4 ▶ **1.1** Watch the third part (7.31–9.18) of the talk. Choose the correct option to complete the sentences.

1 19th-century public education systems were designed to meet the needs of *industrialism / the government*.
2 People were steered away from subjects like *history / music* that wouldn't directly result in a job.
3 Ken Robinson says that the result of this is that many talented people feel they are not *talented / employable*.
4 In the past, if you had a degree, you had *status / a job*. Now, Ken Robinson says degrees aren't worth anything.
5 There is a process of academic *evolution / inflation*. Each job requires a higher degree.

▶ tea towel **BR ENG**
▶ dish towel **N AM ENG**

▶ maths **BR ENG**
▶ math **N AM ENG**

▶ theatre **BR ENG**
▶ theater **N AM ENG**

5 **1.1** Watch the fourth part (9.18–10.00) of the talk. Complete the three adjectives Ken Robinson uses to describe intelligence. Then match the adjectives with the definitions (a–c).

1 d_____
2 d_____
3 d_____

a The brain is not divided into compartments. Intelligence comes about through the interaction of different parts of the brain.

b Each person is intelligent in an individual way.

c We think about the world in the different ways we experience it – visually, in sound, in movement.

6 **1.1** Watch the fifth part (10.00 to the end) of the talk. Complete the notes about Gillian Lynne. The first letter of each word is given for you.

> **Name:** Gillian Lynne
> **Profession now:** Choreographer (work includes
> ¹ C_____ and *Phantom of the Opera*)
> **School life:** Couldn't ² c_____ ; had
> ³ A_____ ; went to see a ⁴ s_____
> **At the doctor's:** ⁵ S_____ on her hands; doctor
> left her in the room with a ⁶ r_____ on; Gillian
> started ⁷ d_____
> **After the doctor's:** Went to a dance school with others
> who 'had to move to ⁸ t_____ '
> **Career:** Went to ⁹ R_____ Ballet School;
> ¹⁰ f_____ her own company; met Andrew Lloyd
> Webber; became a ¹¹ m_____
> **Conclusion:** Another person might have put Gillian on
> medication and told her to ¹² c_____
> ¹³ d_____

VOCABULARY IN CONTEXT

7 **1.2** Watch the clips from the TED Talk. Choose the correct meaning of the words and phrases.

8 **1.3** Watch the clips from the talk. Complete the collocations. Then discuss your answers.

9 Work in pairs. Complete the sentences in your own words.

1 I had never … before, but I had a go.
2 What strikes most visitors to my country is …
3 Anyone who thinks that … is profoundly mistaken.
4 … is quite a protracted process.

CRITICAL THINKING The speaker's aims

10 Work in pairs. In his talk, do you think Ken Robinson's main purpose was to entertain, persuade, inform or something else?

11 Read these comments* about the TED Talk. Do you agree with the viewers' comments? Were their opinions the same as yours?

> **Viewers' comments**
>
> **K** **Kris** – Ken Robinson is right when he says that most education systems don't value individual talent. They just seem intent on producing people in the same mould. That's actually quite depressing, but the way he presented it kept me engaged. His humour shows the absurdity of the current education system.
>
> **Y** **Yuki** – Sir Ken Robinson made us laugh but at the same time made us reflect: we must all ignore the rat race of the school/college system and follow our real dreams.

*The comments were created for this activity.

PRESENTATION SKILLS Using humour

12 Work in pairs. What are the benefits of using humour in a talk? What could be the dangers?

13 Look at the Presentation tips box. Compare your ideas from Exercise 12 with the points in the box.

> People use humour in presentations for the same reason they use stories or strong images – as a way to connect and to help their audience relate to their argument. You don't have to use humour, but if you do use it, remember these points:
>
> • Its purpose is to relax people. If you feel unnatural or nervous using it, then it probably won't be relaxing.
> • It should illustrate your point and not distract from it.
> • It should not offend any group or individual.
> • It helps if the humour is based on a personal anecdote which others can easily relate to.
> • It's a good idea to test any jokes on friends or colleagues before your presentation.

14 **1.4** Watch the clip from the TED Talk. Which of the points in the Presentation tips box do you think are true of the joke Ken Robinson tells?

15 You are going to talk about an aspect of your school life. Choose one of the topics below or think of your own idea. Make some brief notes about the point you want to make. Then think of a (funny) story that illustrates the point.

• the way you were taught
• the way children behaved
• school rules
• sports activities

16 Work in small groups. Take turns to present your point. Did your audience relate to the story you told? Did telling the story help you to connect with your audience?

▶ carry on / continue **BR ENG**
▶ continue **N AM ENG**

▶ status /ˈsteɪtəs/ **BR ENG**
▶ status /ˈstætəs/ **N AM ENG**

1.2 What've you been up to?

CREATIVITY SURVEY

SURVEY OF 7,000 ADULTS IN THE UNITED STATES, UNITED KINGDOM, GERMANY, FRANCE AND JAPAN

WHAT THEY SAY

80% of people surveyed feel creativity is key to economic growth

66% say creativity is valuable to society

75% say they are under pressure at work to be productive rather than creative

59% say the education system stifles creativity

39% say they are creative

25% say they have realized their creative potential

52% of Americans say they are creative

WHAT THEY DO

50% of those surveyed have received some element of creative or arts education in their lives

People spend **25%** of their work time being creative

32% took an arts class at school

OF THE AMERICANS SURVEYED, AT LEAST ONCE IN THE LAST 12 MONTHS:

 50% have created, performed or shared art or music of various kinds

 32% have danced at a social event

 15% have shared their own photographs

 13% have knitted, sewn or woven something

 12% have played a musical instrument

 9% have sung solo or in a group

 8% have fashioned (made) something from leather, metal or wood

 7% have tried their hand at creative writing

GRAMMAR Definite and indefinite time

1 Work in pairs. Write down:

  1 three creative activities that people do at work or in their studies.
  2 three creative activities that people do outside work or studies.

2 Work with another pair. Compare your answers from Exercise 1. Did you have similar ideas? Do you think it's important to have creative activities in your life? Why?

3 Look at the infographic and answer the questions.

  1 How important do people feel creativity is? How is this recognized at work and in school?
  2 Are you surprised by any of the statistics about participation in creative activities? Which ones and why?

4 Read the sentences (1–6) in the Grammar box. Answer the questions (a–e).

DEFINITE AND INDEFINITE TIME

1 *A quarter of people say they **have realized** their creative potential.*
2 *One in two respondents **have received** some element of creative or arts education in their lives.*
3 *32% **took** an arts class at school.*
4 *She **has been singing** in a choir since she was ten.*
5 *One 18-year-old said, 'I've just **written** my first novel.'*
6 *6% of people changed jobs last year, because they **weren't realizing** their creative potential.*

a Which two sentences refer to finished events at a definite time in the past?
b Which two sentences refer to an indefinite time in the past?
c Which sentence refers to a recent past action?
d Which sentence refers to something that started in the past, and is still continuing?
e In which sentence is the action finished, but the time referred to unfinished?

Check your answers on page 74 and do Exercises 1–4.

5 Read the sentences. How does the meaning of each sentence differ with each option?

1 *She's written / She wrote* over twenty books.
2 Thanks, *I've had / I had* a great time.
3 *I've been practising / I've practised* the piano this morning.
4 *I've had / I had* the camera for five years.
5 What *have you been doing / have you done* today?
6 *I was talking / I've been talking* to him recently about it.

6 Complete the conversation with the most natural form of the verbs: present perfect simple, present perfect continuous, past simple and past continuous.

A: ¹ _____ (you / ever / make) anything from wood or metal?

B: Not really. I ² _____ (make) a metal box once at school and I ³ _____ (build) a few things for our house over the years.

A: I ⁴ _____ (not / do) anything like that for years, but I've been thinking of joining a craftwork evening class.

B: What kind of crafts ⁵ _____ (you / have) in mind?

A: Well, my neighbour ⁶ _____ (go) to a knitting class lately. She ⁷ _____ (tell) me about it the other day. It sounds really good fun.

B: ⁸ _____ (you / ever / knit) anything before?

A: No, but my neighbour ⁹ _____ (knit) all sorts of things. In fact, she ¹⁰ _____ (experiment) with all sorts of new designs.

7 Choose the correct option to complete the sentences.

1 Have you *ever / before* wondered about applying for a more creative job?
2 I've been writing poetry *for six years / since six years*.
3 He's only had one woodwork lesson *yet / so far*, but he's keen to carry on.
4 The number of creative subjects has fallen significantly *for the last ten years / over the last ten years*.
5 She's *lately / just* finished a degree in design technology.
6 I haven't written the talk *yet / already*, but I've got a lot of good ideas for it.
7 We've been learning how to make clay pots at evening class *this week / last week*.
8 I've never done anything like it *before / already*.
9 I've lived in London *since all my life / all my life*.
10 She's been taking dancing lessons *lately / so far*.

8 Put the time expressions you used in Exercise 7 in the correct category (1–3).

1 Indefinite time (an unspecified time in the past): e.g. *already, never*
2 Unfinished time (a time started in the past and continuing now): e.g. *since Tuesday, so far*
3 Recent time (in the recent past): e.g. *recently*

LANGUAGE FOCUS Expressions with statistics

9 Choose the correct option to complete the expressions about statistics.

1 The vast *majority / minority / extent* of people at the open day were newcomers.
2 A significant *handful / deal / proportion* of the respondents in the survey were retired people.
3 Only a small *share / handful / amount* of people took creative studies beyond secondary school level.
4 The percentage of people who can read music is a tiny *fraction / branch / element* of the total population.
5 The number of people who follow a creative career is almost *unimportant / tiny / negligible*.
6 A *little / small / trivial* minority of people said creativity had no place in education.
7 There were *relatively / significantly / barely* few takers for the knitting course.
8 *Virtually / Almost / Hardly* anyone considers themselves to be completely lacking in creative talent.
9 Three out of *every / all / each* five wished they had had a more supportive teacher.
10 About one *from / in / of* four people responded negatively.

See page 75 for more information about expressions with statistics, and do Exercise 5.

10 Make three sentences based on the statistics in the infographic using the expressions in Exercise 9. Then compare sentences with your partner.

SPEAKING Creativity survey

11 **21st CENTURY OUTCOMES**

Work in pairs. Ask and answer the questions in the survey.

1 Did your school(s) emphasize the creative arts (music, drama, dance, creative writing, photography, etc.)?
2 What proportion of your own daily work or study would you say is 'creative'?
3 Do you feel that more or less of your time is devoted to creative activities now than when you were a child?
4 How much of your time outside work or study is taken up with creative pursuits?
5 What have you produced or created in your life that you are most proud of?
6 What creative skill or ability would you most like to possess?

12 Listen to the answers to the survey of other students in the class. Then write two or three conclusions. Use language for expressing statistics.

1.3 How talent thrives

READING What I talk about when I talk about running

1 Many talented people never realize the potential of their talents. Why do you think talent translates into success for some people and not for others? Discuss possible reasons.

2 Read the extract from the book *What I talk about when I talk about running* by Haruki Murakami. What three keys to successfully exploiting your talents does Haruki Murakami identify? Define each key in your own words.

3 Read the article again. Choose the best answer (a–c).

1 Which adjective best describes the nature of talent, according to Murakami?
   a rare
   b unpredictable
   c unfairly distributed
2 According to Murakami, having focus is:
   a more important than having talent.
   b indispensable to success.
   c the key to thinking critically.
3 According to Murakami, when you apply your talents with focus and endurance, you will begin to notice that:
   a your body changes.
   b your mind becomes sharper.
   c your capacity for good work increases.
4 What does the example of the writer Raymond Chandler tell us?
   a Discipline is very important.
   b Even talented people make mistakes.
   c We need to be in the right place at the right time.

4 What overall lesson do you think we should take from Murakami about jobs which use our talents? Do you agree with this? Why? / Why not?

5 Find the words and expressions in bold in the article. What do you think they mean? Then answer the questions.

1 What are the **pre-requisites** for a happy marriage?
2 Tears, anger and joy are all examples of things that can **well up**. What usually happens next when an emotion wells up inside us?
3 Would it be fun to play tennis with someone whose game was **erratic**? Why? / Why not?
4 If someone won a game or match **hands down**, how easily did they win?
5 If you return to a country ten years after first visiting and it has changed **imperceptibly**, how much has changed?
6 For what tasks or jobs is patience **a must**? Why do you say this?

VOCABULARY Creativity collocations

6 Match the verbs (1–9) with the nouns or pronouns (a–i) to make expressions about creativity and originality.

Verbs	Nouns / Pronouns
1 have	a yourself freely
2 come up with	b yourself to your work
3 express	c your own path
4 come at	d a new idea
5 take up	e a flash of inspiration
6 devote	f the experience of others
7 break with	g something from a different angle
8 follow	h a new hobby
9 build on	i convention

7 Complete the collocations. Use the verbs from Exercise 6.

1 In 1825, James Clark, who worked in his brother's tannery making sheepskin rugs, _____ a brainwave. Why not use all the sheepskin offcuts to … ?
2 In the 1970s, Cadbury's, the chocolate bar manufacturer, _____ tradition and produced a bar that had …
3 Bob Simon _____ motorcycling at the age of 70, saying that taking risks is a good way to …
4 Sarah Tansley, the headteacher at Kendal Primary School, is new to education having _____ it from an unusual direction. For forty years she …
5 Terezinha da Silva has _____ an invention to bring clean water to people living in the slums of São Paulo, using dirty rainwater from people's roofs. Da Silva …

8 Work in pairs. Discuss possible ways of completing the sentences in Exercise 7. Compare your answers with another pair and then check with the information on page 89.

SPEAKING Learning from experience

9 **21st CENTURY OUTCOMES**
What lessons have you learned from your work, studies or creative / leisure activities? Think about these areas and make notes.

- How to be efficient / good at a particular activity
- How to improve / make progress
- How others can help you in this activity / How to collaborate successfully with others
- How to balance this activity with other things in your life

10 Work in small groups. Discuss the lessons you have learned and the experiences that helped you discover these things. Which lesson did you find most useful?

What I Talk About When I Talk About Running

In every interview I'm asked what's the most important quality a novelist has to have. It's pretty obvious: talent. No matter how much enthusiasm and effort you put into writing, if you totally lack literary talent you can forget

5 about being a novelist. This is more of a pre-requisite than a necessary quality. If you don't have any fuel, even the best car won't run.

The problem with talent, though, is that in most cases the person involved can't control its amount or quality. ...

10 Talent has a mind of its own and wells up when it wants to, and once it dries up, that's it. Of course certain poets and rock singers whose genius went out in a blaze of glory – people like Schubert and Mozart, whose dramatic early deaths turned them into legends – have a certain appeal,

15 but for the vast majority of us this isn't the model we follow.

If I'm asked what the next most important quality is for a novelist, that's easy too: focus – the ability to concentrate all your limited talents on whatever's critical at the

20 moment. Without that you can't accomplish anything of value, while, if you can focus effectively, you'll be able to compensate for an erratic talent or even a shortage of it. I generally concentrate on work for three or four hours every morning. I sit at my desk and focus totally on what

25 I'm writing. I don't see anything else, I don't think about anything else. ...

After focus, the next most important thing for a novelist is, hands down, endurance. If you concentrate on writing three or four hours a day and feel tired after a week of this,

30 you're not going to be able to write a long work. What's needed for a writer of fiction – at least one who hopes to write a novel – is the energy to focus every day for half a year, or a year, two years. ...

Fortunately, these two disciplines – focus and endurance – are different from talent, since they

35 can be acquired and sharpened through training. You'll naturally learn both concentration and endurance when you sit down every day at your desk and train yourself to focus on one point. This is a lot like the training of muscles ... gradually you'll expand the limits of what you're able to do. Almost imperceptibly you'll make the bar rise. This involves the same process as jogging every day to strengthen your muscles and develop a runner's physique. ... Patience is a must in

40 this process, but I guarantee the results will come. ... The great mystery writer Raymond Chandler once confessed that even if he didn't write anything, he made sure he sat down at his desk every single day and concentrated. ...

Most of what I know about writing I've learned through running every day. These are practical, physical lessons. ... I know that if I hadn't become a long-distance runner when I became a

45 novelist, my work would have been vastly different.

1.4 It's not really my thing

READING Sing while you work

1 Work in pairs. Discuss the questions. Then read the extract from the article and compare your answers.

    1 When people feel bored or disengaged at work, how does this affect the company they work for?

    2 What kind of things can companies offer employees to keep them engaged?

2 What do you think the 'benefits' mentioned in the last sentence of the article are? Make a list. Then compare your answers with the statements on page 89.

Sing while you work

Statistics tell us that around seventy per cent of employees are disengaged in their jobs and that 36 per cent dream of having more creative roles and are considering moving to another company. For companies those are worrying, and potentially expensive, statistics. Because disengagement from work is high, companies are constantly on the lookout for new ways to keep employees motivated and to switch their focus from the frustrations of more humdrum work tasks.

One such idea is forming a company choir. This was the subject of a TV series in the UK, *The Choir: Sing while you work*, where a professional choirmaster, Gareth Malone, attempted to turn a group of employees with little or no singing experience into a respectable choir. The choir is composed of employees from all parts of the company and once they have been trained to a certain standard they then represent the company in singing competitions against other company choirs. The benefits to both employees and the company are numerous. For example, participants said that …

LISTENING A company choir

3 🎧 **3** Listen to a conversation between two employees at a company where a choir has been set up. Complete the table.

Who	Speaker A (Woman)	Speaker B (Man)
likes the idea?		
can sing?		
wants to participate?		

4 🎧 **3** Listen to the conversation again. Look at the Useful language box. Which expressions do the speakers use? Discuss with your partner what the speakers used the phrases to talk about.

DESCRIBING LIKES AND TALENTS

Describing likes and dislikes

I'm (really) in favour of / against …
I'm a (big) fan of …
I'm (quite) keen on / fond of …
I'm (not) really into …
I (do / really) like / love …

It's / That's not (really) my (kind of) thing …
I can take it or leave it.
I can't (really) get excited about …
It appeals / It doesn't really appeal to me.
I'm not so keen on …

Describing talents and abilities

I'm (quite) good at …
He's a born (linguist).
You're a natural.

I'm no good at … / I'm not great at …
I can't … to save my life.
I have a / no talent for …
I'm hopeless at …

Pronunciation Emphasis and de-emphasis

5a 🎧 **4** Read the sentences. Listen and underline the stressed words.

    1 I do love a good musical.
    2 The idea quite appeals to me, actually.
    3 I really have no talent for playing music.
    4 Classical music's not really my thing.
    5 I'm quite good at singing, but I'm not keen on dancing.

5b What is the difference in meaning when *quite* is stressed and when it isn't?

SPEAKING Describing likes and talents

6 Work in pairs. Think of an activity that could benefit people working for an organization similar to the activity you read about on page 16. Discuss how the activity would be organized.

7 Work with a new partner. Take turns to present your activities. Then discuss if your talents are suited to the activities and if you would like to sign up. Act out conversations like the conversation in Exercise 3. Use the expressions in the Useful language box on page 16 to help you.

WRITING A progress report

8 Read the progress report about a new company initiative to make the workplace more fun. Did the initiative have the desired results? Do you like these ideas?

This is a short report on the progress we have made since the decision (EGM, 12th Nov) to hold monthly theme days within the company.

We have held two theme days so far, in January and April. The first was a healthy eating day, where employees were asked to bring in a healthy lunch for a colleague in another department. Our aim was to raise health awareness and also to encourage inter-departmental collaboration.

The second was a 'Brighten a Space' day where employees worked together to make photo displays in areas of the building that seemed dull. The purpose of this was to make the office a more pleasant place and to create images that reflected the company's values.

There was an extremely positive response to both initiatives – participation rates were around 90% and 75%. In the follow-up questionnaires, 94% of participants expressed appreciation of the theme days and 88% said they would be keen to do more. Even more significantly, two employees have since started their own healthy eating campaign, posting recipe ideas on the company's intranet. A 'Happy Work Environment' group has also been formed to come up with improvements for the office space. No specific research has been conducted yet on improvements in collaboration or on whether people feel more inspired in their environment, but anecdotal evidence points to both these results.

The next planned theme day will be in June on the theme of 'Team Exercise'. Details have to be finalized, but our intention is to organize a contest involving physical activities.

9 Work in pairs. Read the report again. Look at each paragraph in the report. What is the function of each one?

Writing skill Nominalization

10a Look at the sentence from the report and notice how the meaning of the underlined noun can be expressed using a verb. Then rewrite the sentences (1–4). Change the underlined nouns to phrases with verbs.

> Our <u>aim</u> was to raise health awareness.
> We *aimed to raise health awareness*.
>
> **1** There was an extremely positive <u>response</u> to both initiatives.
> Employees _____ .
> **2** 94% of participants expressed <u>appreciation</u> of the theme days.
> 94% of participants said they _____ .
> **3** A group has also been formed to come up with <u>improvements</u> for the office space.
> A group has also been formed to come up with ways we _____ .
> **4** Our <u>intention</u> is to organize a contest involving physical activities.
> We _____ .
>
> *See page 75 for more information about nominalization, and do Exercises 6 and 7.*

10b Rewrite the sentences. Nominalize the underlined verb phrases. You may need to make other changes.

1 We <u>were attempting</u> to encourage more collaboration.
It was _____ .
2 Participation rates <u>have increased</u> significantly.
There has _____ .
3 Some people <u>resisted</u> the idea at first.
There was _____ .
4 We <u>don't intend to repeat</u> this exercise.
We have _____ .
5 It <u>was decided</u> to test the idea on a small section of employees.
A _____ .
6 It was interesting to see how employees <u>reacted</u> to the initiative.
It was interesting to see _____ .

11 **21st** **CENTURY OUTCOMES**
Write a progress report on one of the initiatives that you discussed in Exercises 6 and 7. Include details of the activity, the results (its success) and the next steps. Write 200–300 words.

12 Work in pairs. Exchange your reports. Use these questions to check your partner's report.

- Have they introduced the subject of the report?
- Have they explained the results?
- Have they outlined the next step or steps?
- Are there one or two examples of nominalization?

2 Hopes and fears

BACKGROUND

1 You are going to watch a TED Talk by Megan Washington called *Why I live in mortal dread of public speaking.* Read the text about the speaker and the talk. Then work in pairs and discuss the questions.

   1 What facts in the text indicate Megan Washington's success as a singer?

   2 What is a stutter? How do you think a stutter would affect a person who has one?

3 How do you feel about public speaking? Is it something you dread? Why? / Why not? How comfortable do you feel with other means of communication (for example, speaking on the phone, writing letters and reports, speaking in meetings)?

TEDTALKS

MEGAN WASHINGTON is a popular Australian singer and songwriter. She has won two ARIA Awards, the Australian equivalent of the Grammys, and was a judge on the TV singing talent show *The Voice,* in Australia. Her 2010 album *I Believe You Liar* went platinum. In this talk she reveals a secret about herself that she has not shared publicly before – that she has a stutter – and explains how singing helps her with this.

Megan Washington's idea worth spreading is that for all of us there is a way to overcome our fears and find a medium to express ourselves.

Sprinter's prayer at a track
competition, Annapolis,
United States

KEY WORDS

2 Read the questions (1–6). The words in bold are used in the TED Talk. First guess the meaning of the words. Then match the words with their definitions (a–f) and discuss the questions with your partner.

1 What other kinds of **speech impediment** are there apart from a stutter?

2 Why do you think people talk to babies or children in a **singsong** voice?

3 *Megan* and *Sydney* are **proper nouns**. Can you think of other examples of proper nouns?

4 Is it **cheating** to use notes when you're giving a talk?

5 Have you ever been advised **explicitly** about how to speak in public?

6 What do you think is the most **miraculous** thing about the human brain?

a in a clear and detailed way, leaving no room for confusion
b not following (or abiding by) the rules
c remarkable and bringing amazing results
d words that are the names of places or people
e a defect that makes it difficult to speak or produce the correct sound
f where the voice rises and falls in a musical way

AUTHENTIC LISTENING SKILLS Listening to songs

Listening to songs is something that most non-native speakers like to practise. It is beneficial because songs are memorable and are also good for your pronunciation; it is often easier to imitate something when it is sung than when it is said. But understanding the lyrics can be difficult, because the words are vocalized in a way that suits the music rather than in the most comprehensible way for the listener. Fortunately, you can often find song lyrics on the Internet to read while you listen.

3a 🎧 **5** Look at the Authentic listening skills box. Cover the lyrics below and listen to the first two lines of Megan Washington's song. What did you understand?

3b 🎧 **5** Listen to the first two lines from the song again and read the lyrics at the same time. Complete the lyrics.

I would be a beauty but my [1] _____ is slightly too big for my face

And I would be a dreamer but my [2] _____ is slightly too big for this [3] _____

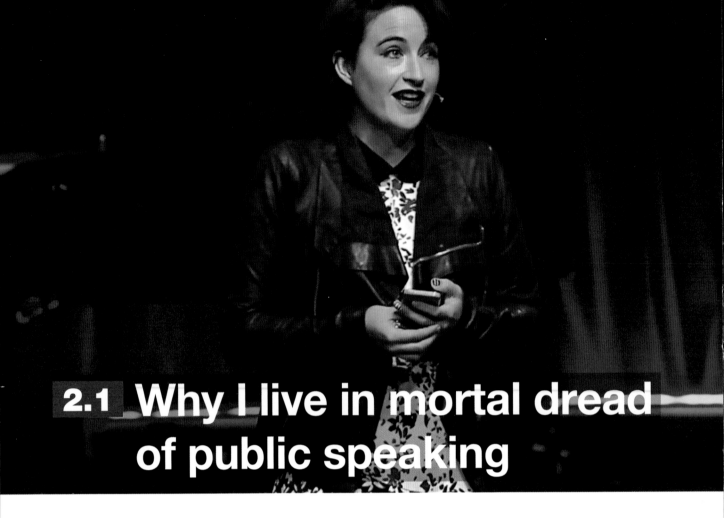

2.1 Why I live in mortal dread of public speaking

TEDTALKS 🏠 Watch at home

1 ▶ **2.1** Watch the TED Talk. What message did you take away from the TED Talk? Discuss with your partner.

2 ▶ **2.1** Watch the first part (0.00–2.47) of the talk again. Then work in pairs and answer the questions.

  1 How does Megan Washington rate the seriousness of her problem?
  2 What is she fearful of? What is she not fearful of?
  3 What things did she hope would happen when she grew up?
  4 What has she decided to do, now that she's 28?

3 ▶ **2.1** Watch the second part (2.47–5.22) of the talk again. Complete the sentences.

  1 The other stutterer Megan Washington met, Joe, thought she was *in love with him / making fun of him*.
  2 Many people think she's *stupid / drunk*.
  3 For Megan Washington, the most difficult thing as a stutterer is saying *proper nouns / people's names*.
  4 If Megan Washington thinks she's going to stutter, she *starts the sentence again / thinks of a synonym or paraphrase*.
  5 She solved the problem of saying her band member Steve's name by dropping *the 's' / the 't'*.

4 ▶ **2.1** Watch the third part (5.22–8.36) of the talk again. Complete the summary with these words.

cheating	fluent	medication	nice
singsong	smooth	TV	understood

One technique that therapists use with stutterers is called
¹ _____ speech where they get the person to speak
in a ² _____ way. The problem is that it makes the
person sound as if they are on ³ _____ . Megan
Washington uses this technique when she's on
⁴ _____ , but it feels like ⁵ _____ .

Singing is not just about making ⁶ _____ sounds
or feeling ⁷ _____ ; it's the only time she can really
express herself. When she sings, it is the only time she feels
⁸ _____ , because for some reason the brain
won't allow you to stutter when you sing.

▶ often /ˈɒf(ə)n/ **BR ENG**
▶ often /ˈɔf(ə)n/ **N AM ENG**

▶ awkward /ˈɔːkwə(r)d/ **BR ENG**
▶ awkward /ˈɔkwərd/ **N AM ENG**

5 ▶ **2.1** Work in pairs. Look at the lyrics of Megan Washington's song and try to complete the missing words. The words at the end of a line rhyme with the last word in the line before. Then watch the fourth part (8.36 to the end) of the talk again and check your answers.

> I would be a beauty but my nose is slightly too big for my face
> And I would be a dreamer but my dream is slightly too big for this ¹ ____*space*____
> And I would be an angel but my halo it pales in the ² _____ of your ³ _____
> And I would be a joker but that card looks silly when you play your ⁴ _____
>
> I'd like to know: Are there stars in hell?
> And I'd like to know, know if you can ⁵ _____
> That you make me lose everything I know
> That I cannot choose to or not let ⁶ _____
>
> And I'd stay forever but my home is slightly too far from this place
> And I swear I try to slow it down when I am walking at your ⁷ _____
> But all I could think idling through the cities
> Do I look ⁸ _____ in the rain?
> And I don't know how someone quite so lovely makes me feel ⁹ _____
> So much ¹⁰ _____

VOCABULARY IN CONTEXT

6 ▶ **2.2** Watch the clips from the TED Talk. Choose the correct meaning of the words and phrases.

7 ▶ **2.3** Watch the clips from the talk. Complete the collocations. Then discuss your answers.

8 Complete the sentences in your own words. Then compare your sentences with a partner.

1 My best friend / mother / boss manages to stay serene and calm, even when …
2 For me, speaking good English and … are inextricably linked.
3 When you're giving a public talk, you can't get away with …
4 After talking to people all day at work, … is sweet relief.

CRITICAL THINKING Winning your audience over

9 Judging by the applause at the end, Megan Washington clearly won her audience over. Work in pairs. Discuss how you think she was able to do this. What techniques did she use?

10 Read this comment* about the TED Talk. Do you agree with the viewer's comment? Were her reasons the same as yours?

Viewers' comments

J **Joss** – I almost cried watching this. Her vulnerability, grace and humility completely charmed me. It's a very courageous thing to stand up on stage in front of a group of strangers and expose your flaws and insecurities.

*The comment was created for this activity.

PRESENTATION SKILLS Being authentic

11 Work in pairs. How can you ensure when you give a talk that you speak from the heart and allow the audience to see your true personality?

12 Look at the Presentation tips box. Compare your ideas from Exercise 11 with the points in the box.

> **TIPS**
>
> When you give a talk, there's a temptation to see the stage as an acting stage and play a different character from the person you really are. Try to resist this temptation: the audience want to see you, not an actor. Follow these tips:
>
> • Be yourself. Write your talk yourself. Use words and expressions that you would normally use. Make sure your words convey your personality and your curiosity about the topic.
> • Be personal and relatable. Pepper your talk with stories, examples and applications of your idea – make sure your talk isn't overly conceptual.
> • Be passionate. Whenever possible, choose a topic that you feel passionate about. Your excitement translates from the stage and becomes contagious.
> • Be comfortable. Wear something you would normally wear and feel comfortable in.

13 ▶ **2.4** Watch the clip from the TED Talk. Which of the techniques in the Presentation tips box can you see in Megan Washington's talk?

14 You are going to give an introduction to a talk on 'How I overcame a fear'. Use the ideas below or your own idea. Make brief notes for an introductory paragraph and practise presenting your introduction.

• fear of flying
• fear of heights
• fear of driving at night
• fear of making mistakes (e.g. when speaking English)

15 Work in small groups. Take turns to present your introductions. Which techniques from the Presentation tips box did you use? Were these techniques successful in helping you to 'be authentic'?

▶ wanted /wɒntɪd/ **BR ENG**
▶ wanted /wɑnɪd/ **N AM ENG**

2.2 Optimist or pessimist?

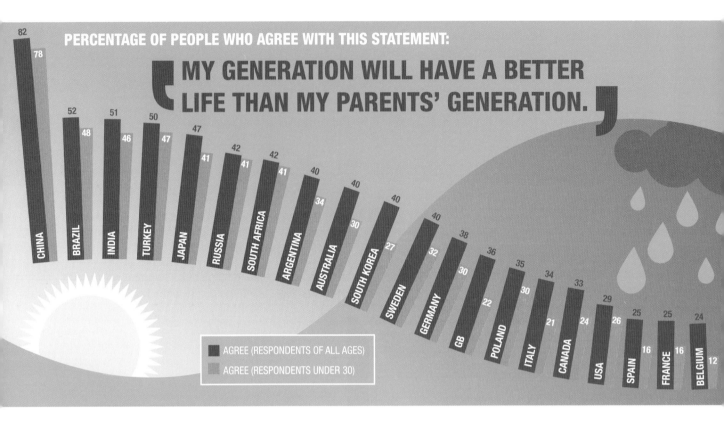

PERCENTAGE OF PEOPLE WHO AGREE WITH THIS STATEMENT:

MY GENERATION WILL HAVE A BETTER LIFE THAN MY PARENTS' GENERATION.

AGREE (RESPONDENTS OF ALL AGES)
AGREE (RESPONDENTS UNDER 30)

CHINA 82 78 · BRAZIL 52 48 · INDIA 51 46 · TURKEY 50 47 · JAPAN 47 41 · RUSSIA 42 41 · SOUTH AFRICA 42 41 · ARGENTINA 40 34 · AUSTRALIA 40 30 · SOUTH KOREA 40 27 · SWEDEN 40 32 · GERMANY 38 30 · GB 36 22 · POLAND 35 30 · ITALY 34 21 · CANADA 33 24 · USA 29 26 · SPAIN 25 16 · FRANCE 25 16 · BELGIUM 24 12

GRAMMAR Future forms

1 Work in pairs. When you compare life today to life fifty years ago, do you think people have:

a a better life? **b** a worse life?
c a life that is better in some respects but worse in others?

2 Look at the infographic. Answer the questions.

1 Overall are people optimistic or pessimistic about having a better standard of living than their parents?
2 Which countries are more optimistic? Which are more pessimistic? Do these countries have anything in common?
3 Are the younger generation more or less optimistic than the overall population?
4 Why do you think China is exceptionally optimistic?

3 🎧 **6** Listen to an economist's commentary on the statistics in the infographic. Complete the sentences.

1 The economist describes the statistics as just a _____ of how people feel at the moment.
2 He describes China, Brazil and India as _____ industrialized countries and the US, Spain and France as _____ industrial economies.
3 He says in future, Western economies will not rely on _____ sector industries.
4 Instead the economies will be based on _____ thinking and technology. This change will result in a better quality of _____ for everyone.

4 Read the sentences (1–8) in the Grammar box. Answer the questions (1–2).

FUTURE FORMS

1 *In China and India people feel things **are going to get** better.*
2 *In the US, Spain and France people think that in thirty years, things **will have got** worse.*
3 *In thirty years or so, Western economies certainly **won't be doing** the same things they are doing now.*
4 *I'm not saying that things **are about to change.***
5 *If we **are to progress**, the post-industrial economy will have to evolve.*
6 *I think we **will use** creative thinking and technology to overcome the problems.*
7 *A better standard of living in the post-industrialized nations **may** or **may not come** out of that.*
8 *I'm **speaking** at the conference on Tuesday.*

1 Which sentence:
   a describes a continuous event in the future?
   b describes a completed event in the future?
   c describes a future arrangement?
   d expresses uncertainty about a future event?
   e describes a change in the very near future?
   f describes a pre-condition for a prediction?

2 Which two sentences simply predict a future event?

Check your answers on page 77 and do Exercises 1–3.

5 Complete the sentences. Use an appropriate future form. Sometimes more than one form is possible.

1 It's impossible to predict what _____ (happen) in the next thirty years. We _____ (be) better off, we _____ (be) worse off.

2 At the rate I'm going, I _____ (still / live) with my parents when I'm forty!

3 My partner and I have decided that we _____ (move) to an area where the cost of living is lower.

4 The idea that we _____ (save) enough to retire by the time we're sixty like my parents did is a joke.

5 We _____ (never / be) able to buy our own house, I don't think.

6 You have to look on the bright side. We _____ (earn) as much money as our parents did, but I think we _____ (be) better off in other ways.

7 This time next year, I _____ (pay) off all my student debts.

8 I _____ (do) a course in money management next week. My friend did it and said it was really good.

6 The last example in the Grammar box uses a present tense to talk about future time. Work in pairs. Look at these other uses of present and future tenses. Which sentences refer to future time? Which sentences refer to present or general time?

1 Sorry, I have to go. My train **leaves** in half an hour.

2 Can you slow down? We**'re going** too fast.

3 There's no point calling San Francisco now. No one **will be** at work yet.

4 Oh no! I forgot to put a parking ticket on my car. I**'ll be** back in a moment.

5 Is it five o'clock already? Sorry, I have to go. My wife **will be waiting** outside in the car.

6 We**'re getting** married on 4th July, American Independence Day.

7 He **will keep** interrupting when others are speaking.

8 Exercise **works** best for me when I do it early in the day.

9 If we **are** to get a good price, we'd better book the flight soon.

7 Work in pairs. Talk about these ideas.

• a future plan or ambition you have, e.g. *'One day I …'*

• an arrangement you've made, e.g. *'Next weekend / month / year …'*

• a prediction about your future, e.g. *'I expect …'*

• a thing you know someone else is doing at this very moment in another place, e.g. *'Right now …'*

• a thing you know you will be doing in the future, e.g. *'In two months …'*

LANGUAGE FOCUS Expressions of certainty

8 Look at the two sentences from the economist's commentary in Exercise 3. How certain is the speaker that these things will happen?

> **1** *These statistics are just a snapshot of how people feel at the moment. But the situation **is very likely to change**.*
>
> **2** *We will use creative thinking and technology to overcome the problems that we **are** all **bound to face** in the future.*

See page 78 for more information about expressions of certainty, and do Exercise 4.

9 Look at these phrases and grade them by order of certainty (A, B, C or D)

```
              A          B         C         D
won't happen__|_____|_____|_____|_will happen
```

1 It's highly unlikely to happen.
2 In all likelihood, it will happen.
3 It may well happen.
4 It's very likely to happen.
5 It's bound to happen.
6 It's anyone's guess whether it will happen.
7 It's a foregone conclusion.
8 It's by no means certain.

10 Work in pairs. What do you think the probability of these things coming true is? Give reasons.

• people will live to be 150 years old
• driverless cars will become common
• the global population will reach 10 billion (currently it's 7 billion)
• global warming will be reversed

SPEAKING Attitudes towards the future

11 **21st CENTURY OUTCOMES**

Work in pairs. Ask and answer the questions to complete this questionnaire.

1 Do you think you will be better or worse off than your parents in your lifetime?

2 Do you think the world in general will have become a better or a worse place in fifty years' time?

3 Are you (or your children) likely to be living in your own home by the time you (or they) are thirty?

4 Do you think that having a lower income necessarily means a worse quality of life (and vice versa)?

5 Do you think a richer generation should help their children financially when they are adults?

12 Work with another pair. Discuss your answers to the questions in Exercise 11. Are you optimistic for the future?

2.3 Expanding your horizons

READING Outside the comfort zone

1 Work in pairs. Discuss the questions.

  1 What does *comfort zone* mean? In what situations do you feel outside your comfort zone?

  2 What feelings – physical and emotional – do you experience when you are outside your comfort zone?

  3 Do you think it's good to sometimes be in these situations? Why? / Why not?

2 You are going to read an article about being outside the comfort zone. Read the first paragraph. Tick (✓) the two sentences that you think reflect the points of view that are expressed.

  1 There are few things of value within our comfort zone.

  2 The general belief is that stepping out of your comfort zone is a useful thing to do.

  3 Stepping out of the comfort zone is not for everyone.

  4 Too many of the tips you find on the Internet are about self-improvement.

3 Read the rest of the article. Choose the best option to complete the sentences.

  1 Being stuck in an overcrowded lift is given as an example of *an everyday / an unpleasant* situation.

  2 According to the article, getting out of the lift gives us a feeling of *accomplishment / liberation*.

  3 We get a feeling of achievement when we manage *frightening situations / everyday difficulties*.

  4 Overcoming your fear in a particular situation makes you *keener to do it again / less afraid in other situations*.

  5 The example of the prison visit is used to show how being taken out of your comfort zone can *build understanding within communities / help business leaders to manage teams*.

  6 Julia Middleton believes putting people in unfamiliar situations teaches them to *be less suspicious of others / break out of their own small worlds*.

4 Find the words in bold in the article. Then answer the questions.

  1 If there's an **overwhelming consensus**, roughly what percentage of people are in agreement? (para 1)

  2 If someone said to you 'Do you get my **drift**?', what would they be asking you? (para 1)

  3 What does '**which**' refer to in line 21? (para 2)

  4 What things can you **overcome**, other than fears? (para 2)

  5 What kinds of things do '**adrenaline junkies**' do to get their excitement? (para 2)

  6 What adjective with the word 'day' in it means the same as **mundane**? (para 2)

  7 What's another word for **inmates**? (para 3)

  8 If a building is **insulated** against the cold, what kind of measures have been taken? (para 4)

5 Which of the examples in the article of ways that people could be taken out their comfort zones appealed to you personally? Why? Discuss your ideas with your partner.

VOCABULARY Hopes and fears

6 Complete the idioms about hopes and fears with these words.

| butterflies | dark | dashed | feet | get |
| give | nerves | pinned | plucked | sky |

  1 I'll help you look for your ring, but don't _____ **your hopes up** – I may not find it.

  2 His **hopes** of becoming a firefighter **were** _____ when he learned that – at fifty – he was too old.

  3 She had _____ **her hopes** on getting the job, so she was disappointed when they told her that they had hired someone else.

  4 The thing that sets great sports people apart from ordinary ones is that they never _____ **up hope**.

  5 She's so talented – she can go anywhere she wants. **The** _____**'s the limit**.

  6 He wanted to ask her for her autograph, but he **got cold** _____ .

  7 Poor Jake. He was **a bundle of** _____ before his talk.

  8 After some hesitation, she _____ **up her courage** and jumped across the gap.

  9 I **get** _____ **in my stomach** every time I think of my interview next Monday – I'm so nervous!

  10 We really had no idea what our new life in Australia would be like. It was **a leap in the** _____ .

7 Work in pairs. Discuss what each idiom in Exercise 6 means. Then choose four idioms to describe situations that you have been in.

SPEAKING Comfort zone

8 **21st** CENTURY OUTCOMES

Work in pairs. Look at the suggestions (1–5) for taking people out of their comfort zones. Then discuss the questions (a–c) on page 25.

  1 Volunteer to work at a soup kitchen, handing out food to the homeless.

  2 Try to eat a kind of food that you normally avoid eating.

  3 Go out of your way to thank or show appreciation to someone in your life whom you respect and admire.

  4 Visit a part of your city that you never normally visit (without any map or GPS help). Get acquainted with the area by asking strangers for directions.

  5 Give a short performance – a song, a story, a poem – at a local 'open mic' event.

THE COMFORT ZONE

Google 'out of your comfort zone' and, along with a host of tips on how to get there, you will find an overwhelming consensus that this is something we really all ought to be doing. The general drift is that if you stay in your own comfortable little box, never seeking new experiences or taking risks, your life will be pretty dull and unfulfilling. If, on the other hand, you step out of this familiar world, something magical will happen: not only will you grow as a person, but whole new vistas of opportunity will open out before you. However, where a lot of the advice, whether from bloggers or personal coaches, falls short is how being taken out of your comfort zone can profit not just you, the individual, but others too.

At its simplest level, being out of your comfort zone means doing things that make you feel uncomfortable or anxious, such as driving at night in the pouring rain or being stuck in an overcrowded lift. No one, of course, actually advocates seeking out these kinds of situation as a route to self-improvement. Rather, they advise that we place ourselves intentionally in challenging situations, mastery of which will give us not just a sense of relief (as in the case of escaping the crowded lift), but a sense of real achievement. We have managed a difficult situation, overcome a fear, and are now better placed to deal with it the next time. Canoeing on white water for the first time and managing to negotiate some treacherous rapids would offer such a feeling of accomplishment. But it doesn't have to mean seeking adventure or becoming an adrenaline junkie. It could equally be something more mundane, like a person who has no experience of cooking preparing a meal for ten guests. The principle is the same: the more you attempt to do things that scare you, the more confident you will become and the more your fear, in general, will begin to fade. You'll go for that job you thought you had no hope of getting; you'll go travelling on your own; you'll learn a new language.

There is no doubt that these kinds of achievement bring a greater sense of self-empowerment, but there still seems to be something lacking here. The key perhaps is in the word 'self'. Where is the benefit to others? I was struck the other day reading an article about a leadership training company called 'Common Purpose' which offers a more socially-minded approach to taking people out of their comfort zones. One of their programmes involved participants visiting a local prison and speaking to inmates about how they had got there and what the challenges of being 'inside' were. A managing director of a local company who took part said, 'What I gained from this experience in a business sense might be indirect, but in a social sense it was priceless – and like any business, [my company] exists in a social setting.' This experience wasn't so much about confronting one's demons as opening one's eyes to the situation of others. That can be uncomfortable, but ultimately, it is something that benefits more than just the individual concerned.

We all operate within the confines of certain worlds and our own thoughts and actions are limited by them. The kind of programme offered by Common Purpose removes this insulation and extends our knowledge not just of our own limitations, but of the restrictions and difficulties that others face. As Julia Middleton, the founder of Common Purpose, puts it, 'Most people tend to stay within their limits … they often don't recognize that a different approach is needed … As professionals we cannot afford to be isolated from fellow decision-makers, and as people, we cannot continue to be insulated from our fellow citizens.'

Questions

a Would you feel uncomfortable doing this or being in this situation?

b What personal benefit could come from doing this?

c What benefit could it bring to the community or others?

9 Think of another activity and answer the questions (a–c) from Exercise 8 for this activity. Then compare your idea and its benefits with another pair.

2.4 Worst-case scenario

READING Being prepared

1 Work in pairs. Discuss the questions. Then read the extract from an article and check your answers.

  1 What is a worst-case scenario?
  2 What is 'scenario planning' and who uses it?

2 Match the verbs in box A with the nouns in box B to make collocations. Then discuss which of these things you regularly do (or would do) when you travel abroad.

A

allow	carry	confirm	get	hang on to
pack	read up on	take out	wear	

B

your booking	a first aid kit	insurance	jabs
local laws / customs	a map	a money belt	
plenty of time	receipts		

Worst
case scenario

Any forward-looking business or government will put plans in place for all possible scenarios: best-case, worst-case, probable case. Scenario planning doesn't mean predicting the future – it just means being prepared. Unfortunately, many of us as individuals think we're immune to bad things happening. Bad things can happen to anyone, but they happen a lot less if you take proper precautions.

This applies in particular to travellers, because there are an awful lot of things that can go wrong when you are outside your familiar environment. Worst-case scenarios include things like having an accident in your hire car, leaving all your valuables in a taxi, being stranded by a natural disaster, or realizing you aren't covered by your insurance following an accident. The following tips are from people – travel agents, guidebook writers and embassy officials – who routinely deal with these situations and help people to avoid them.

LISTENING Travel advice

3 🎧 **7** Listen to two people giving advice for two of the worst-case scenarios described in the article. Make notes for each scenario using these headings.

  1 The worst-case scenario mentioned
  2 Preventative measures
  3 Actions in the event of this happening

4 🎧 **7** Listen to the advice again and look at the expressions in the Useful language box. Tick (✓) the expressions the speakers use. How do they complete these expressions?

GIVING AND JUSTIFYING ADVICE

Giving advice

Be aware that … / Be aware of …
For your own peace of mind, …
Take time to …
…-ing … is also advisable / a good idea.
Opt for … / Choose … over …
Avoid …-ing
I'd (strongly) advise against …-ing
The best thing is to …
In the event that / In the event of …
Consider …-ing …

Justifying advice

The chances are that …
It may be helpful if / when …-ing
It can be invaluable when …-ing
That way, you'll / you won't …
That will ensure that …

Pronunciation Consonant clusters

5 🎧 **8** How do you think the underlined consonant clusters are pronounced? Discuss with a partner. Then listen and check.

al**th**ough	a**sk**ed	chan**g**ed	clo**thes**	cri**sps**
ex**pl**ain	fi**fth**	hel**pf**ul	len**gth**y	mon**ths**
si**xth**	**spl**ash			

SPEAKING Giving advice

6 Work in pairs. Choose two of the scenarios (1–4) on page 27. Decide on your roles and act out the conversations.

Conversation 1: Advise the other person about how to minimize the risk of this situation happening

Conversation 2: Help someone to deal with the situation when this has happened

Scenarios

1 Someone overcharging you for something you have bought (e.g. a shop owner and a customer)
2 Your hotel cancelling your reservation (e.g. a hotel receptionist and a guest)
3 Having an accident in your hire car
4 Getting bitten by a disease-carrying insect

7 Work with a new partner. Act out two more conversations. Then discuss what the most useful advice was that you received.

WRITING An account of an incident

8 Read this account from an online travel forum of escaping a tricky situation. How did the writer get out of the situation? Did he follow any of the advice you heard in Exercise 3 on page 26?

 Three weeks ago I was returning from a business trip in Krakow in Poland. It was a Friday and I was supposed to be back in London for my sister's wedding the following day. Ironically, I was originally going to come back on the Thursday because my Friday meeting had been cancelled, but I thought it would be more relaxing to stick to my original schedule. What a mistake! Overnight, it snowed very heavily and I woke to a thick blanket of snow. I telephoned the airport immediately to see what the situation was. They told me that no flights would be taking off until the morning after at the earliest.

At that point I went into military mode. My only concern was how I was going to get back in time for the wedding. What were my options? Obviously, I couldn't hire a car. It was an eighteen-hour drive to the UK even in good conditions. I went online and researched the weather situation at other airports. Warsaw, Poznań and Berlin all had the same problems. Knowing that the cheaper airlines flew to more obscure places, I checked their websites. Luckily, Ryanair had a flight that evening from Ostrava to London. Ostrava was only 160 kilometres away and, amazingly, the flight was only £20. With my heart in my mouth, I picked up the phone and called Ostrava airport. Yes, flights were operating as normal and the road to the airport was clear.

I rang hotel reception and asked them to find a taxi that could take me to Ostrava. Imagine my joy when they said that two other people had made the same request and that a taxi would be coming in half an hour. Better still, we could share the cost. Not only was I going to get home in time, but I would have company on the journey too.

QUOTE

9 In the account, the writer gives his opinion about certain events by using comment adverbs and phrases. Look at the example in bold. Find four more comment adverbs and phrases in the account and discuss with your partner what each one means.

Ironically, I was originally going to come back on the Thursday because my Friday meeting had been cancelled.'

Writing skill Future in the past

10a Work in pairs. Look at the example of the future in the past. Then find eight more examples of future in the past in the account in Exercise 8.

*Ironically, I **was** originally **going to come** back on the Thursday because my Friday meeting had been cancelled.* (= It was my intention to come back on Thursday.)

See page 78 for more information on future in the past, and do Exercises 5 and 6.

10b Complete the sentences using the verbs in brackets in a form of the future in the past. Then compare answers with your partner.

1 She _____ (come) with us but she changed her mind.
2 The plane _____ (take off) at 7.00, but it was delayed.
3 I thought the taxi _____ (be) expensive, but it turned out to be very reasonable.
4 I expected that he _____ (wait) at the station when I arrived.
5 The insect repellent _____ (be) effective against mosquitoes, but it wasn't.

10c How are these times reported in the future in the past in the account?

1 tomorrow
2 on Thursday
3 tomorrow morning
4 this evening

11 **21st CENTURY OUTCOMES**
Write a similar account about a bad travel experience and how you dealt with it. Use one of the situations you discussed in Exercises 6 and 7, one of the topics below or your own experience. Write 200–300 words.

1 arriving at a hotel to find that they haven't finished building it yet
2 getting on an overnight train to the wrong destination

12 Work in pairs. Exchange your accounts. Use these questions to check your partner's report.

- Is the sequence of events clearly described?
- Does the account use the future in the past correctly?
- Does it include some comment adverbs?

READING

1 Read the article about Pixar. Answer the questions.

  1 What is Pixar's current status in relation to Disney?
  2 What single idea is at the heart of Pixar's philosophy of successful creativity?
  3 How does the company guard against the risk of failure?
  4 In what way has the company physically encouraged interaction between staff?
  5 What does 'the trap of becoming a world unto itself' mean?

VOCABULARY Idioms with *back*

2 Look at the expression *on the back of* (line 2) from the article. Choose the correct meaning (i–iii). Then match the expressions with *back* (1–10) with their meanings (a–j).

  i following on from   ii even in spite of   iii as a reward for

  1 turn your back on
  2 go back on your word
  3 go behind someone's back
  4 put it on the back burner
  5 turn back the clock
  6 take a back seat
  7 know something like the back of your hand
  8 get your own back
  9 go back to the drawing board
  10 be laid back

  a be very familiar with something
  b return to an earlier time
  c start a plan or project from the beginning again
  d break a promise
  e refuse to help
  f take revenge
  g act without consulting someone (often deceitfully)
  h be relaxed
  i have a less active role
  j leave for later (while you concentrate on other things)

3 Complete the sentences with expressions from Exercise 2. Use the appropriate form.

  1 I'm going to _____ in the meeting – it's your idea and you're best placed to make the case for it.
  2 A lot of people find fame difficult to handle but he _____ about it.
  3 One leading critic who was not invited to the official launch of the film _____ by writing a negative review later on.
  4 You can't _____. The economy has changed and we need to adapt to the new environment.
  5 The government made certain financial commitments to pensioners before the election, but now they have _____ and _____ them.
  6 The advertisement we created wasn't approved by the management, so we need to _____ .
  7 My colleague _____ and told my boss that I had applied for a new job.

PIXAR
– AN EXERCISE IN NURTURING CREATIVITY

Pixar is the world's leading computer animation studio. On the back of its box office successes, such as *Toy Story* (1995) and *Finding Nemo* (2003), it was bought by Walt Disney studios – already a film-making partner – in 2006 in a deal worth over US$7 billion. Yet Pixar remained an independent entity, true to its own principles of creative enterprise.   5

Pixar believes that creativity is not about single original ideas; it's a collaborative effort made by a community of people who trust and get on with each other. Movies contain thousands of ideas – about characters, sets, dialogue, lighting, pacing – and each participant must contribute suggestions that will collectively make it a success. So a community of 'good people' is key to Pixar's philosophy. As its founder, Ed Catmull, says, 'a mediocre team can make a mess of a good idea, whereas a great team can make a success of a mediocre idea.'   10   15

But, inevitably, creativity is also about taking risks and because of the enormous costs involved in making a movie, there is always a tension between original creative expression and copying ideas that have been known to deliver commercial success. Pixar's solution to this dilemma is to follow the principle that management is not there to prevent risk but only to ensure that the company's financial recovery is possible if a particular project should fail.   20   25

So Pixar creates an environment where it's safe to have ideas, breaking down barriers between employees and management. Its offices contain large communal spaces where people can bump into each other regularly and have free and open exchanges. To avoid the trap of becoming a world unto itself, it also urges employees to keep an eye on technological innovations in the academic community and on how people are using technology in the wider world. In the words of its Chief Creative Officer, John Lasseter, 'Technology inspires art, and art challenges the technology.'   30   35

GRAMMAR

4 Choose the correct options to complete the summary about animated films.

There ¹ *was / has been* a steady rise in the popularity of animated films ² *over / since* the last fifteen years. Among the top thirty most popular films in the world in 2011, one ³ *in / of* four were animated films. Although a significant ⁴ *element / proportion* of the top thirty films (23%) ⁵ *were / have been* produced outside the USA, all of the animated films were American. *Avatar* has been the highest grossing film (US$2.7 billion) ⁶ *already / to date.* Some say it is not a true animation film, because the makers ⁷ *have used / used* motion capture and CGI (Computer Generated Imagery) when it ⁸ *has been / was being* made. In fact, in the last ⁹ *little / few* years, the ¹⁰ *vast / enormous* majority of action and adventure films have been made using these techniques.

5 Complete the text about Pixar's future with these words.

about to	bound	is going to produce	is to
likelihood	may well	will	will be producing

We've already got *Toy Story 1, 2, 3* and *4* and in all ¹ _____ we will see a *Toy Story 5*. Sequels of other Pixar successes like *Cars* and *Finding Nemo* are also ² _____ to come out. But at what point does the public get tired of sequels? If Pixar ³ _____ realize its founder's ambition – that Pixar ⁴ _____ films long after he is gone – it will need fresh titles too. But this ⁵ _____ be its (and Disney's) thinking: that if it ⁶ _____ creative new films, these will have to be funded by material that is known to work. Is this a risky strategy? Time ⁷ _____ tell. For now it seems to be working, but it doesn't take into account that another innovative film studio could be ⁸ _____ make a breakthrough.

VOCABULARY

6 Choose the correct options to complete the two personal accounts about working in film.

A

'I took ¹ *up / in* filmmaking at college. I had always wanted to come at it from a different ² *side / angle*, to break ³ *out of / with* convention. So when I met Amir at college and saw what he was doing with computers, I thought, 'This is it. If we can use this technology in films, ⁴ *the sky's / the stars are* the limit.' So we set out to make our first animation film together. It was a leap in the ⁵ *dark / night*, but it was very exciting.'

B

'I never meant to get into film work. I had actually ¹ *pinned / nailed* my hopes on becoming a stage actor and I had ² *directed / devoted* myself to achieving that goal. But my hopes were ³ *dashed / devastated* when I failed to get into drama school. Luckily I was living with someone who came

⁴ *up / out* with the idea of making our own short film about life as students and putting it online. It was a ⁵ *flare / flash* of inspiration, because very quickly the first film went viral.'

SPEAKING

7 Work in pairs. For Pixar, the key to creativity lies in collaboration. In what areas of your work, studies or interests do you like collaborating with people? When would you rather be independent? Give reasons.

8 In Pixar's films, toys, fish and cars are given human characteristics and have feelings. Think about an idea for a new animated film which gives human characteristics to something non-human. Then take turns to present your ideas. Try to develop / improve on them with collaboration.

IMPROVE YOUR WRITING Sequencing words and connectors

9 Read the account. Look at the underlined sequencing words, connecting words and comment adverbs. Correct or improve them where necessary.

¹ The last summer we booked a two-week holiday in Greece through a travel agent. ² In the first place we were going to book our flights and hotel directly, ³ like we usually do, ⁴ but my husband thought using a package holiday operator would be easier and ⁵ with the addition cheaper. How wrong he was! ⁶ Even the flight itself wasn't luxurious, ⁷ nevertheless it was reasonably comfortable and, ⁸ with good luck, it arrived on time. ⁹ However, from this moment, things went downhill. ¹⁰ Once the plane arrived at two in the morning, there was no bus waiting to transfer us. It had broken down and we had to wait two hours for a relief bus. ¹¹ When it arrived ¹² at the end, I refused to get on it, ¹³ because of it looked so ancient and unsafe. ¹⁴ Instead, we waited until the car hire firm opened at 8.00 a.m. and ¹⁵ after we booked our own transport.

RATING ★   POSTED **2 days ago**   COMMENTS **9**

10 Work in pairs. Compare your edited versions of the account in Exercise 9. Did you make the same changes?

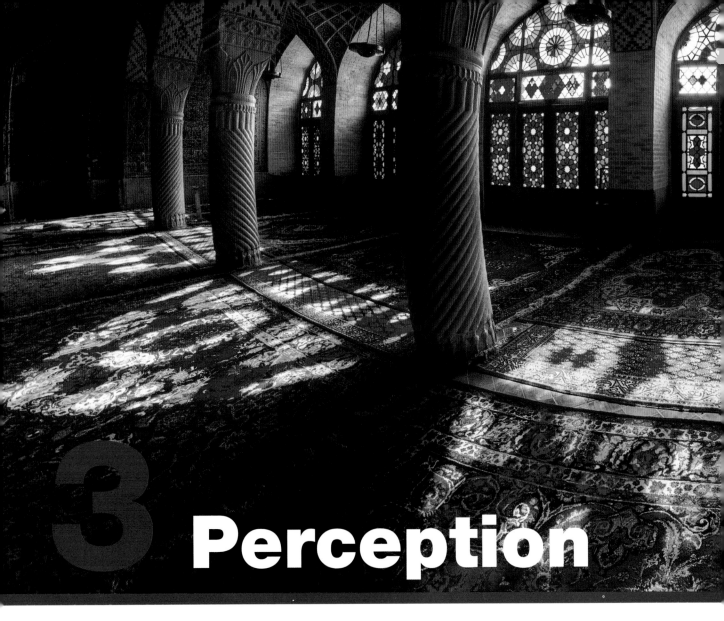

3 Perception

BACKGROUND

1 You are going to watch a TED Talk by Julian Treasure called *The 4 ways sound affects us*. Read the text about the speaker and the talk. Then work in pairs and discuss the questions.

   1 What does Julian Treasure do and what qualifies him to do this?
   2 What is meant by the term 'aural matters'?

3 How do you think sounds affect people – both positively and negatively – in a) offices and b) shops?

TEDTALKS

JULIAN TREASURE is the chair of the Sound Agency, a firm that advises worldwide businesses – offices, retailers, hotels – on how to use sound. He is also the author of the book *Sound Business* and keeps a blog by the same name that discusses aural matters. Before he started his current company, Julian Treasure founded the magazine publishing group, TPD, a business he grew and later sold in 2003. Even earlier in his career, he worked as a drummer for the band *Transmitters*.

Julian Treasure's idea worth spreading is that sound can have a subtle but profound effect on our feelings and behaviour.

Stained glass windows,
Nasir Al-Mulk Mosque,
Shiraz, Iran

KEY WORDS

2 Read the sentences (1–6). The words in bold are used in the TED Talk. First guess the meaning of the words. Then match the words with their definitions (a–f).

1 It's natural to try to **suppress** our negative feelings and focus on the positives.
2 Your body releases cortisol (the stress hormone) as a **fight-flight** response.
3 My Internet has limited **bandwidth**, so the connection keeps getting interrupted.
4 What are the **drivers** of consumer behaviour?
5 When you say one thing and do another, you are not being **congruent** with your values.
6 Every day we are **bombarded** with hundreds of advertising messages.

a in agreement or harmony
b keep down or stop the growth of something
c things that motivate you to act
d the reaction the body has to fear: to attack or to run away
e the amount of data that can be transmitted through a communications channel
f attacked constantly

AUTHENTIC LISTENING SKILLS
Understanding fast speech

The number one reason non-native speakers give for finding authentic listening difficult is speed. Ideas come so fast that it's difficult to keep up. How do you deal with this?

- Make predictions about what you are going to hear based on your own knowledge of the subject.
- Look for visual clues that will aid understanding.
- Enjoy listening: be relaxed and get what information you can without worrying about what you miss.
- Ask questions about what you have heard. If you can't ask the speaker themselves, ask another listener.

3a 🎧 9 Look at the Authentic listening skills box. Read Julian Treasure's idea worth spreading again. Then listen to the introduction to his talk and note down the key ideas you hear.

3b Work in pairs and compare your notes from Exercise 3a. Did Julian Treasure say what you were expecting to hear? Ask questions to get more information.

3c 🎧 9 Answer the questions. Listen again and check.

1 What is Julian Treasure going to do in the next five minutes?
2 What does he say about most of the sounds we hear?

3.1 The 4 ways sound affects us

TEDTALKS 🏠 Watch at home

1 ▶ **3.1** Watch the TED Talk. Write down the examples of sounds that Julian Treasure includes in his talk. Then categorize the sounds into these areas (a–c).

a pleasant sounds
b unpleasant sounds
c powerful sounds

2 ▶ **3.1** Look at the table below. Then watch the first part (0.00–2.55) of the talk again. Complete the table.

3 ▶ **3.1** Complete the sentences with these adjectives. Then watch the second part (2.55–4.10) of the talk again and check your answers.

| dramatic | dreadful | fast |
| hostile | inappropriate | powerful |

1 Most retail sound is _____ and accidental, and even _____.
2 Sound has a _____ effect on sales.
3 Retailers are losing up to thirty per cent of their business with people leaving because the sound is so _____.
4 Music is the most _____ sound there is, because our recognition of it is _____.

4 ways sound affects you	Explanation	Positive / Neutral example	Negative example
Physiologically	Sound affects our hormones, breathing, heart rate, etc.	1 _____	Alarm clock
2 _____	3 _____	4 _____	Sad music
Cognitively	5 _____	Two versions of his voice	6 _____
Behaviourally	We move away from unpleasant sounds towards pleasant ones.	***********	7 _____
			8 _____

▶ behaviour **BR ENG**
▶ behavior **N AM ENG**

▶ centre **BR ENG**
▶ center **N AM ENG**

4 ▶ **3.1** Read the questions. Then watch the third part (4.10 to the end) of the talk again and answer the questions.

   1 All brands use sound, but what do they need to use sound effectively?
   2 What does Julian Treasure suggest the Nokia ringtone is a good example of?
   3 What does Julian Treasure say that the sound a company uses should be congruent with?
   4 What are golden rules two and three for the use of commercial sound?
   Make it _____ to the situation and make it _____ .
   5 Why does Julian Treasure say companies have to test their sounds again and again?
   6 How does taking control of sound help us, according to Julian Treasure?

VOCABULARY IN CONTEXT

5 ▶ **3.2** Watch the clips from the TED Talk. Choose the correct meaning of the words.

6 ▶ **3.3** Watch the clips from the talk. Complete the collocations. Then discuss your answers.

7 Complete the sentences in your own words. Then compare your sentences with a partner.

   1 One song I associate with my childhood is …
   2 The audience left in droves when …
   3 It's difficult to predict the outcome of …
   4 The advertisement had the opposite of the desired effect, which was to …

CRITICAL THINKING Achieving aims

8 The key question for any talk or presentation is: Did the speaker achieve their aim(s)? Work in pairs and discuss the questions.

   1 Did Julian Treasure achieve his aim of making you more aware of how sound affects you?
   2 Which of the techniques that he used to do this were the most helpful for you?
      a examples of individual sounds
      b use of visuals
      c use of persuasive argument
      d use of facts / statistics
      e use of humour
   3 Which fact or example did you find most memorable? Why was this?

9 Read these comments about the TED Talk. Then answer the questions.

   1 Did Julian Treasure achieve his aims with these viewers? Why? / Why not?
   2 What could you do practically in your own daily life to 'take control of the sound around you'?

Viewers' comments

J **Julia** – This talk resonated with me. I work in a hospital where the noise pollution is extreme: constant alarms, paging on loudspeakers, the background noise of machines, etc. After a ten-hour shift I am exhausted, so I hate to think of the negative effects it has on patients who are there for days and sometimes weeks. I wish the hospital management would look at this.

S **Stefan** – I really liked this talk and I'm sure it'll make me more aware of the sounds around me. But practically speaking, I don't think I'm much the wiser about what to do about it. He gave some advice for companies on how to manage sound in a commercial environment, but I'd really have liked more tips for what individuals can do in their daily lives.

*The comments were created for this activity.

PRESENTATION SKILLS Giving shape to your talk

10 Work in pairs. Discuss different ways you can begin and end a talk. What do you think it's important to do at the beginning and end?

11 Look at the Presentation tips box. Compare your ideas from Exercise 10 with the points in the box.

> **TIPS**
>
> There are different ways to structure a talk. Whatever framework you use, think about how you will hold your audience's attention and keep them focussed on the message you want them to take away.
>
> • Begin strong. Think about how you will really grab people's attention from the start.
> • Create a need to listen. At or near the beginning of your talk, explain why you're talking about this topic and why it's important to the audience.
> • Take your audience on a journey. Give your talk a clear route from beginning to middle to end.
> • End powerfully. Summarize your main message and emphasize your emotional attachment to it.

12 ▶ **3.4** Watch the clips from the TED Talk. Which techniques in the Presentation tips box does Julian Treasure follow?

13 Work in pairs. Prepare the introduction to a talk on the topic below, following the points in the Presentation tips box. Write three to four sentences.

'Why we need designated quiet places in our lives: both at work and outside work.'

14 Work with a new partner. Take turns to give the beginning of your talk. Did you like the way your partner began? Why? / Why not? Which techniques were most successful?

▶ on holiday **BR ENG**
▶ on vacation **N AM ENG**

▶ hostile /ˈhɒstaɪl/ **BR ENG**
▶ hostile /ˈhɑst(ə)l/ **N AM ENG**

3.2 Judging by appearances

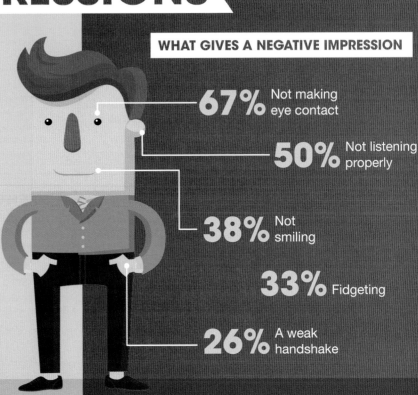

FIRST IMPRESSIONS

HOW WE MAKE FIRST IMPRESSIONS

First impressions are formed within **7–17** seconds

55% is based on a person's appearance

38% is based on quality of voice and manner of speaking

7% is based on what people actually say

WHAT GIVES A NEGATIVE IMPRESSION

67% Not making eye contact

50% Not listening properly

38% Not smiling

33% Fidgeting

26% A weak handshake

GRAMMAR Stative and dynamic verbs

1 Work in pairs. Discuss the following questions.

1 What do you pay attention to when you meet someone for the first time: their appearance, their manner of speaking, their body language? Something else?

2 Do you believe first impressions of people are a good indication of their character? Why? / Why not?

2 Look at the infographic. Summarize to your partner what matters most when we meet someone for the first time. How does this compare with your ideas from Exercise 1?

3 Read the sentences (1–6) in the Grammar box. Answer the questions (a–d).

STATIVE AND DYNAMIC VERBS

1 *Do you **think** it's wrong to make quick judgements about people? **I'm thinking** about when you meet someone for the first time.*

2 *The effectiveness of your speech **depends** less on what you **say** and more on how you say it.*

3 *I**'ve been meaning** to do something about my appearance for a long time. I **don't own** any smart clothes and wearing a suit, for example, **means** you want people to take you more seriously.*

4 *If you don't listen properly, you **are being** disrespectful to the other person.*

5 *Some people **are** always **fidgeting**. It **seems** they're not interested or want to get away.*

6 *His handshake was really strong. It **felt** as if he **needed** to show how powerful he was.*

a Which of the verbs in bold are almost always used in the simple form?

b Look at sentences 1 and 3. What are the different meanings for the simple and continuous forms of a) *think* and b) *mean*?

c In sentence 4, how would the meaning change if the speaker used *are* instead of *are being*?

d In sentence 5, what is the speaker expressing by using the continuous form with *always*?

Check your answers on page 80 and do Exercises 1–3.

4 Work in pairs. Choose the correct form of the verb in these sentences. Where both are possible, say what the difference in meaning is.

1 [a] *Are you / Are you being* judgemental if you form a firm impression of someone in the first few minutes of meeting them? [b] *I don't think / I'm not thinking* so. It's just something we [c] *all do / are all doing* naturally, whether you [d] *like / are liking* it or not.

2 Have you [a] *wondered / been wondering* what impression your online profile photos give? If not, you should, because it [b] *appears / is appearing* that we're very consistent in our reactions to certain characteristics. A smiling face [c] *means / is meaning* someone is approachable; a strong jawline that you [d] *are / are being* a dominant type.

3 It's funny to think that when you got dressed this morning, you [a] *already made / were already making* a personal statement about how you [b] *wanted / were wanting* people to perceive you. [c] *I don't own / I'm not owning* any particularly smart or fashionable clothes and [d] *I suppose / I'm supposing* that says something about me!

4 'First impressions really count' is such nonsense! People [a] *always come / are always coming* up with stuff like this, claiming they [b] *have / are having* scientific proof to show that it's valuable life advice. But it's not. It just reflects the age we [c] *live / are living* in where style [d] *becomes / is becoming* more and more important and the things that really matter less and less important.

5 Complete the conversations. Use these verbs of perception in the correct tense.

feel	look	seem	sound	taste

1 A: How about meeting at 7.00?
B: Yes, that _____ perfect.

2 A: Are you going to Morocco for your holiday?
B: No, the flights were too expensive. It _____ like we'll be driving to Italy instead.

3 A: Why did you follow his advice?
B: Well, it _____ like a good idea at the time.

4 A: Are you hungry?
B: Yes, I _____ a little peckish now.

5 A: Have you started eating already?
B: No, I _____ (just) the soup.

LANGUAGE FOCUS Emphatic structures

6 Look at the example sentences (a–b). Which sentence is more emphatic? Match the two halves of each sentence to make emphatic forms.

> **a** Her incredible energy strikes you.
> **b** What strikes you is her incredible energy.
>
> *See page 80 for more information about emphatic structures, and do Exercise 4.*

1 What strikes you	**a** strikes you.
2 It is her incredible energy	**b** particularly striking.
3 Her incredible energy is	**c** that strikes you.
4 Her incredible energy	**d** strikes you is her incredible energy.
5 Her incredible energy is what	**e** is her incredible energy.
6 The thing that	**f** really does strike you.

7 Rewrite the sentences using emphatic structures. Use the words given.

1 I like the way he always tries to include everyone. (thing)
2 She made a big impression on everyone at the meeting. (did)
3 The fact that he can switch so easily from one language to another is amazing. (what)
4 The blueness of his eyes is very striking. (it)
5 Her manner is abrupt, but actually she's very nice. (particularly)
6 People like that annoy me. (it)

SPEAKING Impressions and judgements

8 *21st* **CENTURY OUTCOMES**

Work in pairs. Look at the list of things below that you might have judged on a first impression. Choose two of them and describe what your first impression was and whether it turned out to be right or wrong.

- a person that you met
- a company or organization that you dealt with
- a building or environment that you worked in
- a country or place that you visited
- a food or a dish that you ate

9 Work with a new partner. Compare your experiences. Were your first impressions accurate or did you make a judgement too quickly? What lesson do you learn from this?

3.3 Lights, music, action

READING Multi-sensory marketing

1 Work in pairs. Look at the title of the article and answer the questions.

1 What methods do retailers use to make products more appealing to customers in shops or online (e.g. special displays)?
2 What do you think multi-sensory marketing means?

2 Read the article. What is the author saying about companies' attitudes to the following?

1 the role of multi-sensory experiences in the retail environment
2 their high street shops
3 online retail

3 Read the article and answer the questions. According to the author:

1 Why is it surprising that multi-sensory marketing is not used more commonly?
2 In a shop, what three things does sensory experience affect?
3 What is the phrase used to describe physical shops in a retail business?
4 Why do retailers seem to prefer the online sales channel?
5 What is the next logical step for the multi-sensory experience?

4 Find words and phrases in the article with the following meanings.

1 failing to take advantage of something (para 1)
2 a published piece of research (para 2)
3 raised (para 3)
4 very importantly (para 4)
5 were successfully aimed (para 4)
6 a thing which is much sought after (para 5)

5 Work in groups. Discuss the possible reasons for the following causes and effects. Would they have the same effect on you?

- slow music ➔ higher restaurant bills
- comfortable chairs ➔ poor negotiating
- eating in the dark ➔ increased restaurant bookings
- pleasant fragrances ➔ increased intention to buy
- dim lighting ➔ increased traffic through the shop of young people

VOCABULARY Feelings and emotions

6 Read the sentence from the article. Find a synonym for *soothing* from box B. Then match the other adjectives in box A with adjectives with a similar meaning in box B.

'The average restaurant bill was 29 per cent higher when slow, **soothing** music was played to diners.'

A

disconcerting	distracting	energizing	infuriating
irresistible	reassuring	rousing	soothing
tempting			

B

comforting	compelling	enticing	maddening
off-putting	relaxing	stimulating	stirring
unsettling			

7 Work in pairs. Discuss the questions, using words from Exercise 6. There may be more than one possible answer.

What adjectives describe the feelings that are evoked by:
1 a country's national anthem at a sporting occasion?
2 the smell of freshly baked bread as you pass a shop?
3 the sound of someone tapping their fingers on the table?
4 the warmth of your own bed?
5 being in a country where you can't read the language?
6 overhearing other people's phone conversations on the bus?
7 a cold shower?
8 the sound of a running stream?

8 Choose three of the adjectives from Exercise 6 and think of other things (sounds, sights, smells, etc.) that evoke these feelings for you. Describe them to your partner.

SPEAKING Creating attractive spaces

9 **21st CENTURY OUTCOMES**

Work in small groups. Look at the following profiles of two different shops and design a multi-sensory environment for them. Think about sights, sounds, smells, etc. and what kind of customers the shop is targeting.

Shop 1: called Fiji. It sells practical objects for the home and home office, e.g. cooking utensils, furniture, stationery. The emphasis is on simple design and natural materials like wood and paper.

Shop 2: called Gametime. It sells video games of different types: sports games, adventure games, puzzle-solving games, etc.

10 Present your ideas to another group. Compare the different elements and discuss which ideas you think work best.

Multi-sensory MARKETING

Much of the conversation that a company has with its customers is conducted through words and images. This is nothing new and it has only been reinforced by the rising share that online sales now play in retail, online being essentially a visual experience. But there is a growing realization among marketers that by ignoring the part that the other senses can play in promoting sales – touch, smell, taste and hearing – companies are missing an important trick.

The use of multi-sensory marketing is much less widespread than one would imagine given that persuasive research into its influence on customer behaviour has existed for some time. As long ago as 1982, Ronald E Milman found a striking link between the music played in retail environments and sales. In his paper 'The Influence of Background Music on the Behaviour of Restaurant Patrons' Milman showed that the average restaurant bill was 29 per cent higher when slow, soothing music was played to diners compared to when the background music was fast. A similar trial in a supermarket yielded even better results.

There is more recent compelling evidence. The *Harvard Business Review* produced a report in 2010 showing that people negotiating the price of a car offered 28 per cent more if they were sitting in a soft, comfortable chair rather than a hard, uncomfortable one. A London restaurant Le Noir saw an increase in bookings when they launched their 'eat in the dark' experience. The idea was that the diners' appreciation of the food's taste and smell would be heightened if visual stimuli were removed.

When it comes to visiting a store, a customer's sensory experience will determine how long they stay, what their feelings are while they are there, and crucially, how much they spend. Nike found that the introduction of pleasant fragrances in the stores increased a customer's intention to buy by as much as 80 per cent. Las Vegas slot machine players spent 45 per cent more in a scented environment than when placed in an unscented one. Clothing company Abercrombie & Fitch also exploit sensory stimuli, using loud music, dim lighting and strong scents in their shops. These features may sound unappealing if, like me, you are in your forties, but with their target market of younger adolescents, they clearly hit the mark.

But there is a wider issue here than simply the use of novel marketing tools. What all this shows us is that too many retailers are underestimating the value that the 'bricks and mortar' side of their business can bring. The sorry state of some of our town centres bears witness to this. Too many businesses view stores as a sales channel just like any other – but one with high attendant costs. Some are even so convinced that the online sales channel is the optimal route, that they model their stores on the customer's online experience. But instead of rushing towards the low-cost holy grail of e-commerce, big brands could be focussing on enticing customers back to the high street with an exciting multi-sensory experience. That could be an attractive proposition, for retailers and consumers alike.

In future this multi-sensory experience will extend beyond the retail environment, believes Charles Spence, a psychology professor from Oxford University, who has helped British Airways develop a music playlist to accompany its in-flight meals. He says that a lot of brands are looking for ways to bring the experience right into consumers' homes. 'Everyone now is selling experience,' he says. 'In five years' time,' he says, 'when you go into a wine store … you'll be able to scan the label on the bottle and get the matching music for your wine.'

3.4 Contrary to popular belief

READING Not what they seem

1 Work in pairs. What do you think are the benefits and drawbacks (to the company and employees) of open-plan offices?

2 Read the extract from an article. Compare your answers from Exercise 1 with the ideas in the article.

LISTENING The reality of the situation

3 🎧 **10** Listen to a conversation between two friends about noise and concentration. Does the first speaker agree with the view about noise levels in the article? What examples does she give to support this?

Not
what they seem

Much loved by bean-counters for their efficient use of space, the idea of open-plan offices was originally conceived in Germany in the 1950s as a way to facilitate communication and the flow of ideas. They are still very common today, but contrary to popular belief, it seems their benefit to worker interaction and productivity is largely symbolic. Recent studies have found that open-plan spaces on the whole have detrimental effects on workers' well-being and productivity, causing problems of low attention span, low creativity and low motivation, not to mention high levels of stress.

But topping these psychological factors is a far more serious physical problem. No, not just the increased risk of the spread of germs from the shared air people breathe, but the issue of noise. As we all know from experience, high noise levels do not help clear thinking.

bean counters company accountants

4 🎧 **10** Listen to the conversation again. Answer the questions.

1 According to the first speaker, what do people generally assume is the best thing for concentration?
2 Why don't young people need peace and quiet to concentrate?
3 Why does the woman's friend have trouble working at her computer?
4 According to the second speaker, what do people believe about the surrounding noise in open-plan offices?
5 What do the woman's neighbours say about their method of getting their baby to sleep?

5 🎧 **10** Listen to the conversation again. Tick (✓) the expressions in the Useful language box that the speakers use to talk about beliefs and facts.

DESCRIBING BELIEFS AND FACTS

Describing beliefs

You would think / imagine that …
Conventional wisdom is that …
The popular belief (now) is that …
On the face of it …
Ostensibly, …
It seems that …
… gives the impression of …
… gives the outward appearance of …
Supposedly, … / Apparently, … / Allegedly, …

Describing facts

But actually / in fact / in reality / in point of fact …
But that's (simply) not the case …
Whereas actually, …
The (sad / painful) truth is that …
If truth be told …
Behind the surface lies …

Pronunciation Stress in contrasts

6a 🎧 **11** Look at the sentences. The two clauses in each sentence present contrasting ideas. Underline the two stressed words in each clause. Then listen and check.

1 It seems cheap, but in fact it isn't.
2 You'd think it would be easy, but in reality it's quite difficult.
3 They say sugar is bad for you, but actually you need sugar.
4 On the face of it he seemed calm, but I don't think he was.

6b Work in pairs. Practise saying the sentences with the same stress.

SPEAKING Describing beliefs and facts

7 Work in pairs. Look at the two ideas (a–b) that are commonly believed to be true. Then follow the steps (1–2).

  a Stress is bad for your health and productivity.
  b Listening to sad music makes you sad.

Student A: Turn to page 89 and read the information.
Student B: Turn to page 94 and read the information.

  1 Read the information carefully and prepare to talk about the beliefs and facts. Think of examples to support the information.
  2 Act out a conversation about the commonly believed ideas. Use the expressions in the Useful language box on page 38 to help you.

WRITING A response to a proposal

8 A company has asked its employees for their views on a proposal to convert the office space into open-plan areas. Read one employee's response and answer the questions.

  1 What is the writer's point of view?
  2 Underline four sentences where the writer presents their view subjectively and circle one sentence where the writer presents an objective fact. Give reasons for your answers.

> From a financial perspective, I completely understand why the company is considering this change to an open-plan office environment. Personally, however, I am far from convinced that its benefits outweigh these savings. Studies show that, as far as social relations are concerned, open environments are a positive thing inasmuch as they foster greater interaction between people. What is far from clear is a) whether those interactions boost productivity and b) whether or not an open-plan office is the only way to achieve this goal. I suspect that the same results could be attained just as easily by providing a few extra communal spaces – for example, comfortably furnished coffee areas. For this reason, I would prefer it if the company first experimented with some smaller-scale measures in creating open-plan spaces, before committing wholesale to the idea.
>
> Lastly, whatever decision is reached ultimately, it is very important, from the point of view of good labour relations, that the measures apply equally to regular staff and to the management of the company. I imagine it would be very damaging for morale if employees thought they were being asked somehow to accept inferior conditions of work.

Writing skill Describing different perspectives

9a Look at this sentence from the response in Exercise 8. Then find three more phrases in the response that describe the perspective from which a situation is viewed.

> '**From a financial perspective**, I completely understand why the company is considering this change to an open-plan office environment.'
>
> *See page 80 for more information about describing different perspectives, and do Exercises 5 and 6.*

9b Rewrite the sentences so they include a phrase to describe perspective. Use the words in brackets. You will sometimes need to change the form.

  1 Putting a lot of people in close proximity with each other is risky. (health)
  2 People who work in offices only do 4–5 hours of efficient work per day, anyway. (individual productivity)
  3 You can't beat an open-plan office for space efficiency. (practical)
  4 Seeing everyone around you working hard can boost your motivation. (psychology)
  5 There are distinct advantages to working in a quiet concentrated manner. (statistic)

10 **21st CENTURY OUTCOMES**

A company is concerned about the effects of chemicals in cleaning and cosmetic products. It has asked staff for their views on the proposal below. Write your response to the proposal, giving both subjective and objective arguments for or against it. Write 150–200 words.

> Artificial fragrances in cosmetics and cleaning products are known to affect one in five people adversely, causing health problems such as nausea and migraines. They are particularly harmful for people with breathing conditions like asthma. Accordingly, the company is proposing a ban on the use of all scented cleaning products (soap, air fresheners, furniture polish, etc.) and on the wearing of perfume or aftershave in the office.

11 Work in pairs. Exchange your responses. Use these questions to check your partner's response.

  • Does the response clearly state their point of view?
  • Does it present subjective and objective arguments for or against the proposal?
  • Does it describe the issue from different perspectives?

4 Human interaction

BACKGROUND

1 You are going to watch an edited version of a TED Talk by Amy Cuddy called *Your body language shapes who you are.* Read the text about the speaker and the talk. Then work in pairs and discuss the questions.

   1 What is Amy Cuddy's field of study? How do you think this field of study belongs in a business school?

2 What are the different elements of nonverbal behaviour? How much of our communication is nonverbal, do you think?

3 Are there any gestures or nonverbal signals that you often use in interactions with others?

TEDTALKS

AMY CUDDY suffered a severe head injury in a car accident early in her college career, and doctors said she would struggle to fully regain her mental capacity and finish her undergraduate degree. But she proved them wrong. Today, Amy Cuddy is a professor and researcher in social psychology at Harvard Business School, where she studies how nonverbal behaviour affects people in a variety of situations – from the classroom to the boardroom.

Amy Cuddy's idea worth spreading is that you can use body language not only to change others' perceptions of you, but also how you feel about yourself.

Hong Kong commute

KEY WORDS

2 Read the questions (1–6). The words in bold are used in the TED Talk. Match the words with their definitions (a–f). Then discuss the questions with your partner.

1 Which of these **hormones** – testosterone and cortisol – is related to stress and which is related to dominance?

2 Is it wrong to **fake** being interested in what someone else is saying?

3 What is an example of a dominant **posture** that people adopt when they want to show they are in control?

4 If you see someone sitting in a **hunched** position, what do you conclude about them?

5 How would you **pose** for a photograph if you wanted to appear as a confident type?

6 Do you ever feel like an **impostor** when you go for an interview?

a chemicals in the body that regulate certain organs and emotions

b the way you hold your body when sitting or standing

c to assume a certain body position, e.g. for a picture

d with the top of your body bent forward or over

e a person who pretends to be someone they are not

f to pretend or give a false impression

AUTHENTIC LISTENING SKILLS Linking: assimilation and reduction

One feature of fast native speech is the linking together of words so that they become merged. In some cases the sounds are assimilated. This means two sounds are merged together and another sound is produced. In other combinations, sounds are also reduced or dropped.

Assimilation: 'You can wait, can't you?' sounds like 'You kn wait, kanchou?'

Reduction: 'I'm going to wait and see.' sounds like 'I'm gonna wait'n see.'

3a 🎧 **12** Look at the Authentic listening skills box. Listen to three sentences from Amy Cuddy's talk. How does she pronounce the underlined phrases?

1 So <u>I want to start by</u> offering you a free no-tech life hack.

2 But before I give it away, I <u>want to ask you to</u> <u>right now</u> do a little audit of your body.

3 So how many of you are <u>sort of making</u> yourselves smaller?

3b 🎧 **13** Listen to the next two sentences and write the words you hear. Then compare answers with your partner.

4 So _____ now.

5 _____ minutes.

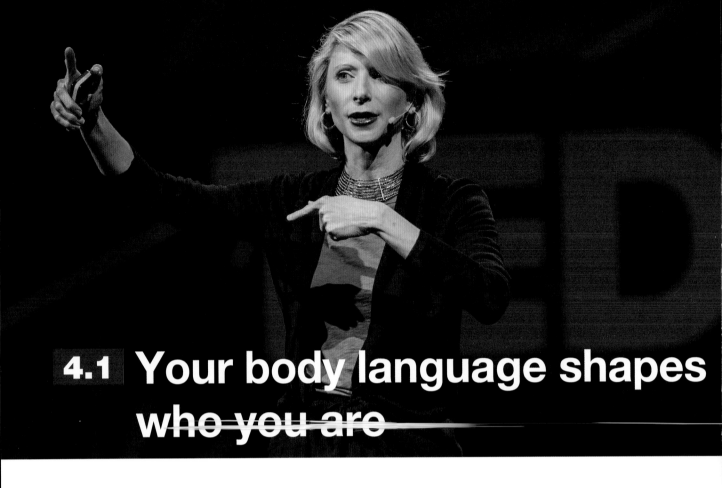

4.1 Your body language shapes who you are

TEDTALKS 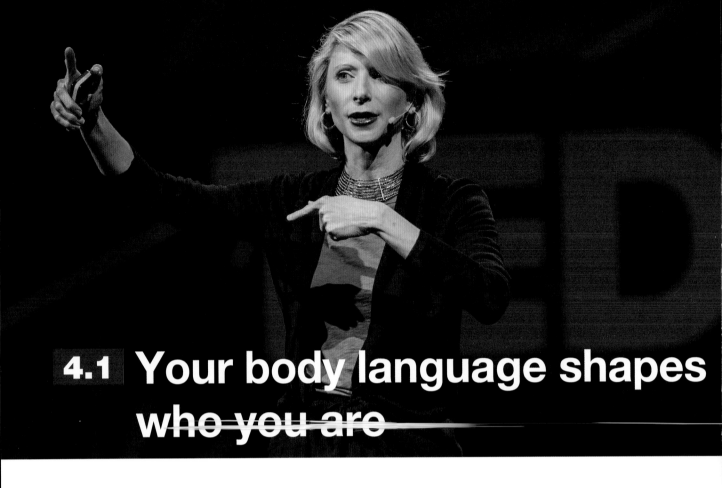 Watch at home

1 ▶ **4.1** Watch the first part (0.00–3.06) of the edited TED Talk. Answer the questions.

1 What does Amy Cuddy ask her audience to do at the beginning of the talk? Why does she do this?
2 What happened with the policeman? What unfortunate impression did it give?
3 When we think about nonverbal signals, what do we consider? What do we often forget to consider?
4 In what environment was Amy Cuddy teaching when she became interested in power dynamics?

2 ▶ **4.1** Work in pairs. Watch the second part (3.06–5.14) of the talk. Explain and demonstrate to each other the following examples of body language.

1 Animals' expressions of power and dominance.
2 The 'pride' gesture shown by all humans, even the blind.
3 How both animals and humans express powerlessness.
4 The meeting of the powerful and non-powerful.
5 Confident and unconfident students in the classroom.

3 ▶ **4.1** Watch the third part (5.14–7.36) of the talk. Complete Amy Cuddy's ideas using one word in each space. The first letter is given for you.

1 W_____ generally feel less powerful than men and this affects their p_____ in class.

2 Can people pretend to feel powerful? Can you f_____ it till you m_____ it?
3 Evidence suggests when we are forced to s_____ we feel h_____ .
4 The second question is: Can our b_____ change our minds? Can we influence our h_____ ?

4 ▶ **4.1** Read the summary. Then watch the fourth part (7.36–9.54) of the talk. Complete the facts.

In the lab, subjects were asked to adopt high and low-power poses for [1] _____ minutes at a time. The researchers took a [2] _____ sample before they did this. Then they gave the subjects an opportunity to [3] _____ : to take a risk. Then the researchers took another sample. The results were that [4] _____ per cent were prepared to take a risk after a high-power pose and [5] _____ per cent after a low-power pose. The former's testosterone increased by [6] _____ per cent, the latter had a ten per cent decrease. In cortisol, the high-power pose subjects had a 25 per cent decrease and the low-power a fifteen per cent [7] _____ . In other words, high-power pose subjects were less likely to feel [8] _____ .

▶ smart **N AM ENG**
▶ clever **BR ENG**

▶ quitting **N AM ENG**
▶ giving up **BR ENG**

▶ college **N AM ENG**
▶ university **BR ENG**

5 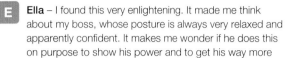 **4.1** Watch the fifth part (9.54–12.21) of the talk. Choose the correct options to complete the sentences.

1 In the next experiment subjects adopted high-power and low-power poses *before / during / after* a job interview.

2 The judges at the interview adopted *high-power / low-power / neutral* poses.

3 The coders *knew / didn't know / guessed* who had adopted which type of pose.

4 The coders chose to hire *the high-power / the low-power / both types of* posers.

5 Many people object to doing the power poses because they would feel like *fools / frauds / failures.*

6 **4.1** Watch the sixth part (12.21 to the end) of the talk. Answer the questions.

1 What happened to Amy Cuddy when she was nineteen? What was she told as a result? How did she feel?

2 How did she turn the situation around?

3 What did her advisor at Princeton say to her when Amy said she was going to quit? Did it work?

4 When Amy Cuddy's student at Harvard came to her feeling unconfident, what two things did Amy Cuddy realize?

5 What is Amy Cuddy's conclusion, which goes beyond 'fake it till you make it'?

VOCABULARY IN CONTEXT

7 **4.2** Watch the clips from the TED Talk. Choose the correct meaning of the words and phrases.

8 **4.3** Watch the clips from the talk. Complete the collocations. Then discuss your answers.

9 Complete the sentences in your own words. Then compare your sentences with a partner.

1 When giving a presentation, try to use slides that complement …

2 It's not important to me what my peers …

3 Listening to Amy Cuddy's theories has given me an opportunity to …

4 If you make a few tweaks to … , you can …

CRITICAL THINKING Avoiding misinterpretation

10 An audience may oversimplify a speaker's message or perhaps even take away the wrong message. Work in pairs. How are these statements, while true, oversimplifications of Cuddy's message?

1 Our body language is important because it shows others how we feel.

2 Power posing and faking confidence can help you, at least temporarily, through a stressful situation.

11 Read these comments* about the TED Talk. Did either of the viewers misinterpret Amy Cuddy's message, do you think? How?

Viewers' comments

E **Ella** – I found this very enlightening. It made me think about my boss, whose posture is always very relaxed and apparently confident. It makes me wonder if he does this on purpose to show his power and to get his way more often.

W **William** – Is there any link here to method acting, I wonder? It seems similar to the technique used by actors when they prepare for a role by 'living' the character they are going to play, putting themselves exactly in their mindset.

The comments were created for this activity.

PRESENTATION SKILLS Structuring a talk

12 Work in pairs. Discuss how Amy Cuddy took us on 'a journey' in her talk. Did you like the way she structured her talk? Why? / Why not?

13 Look at the Presentation tips box. What are the three ways mentioned of structuring a talk? Can you think of other ways?

TIPS

In your talk, you are taking your audience on a journey. You want to lead them from a point of not knowing about an idea to the conclusion that it is an idea well worth thinking about. Think about how you can structure the journey – from beginning through middle to end – to do this. There is not a single right way. You may choose to:

- establish your idea right at the beginning and then unpack it step by step, summarizing the idea again at the end
- create the need for an answer to a question or problem and then lead the listener to the answer nearer the end of the talk
- present certain benefits of your idea and then, when the audience has clearly got these, reveal further or greater benefits that they are unaware of

Whichever structure you choose, the important thing is to think about how the structure of your talk can a) best get your message across and b) keep the audience's attention.

14 **4.4** Watch the clip from the TED Talk. How does Amy Cuddy bring us to the end of the journey?

15 Imagine you have to give a talk on 'How I managed to learn English'. Write a short outline plan of the 'journey' you can take your audience on.

16 Work with a partner. Present your plan. Did your talks follow a similar structure?

▶ grad school **N AM ENG**
▶ postgraduate education **BR ENG**

▶ elevator **N AM ENG**
▶ lift **BR ENG**

▶ (bathroom) stall **N AM ENG**
▶ (toilet) cubicle **BR ENG**

4.2 How we communicate

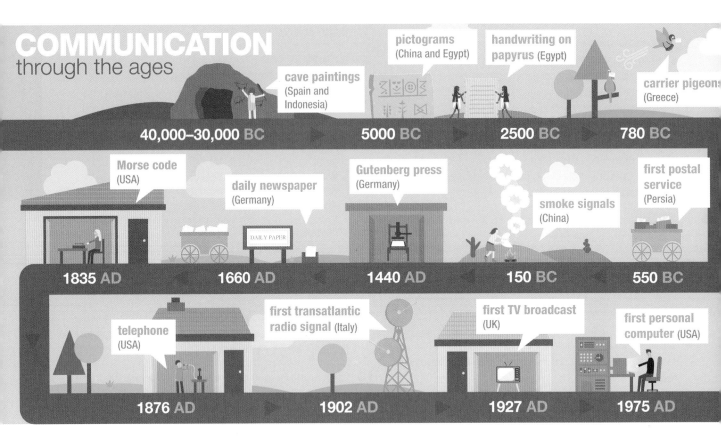

COMMUNICATION through the ages

cave paintings (Spain and Indonesia)

pictograms (China and Egypt)

handwriting on papyrus (Egypt)

carrier pigeons (Greece)

40,000–30,000 BC   5000 BC   2500 BC   780 BC

Morse code (USA)

daily newspaper (Germany)

Gutenberg press (Germany)

smoke signals (China)

first postal service (Persia)

DAILY PAPER

1835 AD   1660 AD   1440 AD   150 BC   550 BC

telephone (USA)

first transatlantic radio signal (Italy)

first TV broadcast (UK)

first personal computer (USA)

1876 AD   1902 AD   1927 AD   1975 AD

GRAMMAR Past forms

1 Work in pairs. Answer the questions.

1 How did people communicate over long distances 2,500 years ago? And 250 years ago?
2 Do you think that human interactions in the past were less satisfactory because means of communication were more limited?

2 Look at the infographic about the innovations in communication through the ages. What do you think was the particular significance of each innovation?

cave paintings = perhaps the first time people recorded their ideas for others to look at

3 🎧 **14** Listen to a short description of the history of communication. Answer the questions.

1 Which mediums of communication from the infographic does the speaker mention?
2 In what way does the speaker say each invention was significant?

4 Read the sentences (1–7) in the Grammar box. Answer the questions (a–e).

PAST FORMS

1 *The real revolution in written communication **came with** the invention of the printing press in 1440 AD.*
2 *40,000 years ago people in Spain and Indonesia **were making** paintings on the walls of caves.*
3 *They conveyed messages far more quickly than people **had been** able to do before.*
4 *Up until then, people **had been reading** handwritten documents.*
5 *Horse riders **used to carry** documents from one posting station to another.*
6 *They **would cover** distances of 2,000 kilometres or more.*
7 *That **must have been** an extraordinary time.*

a Which two sentences describe past actions that happened or were happening at a time even further in the past than the main action / event?
b Which sentence describes a single completed event in the past?
c Which sentence describes a continuing event at a particular time in the past?
d Which two sentences describe a habitual or repeated action in the past? Which of the two past forms used in these sentences cannot be used with stative verbs?
e Which sentence uses a modal verb to speculate about a past event?

Check your answers on page 82 and do Exercises 1–3.

5 Complete the history of the telephone exchange with the correct past tense form of the verb.

Not long after the invention of the telephone, a Hungarian engineer, Tivadar Puskas, [1] _____ (come) up with the idea for a telephone exchange while he [2] _____ (work) for the famous American inventor, Thomas Edison.

People [3] _____ (use) the telegraph system to send telegrams to each other since the 1850s, so the commercial potential of the telephone [4] _____ (be) apparent to all. But, in spite of that, people [5] _____ (not / seem) to appreciate the potential of a telephone switchboard. Instead, in the early days, companies [6] _____ (lease) pairs of phones to subscribers so that they could connect just to each other. But the use of multiplex exchanges [7] _____ (change) all that and by 1904 over three million telephone users [8] _____ (make and receive) calls to various points all over the United States. So strong was the telephone exchange's impact that by the end of the century almost every home had a phone.

6 Work in pairs. Talk about three ways in which you, your parents and / or your grandparents communicated with different people in the past.

When I was younger, I used to write letters to my grandmother because she liked receiving them.

LANGUAGE FOCUS Inversion with adverbial phrases

7 Read the sentence in the box. Answer the questions (1–2).

So strong was the telephone exchange's impact that by the end of the century almost every home had a phone.

1 Where would you normally expect to see the phrase 'so strong' in this sentence? Why has it been placed in this position?

2 What is unusual about the word order in this sentence?

See page 83 for more information about inversion with adverbial phrases, and do Exercises 4–5.

8 Match the two sentence halves which use inversion with adverbial phrases.

1 **Not only** did the radio bring news to people,
2 **Only by** using fresh riders at each station
3 **Not until** smoke signals were used along the Great Wall of China
4 **No sooner** had the printing press been invented
5 **Such** was the impact of television on children

a did people realize long-distance messages could be transmitted so quickly.
b **than** more popular literature started appearing.
c **that** many parents were afraid of having one in their homes.
d it **also** brought music into everyone's homes.
e was it possible for the mail to keep moving.

9 Work in pairs. Answer the questions.

1 In which sentences in Exercise 8 does the inversion occur in the second clause?
2 What kind of word would you have to add in Sentence 5 if you substituted *such* with *so*?

10 Complete the sentences. Then compare sentences with your partner.

1 Not only did the arrival of the Internet …
2 Not until the invention of TV …
3 Only when Skype had become widespread …
4 Such is the popularity of Facebook …

SPEAKING Being hyperconnected

11 21st CENTURY OUTCOMES
In today's world many people are hyperconnected around the clock. Does this describe you? What do you find helpful and what do you dislike about being hyperconnected? Work in pairs and make a list of advantages and disadvantages.

12 Work with another pair. Discuss your lists of advantages and disadvantages from Exercise 11. Draw conclusions about what you think was better and what was not better in the past.

A: There were many more chances for misunderstandings to occur in the past because of slow communication.

B: I don't agree. Not only do misunderstandings still arise with instant messaging, they're probably more frequent, because people often write without thinking.

4.3 Negotiate better

READING Business and life lessons

1 Work in pairs. Discuss when you last negotiated with the following people. What did you negotiate and was the outcome successful? Why? / Why not?

a your employer (e.g. salary, time off, etc.) or tutor (e.g. essay deadline extension)

b a service provider (e.g. bank charges, cost of insurance, mobile phone package)

c a shop or a private seller (e.g. a discount on a product, a second-hand car)

d a friend or a loved one (e.g. where to eat out, where to go on holiday)

2 Look at the six frequently asked questions in the blog about negotiating, but don't read the answers yet. Discuss your answers to each question.

3 Read the blog and compare the answers in the blog with your answers from Exercise 2. Did you mention any of the same things? Did you think your answers or the ones in the blog were more helpful?

4 Read the sentences (1–6). Write A, B or C according to the following criteria:

A the author would probably agree
B the author would probably disagree
C there's not enough information to say what the author would think

1 If you really want something badly, just accept that you are going to have to pay a lot for it.
2 A person who just keeps repeating their position has not thought enough about potential options.
3 Silence is a useful tool because it forces the other person to expand on the reasons for their decision.
4 Asking 'What if' is a way to find out how serious the other person is about making a deal.
5 Personal negotiations are more gentle and unselfish than business negotiations, which can be tough and unprincipled.
6 Staying fairly still and expressionless will prevent the other person from reading your thoughts and feelings.

5 Find words or phrases in the blog with the following meanings.

1 ultimately (question 1)
2 not moving at all (question 2)
3 very confidently (question 2)
4 angry at being treated unfairly (question 3)
5 cause someone to speak freely (question 3)
6 essential (question 4)
7 provoke a reaction (question 5)
8 fail or begin to collapse (question 5)
9 lacking in morals or principles (question 5)
10 revealing (question 6)

VOCABULARY Body language

6 Complete the phrases (1–3) with an appropriate part of the body. Then perform each action.

1 to cross your _____ (or arms)
2 to fold your _____
3 to raise your _____

7 Work in pairs. Look at six more phrases to do with body language. Perform each action. In what situation would you do these things?

| clench your fists | drum your fingers | roll your eyes |
| shake your head | shrug your shoulders | tap your feet |

8 Match the facial expression in bold (1–6) with these emotions (a–f). Then take turns to show your partner what you think each facial expression looks like.

a pleasure   **d** pain
b displeasure   **e** amazement
c contempt   **f** boredom

1 He **winced** when his friend trod on his injured foot.
2 She **scowled** at him from across the table. How could he be so rude?
3 As she **yawned** for the third time in twenty minutes, he realized it was going to be a long evening.
4 'No, thank you,' he said, **sneering** at the offer of advice from someone he clearly thought was stupid.
5 'I think we have a deal,' Jackson said. Sarah couldn't help **grinning**.
6 He stood there **gaping**. 'How did you get here so quickly?'

9 Think of two different gestures or postures and two facial expressions that are a response to the question below. Then work in pairs and act out the gestures and facial expressions. Tell each other what you think they mean.

'So what do you think about our proposal? Are you happy to go ahead?'

SPEAKING Can I have my money back?

10 **21st CENTURY OUTCOMES**

Work in groups of three. You are going to do a negotiation.
Students A and B: You are the negotiators
Student C: You are the observer

- Read the scenario on page 47 and decide on your roles.
- The negotiators have four minutes to try to find a solution.
- After four minutes, the observer can intervene. You then have another three minutes to find a solution.

11 Work with another group and compare results. Did you reach a solution? Did you invent extra or new options to find a solution?

BUSINESS AND LIFE LESSONS

NEGOTIATION – FAQs

Q Search my blog...

Regardless of what some people might have you think, there's no single right way to negotiate, because each situation is unique. But there are a few basic principles you can follow, as you will see from my answers to the following FAQs.

#1 I see a second-hand car that I really want to buy. What's the best way to get a good deal on it and not risk letting it get away?
The trick, as one famous negotiator put it is to 'Care, really care, but not that much.' In other words, imagine you are playing a game. You want to win but at the end of the day, it's just a game. Never get too emotionally attached to something you want. If you do, you're sure to overpay for it.

#2 I'm trying to negotiate with someone, but they just keep repeating their position without budging an inch. What should I do?
At the beginning of a negotiation, you should always outline your general position – what your global interests are – and get your negotiating partner to do the same. Within this framework you can both then explore the options. So if your partner keeps bullishly asserting a specific position, gently remind them of the general goals of the negotiation, so that you can move forward on the specifics in a more principled way.

#3 I always feel uncomfortable when someone makes an offer I can't agree to. I feel like I'm either going to make them resentful of me by saying 'no' or compromise myself by half-agreeing to it. How can I respond in a way that avoids these things?
The writer, Jack Chapman, says that silence is often the best strategy in this situation. Even if the other party makes a pretty reasonable offer, say, in a salary negotiation, staying quiet can help to draw them out further, prompting them to offer more or at least to justify their position. It also gives you an appearance of being cool and calm.

#4 Is there one killer question you can use in any negotiation?
There are two, actually. One is 'What are you really hoping to get out of this?' In a formal business negotiation, you may not actually ask this one directly, but you can ask indirectly, through a series of other questions. The other indispensable question is 'What if?' as in 'What if we doubled our order?' 'What if I took the washing machine now, rather than getting you to deliver it?' 'What if we went there next summer instead?' 'What if' forces the other person to really consider and perhaps re-evaluate their position.

RECENT POSTS

> The key to writing a good presentation

> Dealing with difficult people in meetings

> Raising your online profile

> Brainfood: eating to boost your brainpower

#5 Is there any difference between negotiating with loved ones and business partners?
The big difference is that your nearest and dearest know how to push your buttons – what you really care about, what will make you angry and so on – and vice versa. The key thing is not to let either side use this knowledge to manipulate the other, because the relationship and the future of it are what are important here, not the immediate object of negotiation. A business relationship is unlikely to flounder over a single negotiation, as long as neither side resorts to unscrupulous tactics.

#6 I've read about people having certain body language signals that can give away their real feelings. Is this true?
It is true, but it works both ways. People send all sorts of signals with their bodies. If they fold their arms or cross their legs, for example, they could just be getting themselves more comfortable, but in a negotiation, more likely it's a sign that they are closing off – in other words that they didn't like something you suggested. Look out for inconsistencies in expression which betray someone's true feelings – a smiling mouth but unsmiling eyes – and certain micro-expressions – a momentary wince or a raised eyebrow. And try to avoid giving off any of these tell-tale signs yourself (easier said than done!).

SCENARIO

X bought a home cinema system (large screen, multiple speakers, controls, etc.) from a private seller, Y, for $2,000. It was six months old but new and unused and the retail price was $3,600. When X got the system home, he / she found the screen was too big for the room.

In the meantime, X has found a more suitable one on sale in a shop for $1,800. So X goes back to Y to return the system and get his / her money back. Y spent three weeks and $50 advertising the system and does not want to take it back. As it was a private sale, Y is under no legal obligation to take it back. Negotiate a solution.

4.4 Is that what you meant?

READING Getting things wrong

1 Work in pairs. What mistakes do you remember making (or others making) when you began to learn English? Were they mistakes that affected the meaning?

I thought the event went good...

"WENT WELL!"

But this year there were less people...

"FEWER PEOPLE!"

Getting things wrong

The TV news last night featured a report of a protest in London where a woman was holding up a placard saying 'Stop to arrest innocent people'. Inadvertently, the placard writer had ended up saying the exact opposite of what they had intended. Getting things slightly wrong in a language doesn't usually have such extreme consequences. Often the mistakes are just amusing: 'I put my name and address on the backside to make sure the letter didn't get lost.'; 'Kate and Jake love themselves very much.'

Fixed (and idiomatic) expressions in particular are a minefield for non-native speakers, because you have to get them exactly right. Consider these two mistakes: 'Give a ring to me sometime' and 'It's very good for you to help me.' Mistakes with English are not, of course, confined to those using it as a second language. Increasingly native speakers use language imprecisely or change grammatical forms, for example, 'If I'd have known that before …'

2 Read an extract from an article about language. Look at the five examples of language mistakes mentioned and discuss the questions with your partner.

   1 What do the sentences in the article mean as they stand?

   2 How would you correct the mistakes to give the meaning the speaker intended?

LISTENING Saying the right thing

3 🎧 **15** Choose the options that most appropriately complete the sentences. Then listen to ten short conversations and check your answers.

   1 Thanks, that's very good *for / of* you, but I can manage.

   2 OK. I'll give *her a ring / a ring to her* later.

   3 Thank you, but I really need to speak to her *in person / personally*.

   4 I don't *mind / care* really. Up to you.

   5 Yes, I'd like to *pay / pay for* the room now.

   6 Great. Eight o'clock *suits / fits* me perfectly.

   7 Oh, thank you for doing that. You *mustn't / shouldn't* have.

   8 That's kind of you, but I don't want to put you *off / out*.

   9 Oh, *that's a pity / I'm really sorry to hear that*. I hope he can find another job.

  10 If it's *on / in* your way, that'd be great, thanks.

4 Complete the questions or statements from the conversations you heard in Exercise 3. Use two words per space.

   1 Here – let me give you _____ with that suitcase.

   2 Could I possibly have a _____ with Sarah, if she's free?

   3 I'm sorry. She's _____ at the moment. Perhaps I can help you?

   4 Do you _____ round for a drink later?

   5 Hello, Sir, can I help you _____ ?

   6 When _____ meet?

   7 Thanks for the use of the car. By _____, I filled it up.

   8 Can I _____ anything from the shops?

   9 _____ . My brother lost his job yesterday.

  10 Can I _____ off at the station?

Pronunciation Appropriate intonation

5 🎧 **15** Listen to the conversations again and check your answers to Exercise 4. Notice how expressive the speakers' intonation is in their comments and responses. Practise the conversations with your partner using similar intonation.

SPEAKING Everyday conversations

6 Work in pairs. Act out the following four situations as four-line dialogues. Then make up one more of your own. Use appropriate everyday expressions and responses. Use the expressions in the Useful language box to help you.

1 You're on a bus and someone picks up your jacket and starts to put it on.

2 A friend arrives for dinner with a large box of chocolates.

3 A colleague says they will collect you from the airport when you arrive.

4 A colleague invites you out for dinner and asks where and when you'd like to eat.

EVERYDAY EXPRESSIONS

Question	Response
Can I / Let me give you a hand / a lift?	That's very kind of you, but I think I can manage.
Excuse me. That's my seat.	Oh sorry. I didn't realize.
This is just a little something to say thank you.	Oh, thank you. You shouldn't have.
I'll see Malcolm when I'm in Toronto.	Oh. Please say hello from me. / Please send him my best wishes.
Thanks so much for your help.	Not at all. / Don't mention it.
Sorry I missed your party.	Never mind. Another time.

7 Act out your dialogues in front of another pair. Discuss the differences in your dialogues.

WRITING A formal letter or email

8 Look at the guidelines for clear letter writing. Then read the letter. Match the guidelines with features of the letter. Then compare your answers with a partner.

Guidelines for clear letter writing

1 Greet the recipient warmly but correctly.

2 First establish the purpose of your communication.

3 Use bullet points for action points or points for consideration.

4 Explain further details of the situation concisely.

5 Display any instructions or directions clearly on the page.

6 Highlight the next steps.

7 End the letter by showing appreciation.

Dear Bill,

Thank you very much for your recent email expressing your concerns about the new supplier delivery scheduling system. Here is an update of where we are with it and some reassurances for the future.

- The system is in its testing phase from 11 April to 10 May. Thereafter, we aim to use feedback such as yours to iron out any glitches.

- The full working version will be up and running from 21 May.

- The system is already being used successfully by several of our competitors.

If you would like to be more closely involved in discussions around its development, you would be most welcome to join us at our supplier event at:

11 a.m. Wed February 22: Jackson Conference Centre

If you are not able to attend, please do not hesitate to contact me at any time by phone or email with your ideas or suggestions.

In the meantime, thank you once again for your comments.

Best regards

Michael

---

9 Work in pairs. What do you think the relationship is between Bill and Michael? What indicates this?

Writing skill Checking for errors

10 It is very important to check your writing for errors. Work in pairs. Look at the sentences (1–5) and identify a) the function of each sentence in a letter and b) the mistake it contains.

1 I look very much forward to hearing from you.

2 I will wait to hear what the outcome of these negotiations are.

3 Thank you for taking a time to write to me.

4 This is a brief reminder to the upcoming sales event.

5 Any suggestions for discussion topics must to be sent to …

11 **21st CENTURY OUTCOMES**

Write an email to a business colleague you know well. Include the following points. Write 150–180 words.

- Thank them for inviting you to speak to a group of their employees.

- Outline the topic(s) you will talk about and ask if this is OK.

- Say what day and time would suit you.

- Suggest a phone call to discuss it in more detail.

12 Work in pairs. Exchange emails with your partner. Check that they have included the points in Exercise 11. Then check their email for any errors.

blindekuh

A restaurant with a difference

Blindekuh (named after the game Blind Man's Buff) is a restaurant and cultural venue based in Zurich, where customers eat in complete darkness, served by waiters who are blind or partially sighted. As one of the largest private sector employers of people with visual impairments, Blindekuh helps to open minds and build understanding between those with full sight and impaired vision.

LISTENING

1 🎧 **16** Read the introduction about the restaurant Blindekuh. Then listen to a radio interview and complete the sentences using one word in each space.

1 The idea originally came from people who were working as _____ at an exhibition called 'Dialogue in the Dark'.
2 The exhibition was for _____ -sighted people.
3 Visitors to the exhibition experienced blindness in a number of _____ situations.
4 About seventy per cent of severely visually-impaired people of working age in Europe are _____ .
5 At Blindekuh, the experience of eating and _____ are greatly intensified.
6 The interviewer asks if people are scared that they might _____ their food or drink.
7 To find your _____ , you have to put your hand on the waiter's shoulder.
8 One effect of eating in the dark is that you eat more _____ than normal.

VOCABULARY Body idioms

2 Look at the phrase from the interview. Then complete the other idioms (1–10) with the correct part of the body.

'It's actually quite an **eye-opener**, if you'll forgive the expression.'

back	chest	finger	hand	head
heart	nose	thumb	tongue	tooth

1 Could you give me a _____ with this table? It's really heavy.
2 He helped us with the gardening for an hour and then said he was too tired to carry on. I didn't say anything, but I really had to bite my _____ .
3 Yes, I'd love some pudding. I've got rather a sweet _____ , actually.
4 I think it's a good rule of _____ always to confirm an appointment before turning up for it.
5 You're looking worried. Is there something that you need to get off your _____ ?
6 I didn't understand what Marcus was saying – that kind of technical detail goes straight over my _____ .
7 He's always making jokes about lawyers. It really gets my _____ up, because I'm training to become one.
8 You've put your _____ on it there. They never see the consequences of their actions.
9 No, I don't mind if you leave early today. It's no skin off my _____ .
10 She's got her _____ set on becoming an actress, but it's a very competitive world.

GRAMMAR

3 Choose the correct options to complete a customer review of the Blindekuh restaurant.

Very interesting night out! [1] *I don't think / I'm not thinking* that [2] *I'm / I'm being* disrespectful if I say that the food was not the best [3] *I've had / I've been having*, but people [4] *don't go / aren't going* to Blindekuh for the food particularly – it's the experience they [5] *want / are wanting*. For those who [6] *wonder / are wondering* what Blindekuh is, it's a restaurant where you eat in total darkness – you [7] *don't see / aren't seeing* any light at all – and are served by blind or partially-sighted people.

That makes you focus much more on sound as well as taste. I noticed that our voices [8] *got / were getting* louder and louder as the evening went on. The staff [9] *were / were being* great and by the end of the evening I [10] *really felt / was feeling* that I understood better what it was like to be them. If you are someone who [11] *always looks / is always looking* for new and interesting experiences, I [12] *definitely recommend / am definitely recommending* it.

4 Rewrite the sentences to make them more emphatic.

1 You only realize how important your senses are when you lose one of them.
Only when _____ .

2 Most people don't think about how dependent we are on our sight.
What _____ .

3 We were shown to our table the moment that we arrived.
No sooner _____ .

4 Blindekuh has been so popular that other European cities have copied the idea.
Such _____ .

5 I find it shocking that so many visually-impaired people are without regular work.
The thing _____ .

6 It was not only a great experience, but the food was tasty too.
Not only _____ .

7 You would only find this kind of practical solution to a problem in Switzerland.
Only _____ .

8 I will remember the friendliness of the waiters most.
It _____ .

VOCABULARY

5 Choose the correct verbs to complete the sentences. There are three extra verbs.

clenched	gaped	grinned	raised
rolled	scowled	shrugged	sneered
tapped	winced	yawned	

1 The security man on the door of the restaurant looked very aggressive. He _____ his fists and _____ at us.

2 I don't think she was the least bit interested in the lecture. She turned to me, _____ her eyes and then _____ as if she was about to doze off.

3 Our boss had the nerve to say that our department was lazy and good for nothing. Naomi stood there and _____ in disbelief, but Thierry just _____ his shoulders and walked away.

4 It was a good offer and it _____ a few eyebrows when he refused it – particularly as he _____ at our attempts to reach a compromise.

6 Choose the correct adjective to complete the comments about the situations in Exercise 5.

1 It was a very *unsettling / stirring* experience, because we actually thought he was going to become violent.

2 I found her attitude very *reassuring / off-putting*, because I thought what the speaker was saying was very *rousing / compelling*.

3 It was *enticing / infuriating* that nobody said anything to the boss, but it was *reassuring / disconcerting* that others were as shocked as I was.

4 It was a(n) *enticing / stimulating* offer and I can't imagine why he didn't accept it.

SPEAKING

7 Work in pairs. Answer the questions.

1 Do you like the idea of Blindekuh? Would you like to eat there? Why? / Why not?

2 Think of other experiences (e.g. concerts, food shopping) that could be made more interesting or intense for the customer by depriving them of one or more of their senses. Explain the benefits and how this could work.

IMPROVE YOUR WRITING Checking your work

8 Look at the information about checking your work. Read the letter. Then identify and correct the mistake in each sentence.

Areas where students often make mistakes:

a spelling and typing errors
b mistakes with word order
c grammatical errors
d mistakes with vocabulary and idiom use

Dear Anna

Thank you for the proposal which you sent me last week and I apologize for not answering to you sooner. I needed to consult David Williams before sending you my thinking about it.

In principal, the company is open to the idea of job-sharing. This is particularly true when it allows female employees with children to make a better balance between their work life and home life. From a financially perspective, job-sharing could also in some cases be beneficial to the company. However, in this case we are not convinced that it should make practical sense. Louise, with whom you are proposing to combine roles, has already a very heavy workload already and could not be expected to take on more work. Having said all this, we recognize that the company needs to do something to take in account your family situation. Accordingly, David has suggested to meet on Thursday at 2 p.m. in his office to discuss possible solutions. Please inform me that this suits you.

Kind regards

Beatrice

9 Work in pairs. Compare your corrections to the letter in Exercise 8. Did you find the same mistakes and did you correct them in the same way?

5 Economic resources

A new LED vegetable farm is unveiled in Tagajo, Japan

TEDTALKS

HANS ROSLING began his career as a physician, spending many years in rural Africa tracking a rare paralytic disease. He co-founded Médecins Sans Frontières, Sweden, wrote a textbook on global health, and as a professor of International Health at the Karolinska Institutet, Stockholm, initiated key international research collaborations. He is best known for his unique style of presenting economic data. He developed this style through his non-profit organization, Gapminder, with a piece of breakthrough software, which Google purchased in 2007.

Hans Rosling's idea worth spreading is that even technology that we take for granted, such as the washing machine, is important because it frees people's time for more educational and life-changing pursuits.

BACKGROUND

1 You are going to watch a TED Talk by Hans Rosling called *The magic washing machine*. Read the text about the speaker and the talk. Then work in pairs and discuss the questions.

  1 What are Hans Rosling's interests?
  2 What enables him to give distinctive presentations?
  3 Can you think of any other devices / machines apart from the washing machine that have freed people's time for more productive pursuits?

KEY WORDS

2 Read the sentences (1–6). The words in bold are used in the TED Talk. Match the words with their definitions (a–f). Then work in pairs and answer the questions.

  1 What machines or technology are you **mesmerized** by?
  2 One definition of being below the **poverty line** is not being able to afford the necessities to live a healthy life. Can you think of any other definition?
  3 Why is it important to subject economic data to close **scrutiny**?
  4 Which **fossil fuel** is the most polluting?
  5 What do you think are the main causes of child **mortality** in the world?
  6 Where in the world would you find a **favela**?

  a the point at which people are considered to be poor
  b to have your attention completely captured by something
  c material formed from ancient plants and animals (coal, oil, gas) that are burned to produce energy
  d the number of deaths
  e (from the Portuguese) an area of very poor and crowded housing
  f very close and critical examination

AUTHENTIC LISTENING SKILLS
Prediction

> Thinking about what a speaker is going to say about a topic before they speak helps you as a listener in several ways:
>
> • It gives you a reason to listen.
> • You begin to think about the topic-related vocabulary that you are going to hear.
> • You form ideas that may or may not be confirmed by the speaker.
>
> These things help before you listen, but once the speaker has begun speaking, listen carefully to what they are saying. If you continue to predict while listening, it may distract from what you are actually hearing.

3a Work in pairs. Look at the Authentic listening skills box. You are going to watch a TED Talk called *The magic washing machine*. Write four key words related to washing clothes. Then compare your words. Did you write the same words?

3b 🎧 **17** Work in pairs. Why do you think the invention of the washing machine was so significant? Discuss with your partner. Then listen to the introduction to Hans Rosling's talk and answer the questions.

  1 Does Hans Rosling give or suggest the reason why the invention of the washing machine was so significant?
  2 Did he use any of the words you wrote in Exercise 3a?

5.1 The magic washing machine

TEDTALKS 🏠 **Watch at home**

1 ▶ **5.1** Watch the TED Talk. Answer the questions.

  1 What have been the benefits of the washing machine, according to Hans Rosling?

  2 What conditions will be necessary for everyone in the world to have a washing machine?

  3 What kind of energy would Hans Rosling like to see being developed?

2 ▶ **5.1** Watch the first part (0.00–5.32) of the talk again. Answer the questions.

  1 How did Hans Rosling's grandmother wash clothes in the past?

  2 How does Hans Rosling define the world's richest and poorest in terms of daily spending?

  3 What are the four categories by which Hans Rosling differentiates the world's population? What are the 'lines' that separate them?

  4 According to Rosling, at the time of this talk how many people were still without a washing machine?

  5 How does he describe the work of washing clothes by hand?

  6 How many of his students don't use a car? And a washing machine?

3 ▶ **5.1** Watch the second part (4.38–6.40) of the talk again. Complete the sentences with the statistics Hans Rosling shares.

- Total number of people in the world: [1] _____
- Total number of fossil-fuel energy units consumed: [2] _____
- The richest [3] _____ people use [4] _____ units ([5] _____ of the total energy).
- The people with washing machines use [6] _____ units (of energy).
- The 'bulb' people use [7] _____ units per billion people.
- The [8] _____ billion poorest people use only one unit.
- By the year [9] _____ the population of the lowest category will grow; they have [10] _____ children because of high child mortality.
- At the same time because of economic growth, the two lowest categories will each [11] _____ their energy use.
- Overall, energy use will increase to [12] _____ units.

▶ behavior **AM ENG**
▶ behaviour **BR ENG**
▶ labor **AM ENG**
▶ labour **BR ENG**

4 ▶ **5.1** Watch the third part (6.40 to the end) of the talk again. Are the sentences true (T) or false (F), according to Hans Rosling?

1 People in more developed economies need to advise the less developed countries how to be more energy-efficient.

2 Dilma Rousseff widened access to electricity in Rio de Janeiro in Brazil.

3 Dilma Rouseff's policies on energy helped her to become president of Brazil.

4 With the new free time available to her, Hans Rosling's mother was able to educate herself.

5 According to Hans Rosling, we should feel grateful for heavy industry – energy, steel, chemical processing, etc.

VOCABULARY IN CONTEXT

5 ▶ **5.2** Watch the clips from the TED Talk. Choose the correct meaning of the words and phrases.

6 ▶ **5.3** Watch the clips from the talk. Complete the collocations. Then discuss your answers.

7 Complete the sentences in your own words. Then compare your sentences with a partner.

1 You have to be a hardcore environmentalist to …

2 A lot of my fellow students …

3 … is a very time-consuming activity.

4 There's a high probability that …

CRITICAL THINKING Reading between the lines

8 It is important when listening to an argument to think about what is implied as well as what is explicitly said. Work in pairs. Which of these views do you think were implied by Hans Rosling in his talk?

1 Technology is a wonderful thing.

2 Restricting energy consumption in developing countries will restrict their progress.

3 Overpopulation will be a serious problem in 30–40 years' time.

9 Read these comments* about the TED Talk. Do you agree with the inferences the viewers have drawn from Hans Rosling's talk? Why? / Why not?

Viewers' comments

H **Hannah** – I think Hans Rosling is saying that we must not judge people in developing countries if they use machines which pollute, because they just want a better life and what people in the developed world already have. He chose the example of the washing machine, because it is a necessary, not a wasteful, use of energy.

R **Rama** – Hans Rosling wants us to see that technological progress and education are strongly linked. It is true that machines give us more time. It is how we choose to use that time that is important. I think the point he is making is that we should use this time to educate ourselves as he and his mother did. He is kind of implying too that we often use the time we gain with machines to pursue less productive activities.

The comments were created for this activity.

PRESENTATION SKILLS Presenting statistics

10 Work in pairs. How can statistics help you to present your ideas? What are the dangers in presenting a lot of statistics in a talk? How can these risks be minimized?

11 Look at the Presentation tips box. Compare your answers from Exercise 10 with the ideas in the box.

TIPS

Be strategic about visuals (e.g. charts, diagrams and pictures) that present statistics. Don't overuse them or you will overload your audience with information. Use visuals selectively and make sure each visual is bright, clear, simple and easily comprehensible. For example:

• a single sentence stating a striking statistic
• a graph or chart that shows a clear trend or deviation from a trend
• an infographic that illustrates data with icons or images
• an arresting photo that backs up a statistic you have given

If you are using a graph or infographic to explain a dynamic situation, try to make the visual itself dynamic so that it changes as you describe the development, rather than using a sequence of slides. The audience may remember the development better that way.

12 ▶ **5.4** Watch the clip from the TED Talk. Which of the techniques in the Presentation tips box does Hans Rosling use? Are they effective?

13 Work in pairs. Turn to page 89 and look at the information.

• Discuss how you would present the information in a dynamic slide.
• Make a sketch of your slide. Use the ideas in the Presentation tips box to help you.
• Write a few sentences to explain the idea.
• Practise presenting the idea with the slide.

14 Work with a new partner. Take turns to present the idea and the slide. Did you have similar ideas?

▶ laundry **AM ENG**
▶ washing **BR ENG**

5.2 Energy-hungry world

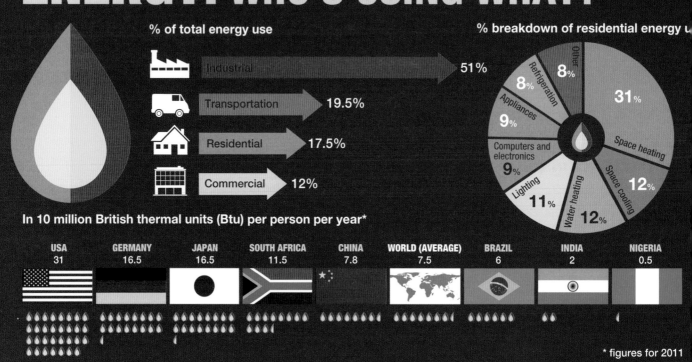

GRAMMAR Passive forms

1 Work in pairs. Discuss the questions.

1 Compared to other people in the world, do you think your energy use is above or below average?

2 How do you consume this energy: at home, getting around, in the products you buy, or some other way?

2 Look at the infographic and answer the questions. Do the facts surprise you? Why? / Why not?

1 Which country uses the most energy per person? And the least?

2 Which sector is the biggest user of energy? And the smallest?

3 What are the three largest uses of energy in the home?

4 What proportion of a household's energy is used by household appliances and electronic devices?

3 🎧 **18** Listen to an energy expert speaking about the statistics in the infographic. What reasons does she give for the following?

1 the level of energy consumption in the USA

2 transport being a big issue for the future

3 people not doing more to save energy in their homes

4 Read the sentences (1–7) in the Grammar box. Answer the questions (a–c).

PASSIVE FORMS

1 *The disparity in energy use between different countries **is linked** to their level of economic development.*

2 *In the United States much more energy **is being consumed** by each person.*

3 *American energy consumption **could be reduced** if greater priority **was given** to energy efficiency.*

4 *I'm confident that efforts **will be made** in this direction, particularly by industry.*

5 *People in developing countries **have been restricted** by the cost up to now.*

6 *The main area which needs **to be addressed** is heating and cooling.*

7 *The solution is relatively cheap and simple. It just means homes **being insulated** properly.*

a What tense or form of the verb is used in each passive verb in bold?

b Which sentences specify the agent of the action, and who or what is it?

c In the other sentences, why is the agent not mentioned?

Check your answers on page 84 and do Exercises 1–2.

5 Rewrite the sentences as passive sentences. Decide if the agent needs to be mentioned or not.

1 Experts expect electricity consumption to double by 2050.
2 Coal power plants generate 25 per cent of the world's electricity.
3 If we are to reduce CO_2 emissions, we need to find alternatives to fossil fuels.
4 Whoever first used a sailing boat discovered wind power – probably around 5,000 years ago.
5 If scientists can find a solution to the problem of electricity storage, wind power will be more practical.
6 People could save a lot of energy if they were more careful about switching off lights and appliances.
7 The use of smart appliances, like intelligent fridges, will reduce energy consumption in future.
8 It wouldn't surprise me at all if people were still discussing these issues in thirty years' time.

6 Choose the most appropriate option (active or passive) to complete the text.

[1] *Millions of homes across Europe could be powered by African sunshine / African sunshine could power millions of homes across Europe* by 2020 under a new $12bn plan to build a giant solar farm in the Sahara Desert. [2] *The electricity generated by the farm will be shipped / Operators will ship the electricity generated by the farm* to Europe through an undersea cable which will stretch 450 km from the coast of Tunisia to Italy. From there [3] *it would be distributed / they would distribute it* across the electricity network to various European countries as far as the UK. The farm, which [4] *is known / people know* as the TuNur farm, will be made up of thousands of computer-controlled mirrors that track the sun and [5] *the light is reflected / reflect the light* back towards a central tower. Here, [6] *pipes filled with salt are heated / the light heats pipes filled with salt.* [7] *This salt is used / They use this salt* in turn to heat water, creating steam that drives a turbine and generates electricity.

LANGUAGE FOCUS Nominalization in passive sentences

7 Read the sentences (1–2) in the box. Answer the questions (a–b).

> 1 *American energy consumption could be reduced if people prioritized energy efficiency more.*
> 2 *American energy consumption could be reduced if greater priority was given to energy efficiency.*

a In sentence 2, which verb from sentence 1 has been nominalized (changed to a noun)?
b What other changes have been made?

See page 85 for more information about nominalization in passive sentences, and do Exercise 3.

8 Rewrite the sentences as passive sentences using nominalization. Think about the verb that is needed with each new noun. You may also need to make other changes.

1 They have **agreed** on the main points, but not the details.
2 They **decided** to restrict CO_2 emissions from large industries.
3 They are **researching** the consequences of each possible scenario.
4 They will **confirm** the results after further tests.
5 We have **arranged** for him to be met at the airport.
6 No one **explained** why there was a delay.
7 They **legislated** to ban the burning of coal in people's homes.
8 We will **assist** people with their energy costs.

WRITING AND SPEAKING Headline news

9 **21st** **CENTURY OUTCOMES**
Work in pairs. Complete the headlines below in your own words. Then choose one headline and write, in brief, the story behind it. Use passive verbs where appropriate.

1 **CAR DEVELOPED WHICH CAN RUN ON** _____

2 £10,000 ELECTRICITY BILL RUN UP BY FAMILY WHO _____

3 NEW _____ SAVES ENERGY BY HEATING THE PERSON NOT THE ROOM

4 POLITICIAN COMMUTES TO WORK BY _____ TO HIGHLIGHT ENERGY CRISIS

5 **MILLIONS SAVED BY COUNCIL ON STREET LIGHTING BY** _____

10 Work with a new partner. Take turns to tell your news stories. Ask and answer questions about each story.

5.3 Land for all

READING Land – a fairer system

1 Work in pairs. Look at the online comment. Then answer the questions.

'I have a question. It might seem childish to some, but please think about it anyway. Why do we have to pay to live on our own planet?'

1 Is there any good answer to this question?
2 Do people in your country generally rent or own their homes?
3 Is property and land seen as a good investment?

2 Complete the definitions. Use one word per space.

1 **speculator** someone who risks losses for the possibility of big _____
2 **creditor** someone who _____ money to another person
3 **asset** something which a person or organization _____
4 **commodity** everyday things which are bought and _____

3 Read the article. According to the author, what is the fundamental problem with the current system of land ownership?

4 Read the article again. Are the sentences true (T) or false (F)?

1 The 2008 global financial crash was caused by people speculating in land.
2 The author implies that a similar problem could not happen again.
3 According to Julius Nyerere, landowners profit from the hard work of other people.
4 The author implies that with LVT, the amount of tax you pay will increase if the value of the land increases.
5 People who run a business from a particular piece of land will pay more LVT than those who just live there.
6 LVT is not popular with people who are looking to buy land or property for the first time.

5 Work in pairs. Find the words in bold in the text. Discuss what the words mean. Then answer the questions.

1 What other examples can you give of a) basic **amenities** and b) non-basic public **amenities** in a town? (line 2)
2 If everyone made a **dash** for the exit, how would they be leaving? (line 4)
3 What parts of the body do you use when you are **crawling**? Who normally gets around in this way? (line 8)
4 What responsibilities are **inherent** in owning a property, rather than renting it? (line 11)
5 If an employer rewarded an employee for their **diligence**, what would they be rewarding exactly? (line 35)
6 What **constitutes** lazy behaviour? (line 46)

VOCABULARY Economics

6 Read three people's accounts of their economic situation. Complete the phrases in bold using the verbs given. Then discuss with your partner what each phrase means.

1 A company manager's perspective

cut   expand   go   pay off   take on

'Things are pretty good at the moment – particularly if I think back two years ago when I thought we might
¹ _____ **bankrupt**. But since the government
² _____ **interest rates** last May, we have been able to ³ _____ some of our **debts**. We've also managed to ⁴ _____ our **operations** and even
⁵ _____ a few more **employees**.'

2 An employee's perspective

coming   investing   making   rising

'It's still quite difficult ¹ _____ **ends meet**. I know officially we are supposed to be ² _____ **out of recession**, but we're not feeling it round here. Youth **unemployment is** ³ _____ in our area because no one seems to be ⁴ _____ **in youth training** or apprenticeships.'

3 A politician's perspective

demanding   enjoying   going   setting
stifling   turning

'I think we are slowly ¹ _____ **the economy around**. Manufacturing is ² _____ **a boom** at the moment and more people are ³ _____ **up their own businesses** than ever before. People just need to be patient. I'd urge them to avoid ⁴ _____ **higher salaries** or ⁵ _____ **on strike** or generally ⁶ _____ **the recovery**.'

SPEAKING Economic prospects

7 **21st** **CENTURY OUTCOMES**
Work in pairs. Look at the economic problems (1–4). Think of a solution for each problem. Then discuss the advantages and disadvantages of each solution.

Problems

1 Youth unemployment
2 Weak consumer confidence (people are not spending their money)
3 The government cannot pay for the growing number of pensioners
4 Parents cannot afford to stay at home and look after young children

8 Work with another pair. Compare your answers from Exercise 7. Which solutions did you like?

LAND – A FAIRER SYSTEM

Land – a place to live. Surely it is the most basic of all human amenities. Yet it has also become the principal tool by which people acquire and pass on wealth. The global financial crash of 2008 was precipitated by a credit-fuelled dash for land and property. All over the USA and western Europe people became speculators in land, borrowing vast sums to cash in on rising values until the bubble burst, leaving their creditors, the banks, to go crawling to governments, and us, the tax-payers, to bail them out. Even though the effects of this crash are still being felt today, we seem not to have learned from it. The problems inherent in land as a marketable commodity are still the same as Tanzania's Julius Nyerere described them in his 1967 manifesto, *Ujaama*.

'The African's right to land was simply the right to use it: he had no other right to it … The foreigner introduced … the concept of land as a marketable commodity. According to this system, a person could claim a piece of land as his own private property whether he intended to use it or not. I could take a few square miles of land, call them "mine", and then go off to the moon. All I had to do to gain a living from "my" land was to charge a rent to the people who wanted to use it. If this piece of land was in an urban area, I had no need to develop it at all; I could leave it to the fools who were prepared to develop all the other pieces of land surrounding "my" piece, and in doing so automatically to raise the market value of mine. Then I could come down from the moon and demand that these fools pay me the high value of "my" land …!'

Yet there is a simple solution: a Land Value Tax (LVT). An LVT is a tax on the unimproved value of land, that is to say it is levied not on the value of a property but on the value of the land that the property sits on. Without an LVT, it is possible to buy a piece of land in an undeveloped area and wait for that area to be developed by the government or by the community around you. Through no diligence or hard work of your own, that land will become more valuable by the addition of infrastructure and services – transport connections, schools, shops, etc. A Land Value Tax seeks to collect payment from you on what economists call the 'unearned betterment' of your asset – the part that has nothing to do with your actions as an owner and everything to do with the actions of the community. So if the value of the land is improved by the community, the amount of tax you pay will increase. Should you develop the land yourself, on the other hand, by building or improving a house or running a business from that site, you will not be taxed on those elements, since they constitute productive activity. If, however, you do nothing productive with it, you will pay the LVT regardless. In this way, an LVT discourages idle speculation.

The economists Adam Smith and Milton Friedman both noted the efficiency of a Land Value Tax and it has been implemented in a few countries, such as Denmark, Singapore and Russia. Winston Churchill was also a fan, stating that 'land differs from all other sorts of property'. So why is it not more popular? The main reason, as with many things, is short-term and political. Introducing an LVT would impose fairly heavy costs on today's landowners, who would face a new tax bill and a reduced sale price. The benefit to future generations, however, would be enormous.

5.4 I can well believe that

Fact
or hearsay?

Finding out the true state of the environment and the world's resources isn't easy. Information abounds, but it is often difficult to know whether you are reading objective data or unverified facts that are being used to promote a particular agenda or argument. We are also easily persuaded by what we *want* to hear (perhaps you feel that too much is made of environmental problems or perhaps that they're not taken seriously enough). Look at these statements. Which do you think are accurate?

1 There is enough food in the world to feed everyone.
2 We are the last generation that will harvest wild fish from the seas.
3 A cow in Europe receives twice as much income as a lot of people living in Africa.
4 Only a very small percentage of the world's CO_2 is produced by human activity.
5 The Amazon Rainforest is the world's lung, producing nearly half its oxygen.
6 Deforestation is taking place at a rate of an area equivalent to three football fields every hour.

READING Fact or hearsay?

1 Work in pairs. How careful are you about checking the information you read on the Internet? How can you tell whether what you are reading is reliable or not?

2 Read the extract from an article. Which of the six statements (1–6) in the extract do you think are (probably) true (PT) and which are (probably) false (PF)? Check your answers on page 89.

LISTENING Discussing facts and beliefs

3 🎧 19 Listen to a conversation between two friends. Answer the questions.

1 Which of the statements in the extract in Exercise 2 are the two friends discussing?
2 What argument does the first speaker use the statement to support?
3 What is the second speaker's view of this statement and argument?

4 🎧 19 Look at the expressions in the Useful language box. Do the expressions express belief or disbelief? Write True (T), Probably true (PT), False (F) or probably false (PF). Then listen to the conversation again and tick (✓) the expressions the speakers use.

EXPRESSING BELIEF AND DISBELIEF

I very much doubt that.
I'd be very surprised if that was / were the case.
That doesn't surprise me in the least.
I think they've got that spot on.
That's a common misconception.
That's nonsense.
I suspect that's true.
That's an old wives' tale.
That's what … would have you believe.
I'd take it / that with a (big) pinch of salt.
I can well believe that.
I'd have some reservations about that.

Pronunciation Silent letters

5 🎧 20 In the word *doubt*, 'b' is a silent letter. Look at these words and underline the silent letter. Then listen and check your answers.

architect	biscuit	condemn	guilty
receipt	resign	sandwich	scissors
subtle	thumb	whistle	

SPEAKING Expressing belief and disbelief

6 Work in pairs. Look at the statements and the supporting notes. Prepare to present these ideas.

Student A

1 When you are lost, looking at a tree can tell you which direction to go in.

2 Being lonely in old age is as bad for your health as smoking fifteen cigarettes a day.

Look at the supporting notes on page 89.

Student B

1 Using an automatic dishwasher is more environmentally friendly than washing dishes by hand.

2 Eating carrots helps you see in the dark.

Look at the supporting notes on page 94.

7 Take turns to present your ideas and ask questions about your partner's ideas. Use the expressions in the Useful language box to help you express belief and disbelief. Begin like this: 'Did you know that …?'

WRITING A newspaper report

8 Read the newspaper report. Answer the questions.

1 What has happened?
2 Where and when did it happen?
3 Who was involved?
4 Why did they do this?
5 How did they do this?

9 A good newspaper report should give the key facts (what, who, where, when, why and how) to the reader as soon as possible. Did the report do this? In what order were these questions answered?

Writing skill Passive reporting verbs

10a Look at the example of a passive reporting verb from the report. Find two other examples of passive reporting verbs in the report. Then answer the questions (1–2).

*In an experiment that **is believed to be** the first of its kind, …*

1 Why does the writer use passive reporting verbs rather than active verbs?
2 What are the types of subject a passive reporting verb can have?

See page 85 for more information about passive reporting verbs, and do Exercise 4.

10b Write sentences with passive reporting verbs. Use the verbs in brackets.

1 The technology originated in the USA. (think)
2 They are currently working on a larger-scale version. (say)
3 They are about to launch a prototype in the next few months. (report)
4 There have been several unsuccessful attempts to replicate the results. (believe)
5 The technology will transform the way energy is generated. (hope)

11 21st CENTURY OUTCOMES

Write a short newspaper report using an event that has been in the news recently. Remember to follow the principle of the five Ws and the H questions. Write 150–200 words.

12 Work in pairs. Exchange your reports. Use these questions to check your partner's report.

- Does the report include all the facts?
- Does it answer the five Ws and the H questions as quickly as possible?
- Does it use passive reporting verbs where appropriate?

Breakthrough in energy transmission

The dream of generating solar power in space, where the supply is endless, and transmitting it back to Earth may be a step closer to becoming reality. In an experiment that is believed to be the first of its kind, Japanese scientists managed this week to transmit energy wirelessly.

Researchers at the Japan Aerospace Exploration Agency (JAXA) used microwaves to deliver 1.8 kW of electric power to a small receiver 55 metres away. Although this is a modest amount of energy, enough only to power a small iron, it is hoped that the breakthrough could pave the way for larger-scale and longer distance transmissions in future. JAXA already uses solar energy to power its satellites in space, but has no way of transmitting the energy back to Earth.

The technology is of particular interest in Japan, which now imports large amounts of coal and oil to produce electricity, having been forced to close down nuclear plants after the Fukushima disaster. Other Japanese companies, such as Mitsubishi, are known to be working on similar technology, which could have other useful applications, such as transmitting power to remote areas of the country, or charging electric vehicles from a distance.

6 Practical design

Continuous staircase in the atrium of the London headquarters of financial services company Macquarie, UK

TEDTALKS

ELORA HARDY grew up in Bali with two artist parents. Her creative upbringing led to her becoming a print designer for one of New York's biggest fashion houses. But after some years there, she moved back home and founded Ibuku, a team that builds homes made and furnished almost entirely of bamboo. Using a design process and an engineering system first established at the Green School in Bali, Elora Hardy and her team have found that bamboo offers amazing opportunities to build creatively and sustainably.

Elora Hardy's idea worth spreading is that using traditional natural materials, such as bamboo, in innovative ways can be a force for positive change in the future.

BACKGROUND

1 You are going to watch a TED Talk by Elora Hardy called *Magical houses, made of bamboo*. Read the text about the speaker and the talk. Then work in pairs and discuss the questions.

  1 What is Elora Hardy's background?
  2 What do you think the advantages of bamboo might be?
  3 What other natural building materials can you think of? What benefits do they offer?

KEY WORDS

2 Read the sentences (1–6). The words in bold are used in the TED Talk. First guess the meaning of the words. Then match the words with their definitions (a–f).

  1 The hotel doesn't have regular bedrooms. Each guest sleeps in a small **pod** and uses a separate bathroom.
  2 The first few **shoots** appear in late February, signalling an end to the winter.
  3 The people who repair the stonework on the city's ancient buildings are traditional **artisans**.
  4 We make some standard products but mostly our customers ask us for **bespoke** furniture for their homes.
  5 The insects eat the inside of the tree, leaving the trunk **hollow**.
  6 She revealed her **blueprint** for the redevelopment of the city centre at the council's annual general meeting.

  a without anything inside
  b a small self-contained space for sleeping, washing or living in general
  c custom-made, made-to-measure
  d a design plan
  e craftsmen or women
  f a leaf or stem of a young plant, showing just above the ground

AUTHENTIC LISTENING SKILLS Word boundaries

> When we link words in fast speech, the word boundaries are often blurred, particularly in familiar or commonly used phrases. It is then difficult to hear the individual words in a sentence. For example, when spoken at natural speed, this sentence:
> '***First of all***, *I'd like to **know if** you **can see the** screen*'
> sounds like:
> '***Ferstival**,   I'd like to **nowiff**   you **cn   seether** screen*'
>
> For this reason it is important to:
> - be aware of how words are linked in general
> - become familiar with linking in common phrases

3a 🎧 **21** Work in pairs. Look at the Authentic listening skills box. Listen to the extract from Elora Hardy's talk. Underline the phrases where the words are linked so that boundaries are difficult to distinguish.

'Now, we do have all the necessary luxuries, like bathrooms. This one is a basket in the corner of the living room, and I've got to tell you, some people actually hesitate to use it.'

3b Practise saying the sentences yourself, linking the words in a similar way.

3c 🎧 **22** Listen to the next sentence from the talk and write the words you hear. Then compare answers with your partner.

'So [1] _____ , but one thing I have learned is that bamboo will treat you well if
[2] _____ .'

6.1 Magical houses, made of bamboo

TEDTALKS ⌂ Watch at home

1 ▶ **6.1** Look at the questions. Then watch the TED Talk and make notes. After watching, discuss your notes with a partner. What did you find most impressive about the houses in the talk?

1 What is special about bamboo as a building material?
2 What parts of a bamboo house did Elora Hardy describe in her talk?

2 ▶ **6.1** Watch the first part (0.00–1.51) of the talk again. Complete the facts about the bamboo house.

Feature	Purpose / Advantage
1 Living room on the 4th floor	_____
2 Curving roofs	_____
3 Big tall windows	_____
	Problem
4 'Basket' bathroom	_____

3 ▶ **6.1** Watch the second part (1.51–3.50) of the talk again. Make notes about the features (1–9) of bamboo, as described by Elora Hardy. Why do these features make it such a useful building material?

Features of bamboo

1	Plant type	6	Strength
2	Growing conditions	7	Portability
3	Number of species	8	Appearance
4	Growing time / Growth rate	9	Resistance
5	Length at harvest		

4 ▶ **6.1** Work in pairs. Watch the third part (3.50–7.17) of the talk again. Answer the questions.

1 What is 'Ibuku' and what does the organization do?
2 What are examples of the things Ibuku has built in the last five years?
3 What has been the problem with using bamboo as a building material? How has it affected local attitudes to using it?
4 How did Ibuku solve the physical problem and the public perception of bamboo?
5 What are the 'rules' for building with bamboo, according to Elora Hardy / Ibuku?

▶ tried-and-true **AM ENG**
▶ tried-and-tested **BR ENG**

▶ bug **AM ENG**
▶ insect **BR ENG**

5 ▶ **6.1** Watch the fourth part (7.17 to the end) of the talk again. Complete the summary with these words.

blueprint	boulder	canvas	ceiling	countertops
detail	floor	grow	model	pins
weave				

They make a 3D scale ¹ _____ in bamboo and then use this as a ² _____ to build the house. Elora Hardy questions every ³ _____ and explores each challenge – how can you make a ⁴ _____ without flat boards? ⁵ _____ tiny pieces of bamboo together and put a ⁶ _____ over it. How do you make kitchen ⁷ _____ ? Slice a ⁸ _____ like a loaf of bread. The structure is reinforced by steel joints and the ⁹ _____ , made of bamboo skin, is held together by bamboo ¹⁰ _____ . The result is a building with beauty and comfort in a material that will ¹¹ _____ back.

VOCABULARY IN CONTEXT

6 ▶ **6.2** Watch the clips from the TED Talk. Choose the correct meaning of the words and phrases.

7 ▶ **6.3** Watch the clips from the talk. Complete the collocations. Then discuss your answers.

8 Complete the sentences in your own words. Then compare your sentences with a partner.

1 My parents got me … at a young age.
2 Fairtrade companies try to foster links between … and …
3 When you build a house in an historic area, there are certain constraints, like …
4 My bedroom overlooks …

CRITICAL THINKING Testing arguments

9 Work in pairs. What questions could you ask to test Elora Hardy's argument that bamboo is a promising building material for the future?

10 Read these comments* about the TED Talk. Did the viewers consider similar questions to you?

Viewers' comments

E **Eusebio** – Seems incredible. But can bamboo be made fire-resistant too? And if so, are the chemicals used to make it fire-resistant very harmful to the environment?

A **Alan** – Why stop at houses? Bamboo bikes already exist. And bamboo car bodies also have great advantages: they are strong, can easily be moulded into shape and when dropped from a height, they bounce!

A **Angelica** – It's unfortunate Hardy showed just these houses designed for rich people. What about bamboo transforming the lives of the poor? We didn't see any of those houses. And are they resistant to strong winds too?

*The comments were created for this activity

PRESENTATION SKILLS Persuasive techniques

11 There are certain established ways of using language to make an argument more persuasive. Work in pairs. Look at the techniques (a–c). What are they? Can you think of any other persuasive techniques?

a rhetorical questions
b imagery and metaphor
c repetition of key words

12 Look at the Presentation tips box. Compare your answers from Exercise 11 with the ideas in the box. How do you think you personally would be most likely to use these persuasive techniques in a talk?

TIPS

There are various ways we can use language to make an argument more persuasive. For example:

- emotive words and phrases (e.g. powerful adjectives such as *extraordinary*)
- rhetorical questions (questions we ask without expecting an answer)
- repetition of key words or grammatical structures
- contrasts (*It may not be cheap, but it is needed.*)
- use of imagery and metaphor (*It unlocks the door to a whole world of opportunities.*)

Try to notice how experienced speakers use these techniques and try them out to see which ones you can adopt in a natural way.

13 ▶ **6.4** Watch the clips from the TED talk. Which persuasive techniques does Elora Hardy use? Which ones do you find particularly effective?

14 Prepare to give a short description about the benefits of one of the following ideas. Make notes about what you will say. Use the techniques in the Presentation tips box to persuade your partner of the benefits.

- building houses close to shops and offices
- including a lot of communal space around buildings
- using wood as a building material

15 Work in pairs. Take turns to give your presentation. Discuss which persuasive techniques you found most effective and the most natural to use.

6.2 Get someone else to do it

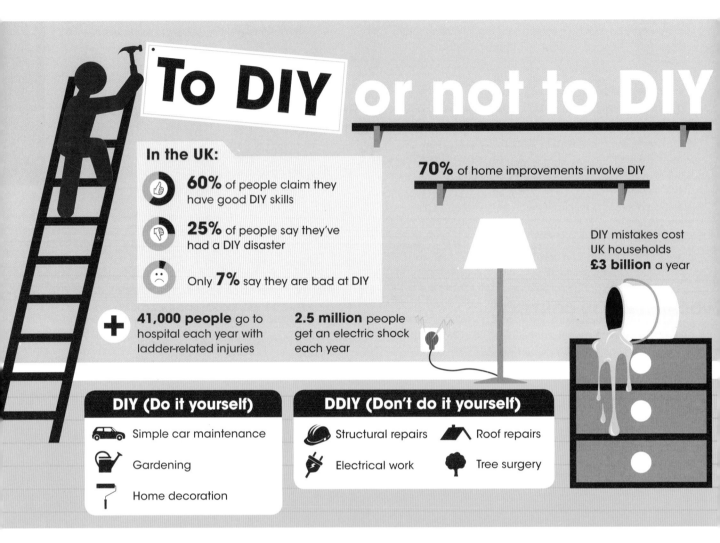

To DIY or not to DIY

In the UK:

- **60%** of people claim they have good DIY skills
- **25%** of people say they've had a DIY disaster
- Only **7%** say they are bad at DIY

+ **41,000 people** go to hospital each year with ladder-related injuries

2.5 million people get an electric shock each year

70% of home improvements involve DIY

DIY mistakes cost UK households **£3 billion** a year

DIY (Do it yourself)
- Simple car maintenance
- Gardening
- Home decoration

DDIY (Don't do it yourself)
- Structural repairs
- Roof repairs
- Electrical work
- Tree surgery

GRAMMAR Causatives

1 Work in pairs and answer the questions.

1 Do you like decorating or fixing things yourself (things at home, bicycles, computers, etc.)? Are you good at DIY?
2 Are there any jobs that you wouldn't do? Why not?

2 Look at the infographic. What is the overall message that it is trying to give? What examples support this message?

3 🎧 **23** Listen to two people discussing DIY facts. Are the sentences true (T) or false (F)?

1 The woman's brother-in-law had an accident with a ladder.
2 He needed to have a minor operation at the hospital.
3 The woman feels it was a job for an electrician.
4 The man is going to have his bathroom professionally painted.
5 The woman never tries to inflate the car tyres herself.
6 The woman's brother-in-law didn't fix the light.

4 Read the sentences (1–7) in the Grammar box. Answer the questions (a–d).

CAUSATIVES

1 *He had to go to the hospital so he could **have his fingers stitched**.*
2 *I wanted to **get our bathroom repainted**.*
3 *He had to **get my sister to drive** him to the hospital.*
4 *It seems crazy to **have a professional do** it.*
5 *He couldn't **get the light** in the attic **to work**.*
6 *He **got his fingers caught** in an attic trap door.*
7 *He managed to **get the light fixed**.*

a In sentences 1 and 2, who will do the 'stitching' and 'repainting'? Are *have* and *get* interchangeable?
b In sentences 3 and 4, what is the difference in the form of the verb that follows *get* and *have*?
c In sentences 5 and 6, can you use *have* instead of *get*? Why? / Why not?
d In sentence 7, what is the difference in meaning if you use *have*?

Check your answers on page 87 and do Exercises 1–3.

5 Rewrite the sentences using a causative form. Use the correct form of the verb in brackets. In which sentences could you use either *get* or *have*?

1 A professional landscape gardener redesigned our garden. (have)
We _____ .
2 The roof is being repaired next week. (get)
We _____ .
3 Our washing machine needs fixing. (get)
We _____ .
4 The car wouldn't start this morning. (get)
I _____ .
5 Someone should look at your boiler, I think. (have)
I think you _____ .
6 Look. The vacuum cleaner's working now. (get)
I'm very proud that I _____ .
7 His head became stuck between the railings and we had to call the fire brigade. (get)
He _____ and we had to call the fire brigade.
8 She finished decorating two walls but not the others. (get)
She managed _____ .

6 Choose the best option to complete the sentences. Give reasons for your choice.

1 He *got / had* his foot wedged under the washing machine while he was trying to move it.
2 I managed to *get / have* all the preparation done, but I haven't started the work itself.
3 I couldn't *have the key fit / get the key to fit* in the lock.
4 I *got / had* my clothes covered in oil when I was fixing my bike.
5 How do you block unwanted calls? I *got / had* it explained to me once, but I've forgotten.

7 Work in pairs. Tell each other about two DIY jobs you are proud of doing and two jobs that you got someone else to do.

8 Complete the details of this anecdote. Then compare anecdotes with another pair.

My _____ broke so I got a
_____ to _____ .
But when he / she was _____ he / she
_____ and _____ . In the
end I had to _____ .

LANGUAGE FOCUS Expressions with *go* and *get*

9 🎧 **23** Look at the sentences (1–3) from the conversation in Exercise 3. Choose the correct option to complete them. Then listen and check.

> **1** Did you know that a lot of people *go / get* injured doing DIY?
> **2** There are always so many little things in the house that *go / get* wrong.
> **3** I *go / get* confused when I have to put air in the tyres.
>
> *See page 87 for more information about expressions with* go *and* get*, and do Exercise 4.*

10 Complete the sentences using the correct form of *go* or *get*.

1 If you work with loud tools and machines all the time you risk _____ deaf.
2 I try not to _____ involved in decisions about interior design – my wife's much better at that.
3 The move was _____ fine until Katya's jewellery box _____ missing.
4 I'm _____ crazy trying to put this wardrobe together. The instructions are really confusing.
5 Don't _____ upset if things _____ wrong.
6 If you _____ started on painting the walls, I'll _____ ready to paint the woodwork.
7 I've been trying to fix this light for hours and I'm _____ nowhere with it.
8 This fridge is so old that it's _____ yellow. It used to be bright white.

SPEAKING Hired help

11 **21st CENTURY OUTCOMES**
Work in pairs. Look at the list of jobs that people pay other people to do. Add four more jobs.

- clothes shopping
- cleaning the house
- walking the dog
- organizing a holiday
- doing the gardening
- organizing your wedding
- cooking

12 Work with another pair. Compare your lists. If money was no object, which jobs would you get someone else to do for you? Which would you still do yourself? Give reasons.

6.3 Better by design

READING Object of desire

1 Work in pairs. What are your favourite functional objects in your home? Why do you like these? Discuss.

I love my toaster. It's based on a classic 1950s design and it makes toast perfectly every time.

2 Read the article about Thonet's Model No. 14 chair. Match the headings (1–6) with the correct paragraph (A–F).

1 An idea worth repeating
2 For rich and poor alike
3 An ethical approach
4 Man on a mission
5 A novel process
6 A timeless object

3 List at least four ways in which the Thonet No. 14 was a revolutionary product.

4 Read the article again. Answer the questions.

1 What exactly was the chair made of?
2 How were the different parts fastened together?
3 How was the special Thonet chair shape achieved?
4 How did Thonet reduce his firm's transport costs?
5 What was an unexpected consequence of Thonet's manufacturing process?
6 Is the chair still available today?

5 Find the words in bold in the article and answer the questions.

1 What other things do we usually describe as **'masterpieces'**? (para A)
2 Can you give an example of two people who are from different **walks of life**? (para B)
3 How would you replace the phrase **never been bettered** using the word 'improved'? (para C)
4 What image does the verb **'spewing out'** create in our minds? (para E)
5 What kind of furniture do you expect to find in an **up-market** furniture shop? (para F)

6 What for you is the most important lesson to take from the Thonet No.14 story? Note your ideas. Then share your ideas with two other students.

VOCABULARY Describing objects: collocations

7 Find these adverb + adjective collocations in the article. Which two adverbs intensify the adjectives (i.e. mean 'extremely')? What do the other two mean?

1 precisely crafted
2 radically innovative
3 amazingly challenging
4 reasonably priced

8 Match the adverbs (1–10) with the adjective (a–j) they frequently collocate with. Then decide if each collocation is positive, negative or neutral in meaning.

Adverb	Adjective
1 reasonably	a expensive
2 shoddily	b used
3 highly	c admired
4 scientifically	d original
5 prohibitively	e put together
6 greatly	f coloured
7 widely	g adequate
8 brightly	h proven
9 beautifully	i priced
10 perfectly	j crafted

9 Complete the sentences using an appropriate adverb + adjective collocation from Exercise 8.

1 The wardrobe we bought was _____ . It lasted six months before one of the doors fell off.
2 Aspirin is _____ to thin the blood and reduce the chance of heart failure.
3 It's not the most beautiful sofa in the world but it's _____ for our needs.
4 German engineering is _____ around the world for its quality.
5 It's considered inappropriate to wear _____ clothing to a funeral.
6 The technique of using steam to bend wood is still _____ today.
7 The Swiss Army Knife has won many awards for its _____ design.
8 We wanted to buy some original Ligne Roset furniture, but we couldn't because it was _____ .

SPEAKING Classic objects

10 **21st CENTURY OUTCOMES**

Work in small groups. Read the scenario and decide on three objects. Consider their design and practicality and how they reflect the age we live in.

> SCENARIO
>
> You have been asked to propose three objects to be included in a 'time capsule'. This will be buried so that a future generation can in a thousand years' time look at what objects both characterized and were prized by the current generation.

11 Work with another group. Present your ideas. Vote on the three best objects.

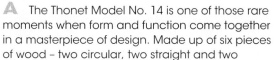

A The Thonet Model No. 14 is one of those rare moments when form and function come together in a masterpiece of design. Made up of six pieces of wood – two circular, two straight and two
5 arched – held together by a few screws and nuts, featuring a woven cane seat, the Thonet No.14 was the first ever mass-produced chair and is believed to this day to have been sat on by more people than any other chair in history.
10 Its maker, Michael Thonet, a German-Austrian cabinet maker of the mid-nineteenth century, was not the only person at the time trying to mass manufacture a chair, but his rivals did not possess his ambition or dedication. After years of technical experiments, Thonet perfected the technique of
15 bending and forming lightweight but strong wood into curved shapes using hot steam. The No. 14 chair was born.

B Thonet's aim had always been to make a chair that could be produced, and thus sold, at an affordable price (three florins, to be precise) and he succeeded. It took very little time from its launch in 1859 for the No. 14 to become popular among people
20 from every walk of life, from school teachers to merchants to aristocrats. By the 1930s, Thonet's company had sold approximately 50 million No. 14 chairs. Its owners include the composer Brahms, the Russian leader, Lenin, and the great architect and designer, Le Corbusier, who said of it, 'Never was a better and more elegant design and a more precisely crafted and practical item created.'

25 **C** What is it about the No. 14 that has appealed to so many of its end users and elicited such high praise from fellow designers? The answers to this question have relevance today as much as they do to the era in which it was created. First and foremost, it fulfils its function admirably, as any well-designed object should: it is comfortable, compact and lightweight. Secondly, it is classically beautiful. According to British designer Jasper
30 Morrison 'It has the freshness of a new product, because it has never been bettered.' For this reason, it is still the default chair of choice for many cafés and brasseries.

D Thirdly, it was radically innovative in its construction. Not only was it made from just a few standard parts, but these parts could be flat-packed and shipped to another destination for assembly by unskilled workers. Indeed it was probably the first truly flat-pack
35 piece of furniture ever made. Added to that, it seems to improve with age. 'As the screws and glue loosen, the structure becomes softer,' Konstantin Grcic, a German furniture designer, said. 'Michael Thonet probably didn't intend that to happen, but it's a beautiful sensation. I've tried to do it with new chairs, but it's amazingly challenging.'

E Fourthly, there are the sustainable and social aspects of Thonet's company. At a time
40 when other factories were spewing out pollution from far dirtier processes, the No. 14 was built in a kinder environment, where workers handled beechwood brought in from local forests. The workers and their families were housed in a kind of company town with access to schools and nurseries, shops and libraries.

F So what of the No. 14 today? The design remains as classic as ever but the prices
45 have lost some of their popular appeal – new models are sold in up-market furniture shops for around £500. But the design (and principle of affordability) has been copied by other furniture makers like Muji and Ikea. Until recently, the latter had a very reasonably priced plastic version called the Ogla, and 'antique' versions can be picked up on eBay for as little as £20.

READING Tricky questions

1 Work in pairs. Think of a job you do or have done. Imagine you have to recruit someone for this job. Look at the list of candidates' qualities. Then discuss the questions (1–3).

Qualities
a ability to think on one's feet
b knowledge of the sector or product
c common sense
d ability to get on with others
e individuality / standing out from the crowd

1 What does each quality mean?
2 Which qualities do you think are most important for the candidate to possess?
3 How would you go about finding out if a candidate possesses these qualities?

Tricky questions

In these days of fierce job competition, interviewers resort to ever more tricky and left-field questions in an attempt to separate the wheat from the chaff: 'On a scale of 1 to 10, how weird would you say you are?' (Zappos clothing); 'If you were a cartoon character, which one would you be?' (Bank of America). Then there are the problem-solving riddles, often based on rather unrealistic scenarios. For example, 'If you had a stack of coins as tall as the Empire State Building, could you fit them all into one room?'

Questions like this one are supposed to test practical intelligence, a recognized aspect of success at work, but do they really reveal anything about a candidate's common sense? Paul Tyma, an engineer and interviewer at Google, famed for its tricky questions, decided to find out. He posed this interview question to his mother: 'Imagine you're given 10,000 sheets of paper, each one an individual university student's record. How would you sort them in order of age?'

2 Read the extract from an article about questions asked at job interviews. Discuss what your answers would be to each of the interview questions.

3 Turn to page 89 and read the comments about the questions in the article. Do you think these are good interview questions? Why? / Why not?

4 Look at two more questions which candidates were asked at job interviews, relating to practical intelligence or common sense. How would you answer them?

1 'What's your best time of day? When are you most productive, would you say?'
2 'You've pushed a cork into a bottle and you want to get it out. How would you go about it?'

LISTENING An interview

5 🎧 **24** Listen to two candidates' responses to the questions in Exercise 4. Are they good answers?

6 🎧 **24** Look at the Useful language box. Then listen to the interviews again and tick (✓) the questions and phrases that the interviewer and candidates use.

INTERVIEW QUESTIONS

Asking interview questions

Do you find …?
When are you most productive, would you say?
Why do you say / think that?
Suppose that / Imagine that … . What would you do?
In a situation where you … , what would you do?
How would you go about it / …-ing?

Answering questions / Buying time

I couldn't tell you really …
That's a tricky question.
That depends … / It depends …
I suppose I'd (probably) …
Let me have a think …
My first instinct is to say …

Pronunciation Word stress

7 🎧 **25** Listen to these words. Where is the stress in each word? What patterns can you identify?

1 translation	situation
2 depend	suppose
3 instinct	schedule
4 productive	effective
5 basic	specific
6 difficult	various

SPEAKING Interview questions

8 Work in pairs. Write some surprising interview questions to test aspects of a candidate's qualities which were listed in Exercise 1. Use the expressions in the Useful language box on page 70 to help you.

9 Work with a new partner. Ask and answer each others' questions. What qualities did your partner show in their answers (e.g. common sense)?

WRITING Posting advice

10 Work in pairs. How do you prepare for interviews? Discuss.

11 Look at the online post written by a candidate who went for an interview with a particular business consultancy firm. Answer the questions.

    1 What were the different stages in the recruitment process?
    2 What advice does she give for each stage?

The first stage was completing the online application form (education, experience, etc.) and doing a short maths and verbal reasoning test. There are examples of these tests online. Then there was a short thirty-minute telephone interview. It's definitely a good idea to read the business news and have a few examples of business stories up your sleeve. The recruiter [1] **asked** me what I thought of Apple's announcement of record profits the day before. Then I had the day at their assessment centre.

In the interview itself on that day, the most difficult part was the business questions again. You have to nominate a company to talk about beforehand, but then they really grill you about it. They [2] **asked** me what the strengths of the company were, why I thought its fortunes had changed recently, and how its problems could be put right – a lot of things I didn't really know the answers to. But the key thing is not to panic. I [3] **said** I needed time to think and they seemed fine with that. Then I just relied on common sense for my answers.

The last part was a role play with a fictional client (he was an actor). I was given some background information about him to read and [4] **was told** I would have a meeting with the client fifteen minutes later. The idea was to get him to agree to work with us. It all went fine until halfway through, when he [5] **said** that he had worked with us before and hadn't been entirely satisfied. He [6] **wanted to know** what guarantees I could give him that things would be different this time. It was a shock, but I got through it OK. The main thing with the role play is to imagine that it's real – really try and 'live' the situation. All in all, it's an enjoyable day … if you prepare. (I got the job, by the way).

QUOTE

Writing skill Reported speech

12a Work in pairs. Look at the examples of reported speech following the verbs in bold in the online post. Write what you think the person actually said at the time.

> **1** The recruiter **asked** me what I thought of Apple's announcement of record profits the day before.
>
> ➔ *'What do you think of Apple's announcement of record profits yesterday?'*
>
> See page 87 for more information about reported speech, and do Exercises 5 and 6.

12b Rewrite the questions and answers using reported speech.

    1 'Is this the only job you're applying for at the moment?'
       The interviewer asked me _____ .
    2 'I've applied for one other job, but I'm not as interested in it as I am in this one.'
       I told him _____ .
    3 'How long do you think you'll stay with us if you get the job?'
       He asked me _____ .
    4 'I imagine I'll probably be here for at least three or four years, if it is working out OK.'
       I said that _____ .
    5 'When did you last have an argument with someone?'
       He asked me _____ .
    6 'I had an argument last week with a shop assistant who wouldn't give me a refund.'
       I said that _____ .

13 **21st CENTURY OUTCOMES**

Write an online post sharing your experiences about a job interview process and giving advice. Either write from your own experience or use the notes on page 89. Write 200–300 words.

14 Work in pairs. Exchange your posts. Use these questions to check your partner's post.

- Does the post outline the stages of the interview clearly?
- Does it give tips or advice for each stage?
- Does it mention some of the questions that were asked at the interview?
- Does it use reported speech correctly?

READING

1 Read the article about Broad Sustainable Building. Then complete the summary.

The Mini Sky City tower is for ¹_____ and ²_____ use. It has ³_____ floors and was ⁴_____ in nineteen days. It was built to withstand ⁵_____ and also to be ⁶_____ friendly.

The problem with tall steel towers is that they are ⁷_____ to build. BSB gets round this problem by using ⁸_____ units and then lifting them into place. The building is also well ⁹_____ from the weather and from air ¹⁰_____ .

VOCABULARY Suffixes -*proof* and -*free*

2 Look at these two words in the article: *earthquake-proof* (line 13–14) and *carbon-free* (line 21). What do the suffixes mean? Complete the sentences (1–10) with these words. There are two extra words.

childproof	crime-free	dust-free
foolproof	maintenance-free	shockproof
showerproof	soundproof	stainproof
stress-free	sugar-free	trouble-free

1 No, the jacket is not completely water resistant, but it is _____ .

2 I just want a _____ job. I'm tired of working to deadlines, and of all the responsibility.

3 The great thing about these uPVC windows is that they're _____ – no painting, no repairing.

4 I know you're not an experienced cook, but believe me, this is a _____ recipe.

5 One of the first things people ask before moving to a different neighbourhood is: Is it _____?

6 I need a _____ room. The neighbours are stomping around upstairs and I can't get to sleep.

7 Why aren't phones more _____? I've had to replace my phone screen three times after dropping it.

8 What do you mean '_____ chocolate'? Surely, that's a contradiction in terms.

9 The main computer server has to be kept in a completely _____ environment.

10 As soon as our baby started to walk, we had all our cupboards fitted with _____ locks.

BROAD SUSTAINABLE BUILDING
– RETHINKING CONSTRUCTION

The future of the high-rise building is modular, according to Zhang Yue, the chairman of the Broad Group and the man behind Broad Sustainable Building (BSB), and looking at the statistics for his 204-metre-tall office and residential tower, Mini Sky City, on the outskirts of Changsha in southern
5　China, it's hard to disagree. While the building itself is unremarkable in its design – a rectangular block of glass and steel – the construction facts are anything but. Employing 1,200 workers, BSB put the 57-storey building together from prefabricated units in just nineteen days. A few years ago, nineteen months would have been considered quick for this type of high-
10　rise tower. But Zhang Yue's motive was not just speed. He wanted BSB to lead a revolution in construction that would combine speed of construction with safety and environmental sustainability.

He chose steel because it was strong, but also flexible and earthquake-proof (an important consideration following the devastation caused by
15　the earthquake in Sichuan Province in 2008). To offset the high cost of traditional steel assembly, he hit upon the idea of pre-fabrication. The steel is cut to length at BSB's factory, numbered, and then slotted together at the site – complete with electric wiring, plumbing and air ducts – into modular units ready to be lifted into position on the tower
20　when the time comes. But in what way is this sustainable?

Firstly, while not carbon-free, the carbon footprint of manufacturing steel and glass is much lower than traditional concrete. Secondly, the windows are made of quadruple-paned glass, which helps insulate the building and make it more energy-efficient. They also guarantee better air
25　quality, keeping out 99 per cent of the polluting particles which are such a problem in many of China's big cities. BSB's next project is to build the world's tallest skyscraper – 220 storeys – in just seven months.

GRAMMAR

3 Rewrite the sentences in the passive form. Use the words in brackets to start your sentences. Sometimes you will need to use nominalization.

1 BSB prefabricates ninety per cent of their buildings' components. (Ninety per cent)
2 People have compared the construction process to the children's toy 'Meccano'. (Comparisons)
3 They only paint the interiors of the buildings on-site. (Only the painting)
4 They leave the client to choose the exact configuration of the building. (The exact configuration)
5 A client might ask to have a gym, for example. (A request)
6 A BSB video shows a magnitude 9 earthquake not affecting the building. (A BSB video shows)

4 Choose the best options to complete the text about Zhang Yue.

Zhang Yue is a highly successful businessman with a personal fortune of $900 million, a man who is used to [1] *having / getting* things done. He is unusual because, seeing the problems of the environment, he [2] *got / went* green at an early stage of his business career. The Broad Group specializes in producing air-conditioning units and from the start, Zhang [3] *had / got* his engineers focus on developing machines that used natural gas, solar power or waste heat for their energy.

He would like more high-rise buildings [4] *to make / made* using his pre-fabricated model, because he believes that if you could get everyone in cities [5] *lived / to live* in high-rise buildings, more land could be left in its natural state. Also, people could then live and work in the same building, so they would not need cars. But not everyone shares his vision or would like to [6] *get / have* their life organized in this way, however green and good Zhang Yue's intentions are. Employees of the Broad Group know this well. Zhang has them all [7] *memorize / to memorize* his handbook called *Life Attitudes of an Earth Citizen*, in which he tries to [8] *have / get* employees to live healthy and environmentally-conscious lives.

VOCABULARY

5 Match the two halves of these phrases.

1	take	a	in youth training
2	invest	b	ends meet
3	go	c	the economy around
4	enjoy	d	a boom
5	come out of	e	your debts
6	turn	f	bankrupt
7	pay off	g	recession
8	make	h	on new staff

6 Complete the sentences. Use the correct adverbs to make collocations describing objects.

1 We wanted to buy a flat near the seafront, but it was _____ expensive.
2 I thought the way they had decorated the flat was fun – _____ coloured walls and interesting lighting.
3 The building has been _____ admired for its engineering, but not its aesthetic looks.
4 Fifteen centimetres of insulation on the walls is _____ adequate in a mild climate.
5 The house itself was well built, but the fixtures and fittings were very_____ put together.
6 Concrete is a _____ used building material.
7 It is _____ proven that 'sick building syndrome' really exists.
8 The flats are very _____ priced – considering they are in such a popular area.

SPEAKING

7 Work in pairs. Think of three things that are commonly said to be good or bad for your health or the environment.

8 Work with another pair. Take turns to tell each other your ideas from Exercise 7. Discuss whether the ideas are believable or not.

IMPROVE YOUR WRITING Using the appropriate style

9 In formal writing, try to use a more impersonal tone (e.g. using passives). Avoid: contractions (*isn't*); a personal tone (*you know*); conversational language (*I reckon*); starting sentences with *and* or *but*; repeating the same words. Read the short report and rewrite it in a more appropriate style.

> Zhang Yue, the Chinese businessman who's famous for the building he put up in a record nineteen days, has just announced his next project. He's going to build the world's tallest building in the same way. A lot of people expected that he'd follow up his other projects with something pretty amazing. But the size of this new building's surprised most of us. He'll build the new tower, called Sky City, in his home town of Changsha and it'll have a hotel, offices, a hospital and five schools. On top of all that, it'll have homes for 17,000 people. To help all these people get up and down the tower, he plans to put 104 lifts in it. People reckon the cost of all this will be around $1.5 billion. But it won't be the world's tallest building for long, because they're building an even taller one in Jeddah in Saudi Arabia.

10 Work in pairs. Compare your edited versions of the report in Exercise 9. Did you make similar changes?

DEFINITE AND INDEFINITE TIME

Present perfect and past simple

We use the present perfect to talk about actions and events that happened at an indefinite time up to the present. The focus of the present perfect (simple or continuous) is the experience and its effect on the present rather than on a sequence of events in the past.

> I**'ve travelled** to a lot of places, but this must be one of the strangest.

The present perfect simple can describe actions which have the potential to be repeated.

> Sonia **has had** 22 different jobs! (there is the potential for her to have more jobs in her life)

We use the past simple to talk about completed actions and events which happened at a definite time in the past.

> I **travelled** to a lot of places as a student and **saw** some amazing things. (relates the experience to a specific time in the past, i.e. when the speaker was a student)
> Sara **had** 22 different jobs. (she is retired or no longer alive)

Past simple and past continuous

We use the past simple to talk about completed actions, often with words for 'finished time'.

> He **served** in the army **from 2008 to 2012**.

We use the past continuous for actions in progress in the past.

> We **were having** a great time **at the party** until a neighbour complained about the noise.

With the past simple and past continuous, the past time of the action is either explicitly stated or strongly implied.

Present perfect simple and present perfect continuous

We use the present perfect simple:

- to talk about finished actions which have a connection with the present (with words for 'time up to now')
  I**'ve** only **had** one apple to eat today.
- with stative verbs for unfinished actions and situations that continue into the present
  I**'ve owned** the car for about two years.
- to talk about repeated actions in the past that may happen again
  He**'s run** several marathons.

We use the present perfect continuous to talk about:

- actions and situations that started in the past and are continuing up to now, often when we want to focus on how long something has been going on or how someone has been spending their time recently
  He**'s been looking** for a job for the last six months.
  So, what **have you been doing** since I last saw you?

- temporary situations and repeated actions
  I can't park outside my house at the moment because some workmen **have been digging** up the road.

If the verb used in these situations is a stative verb (e.g. know, owe, own, want) or if the period is so long as to imply a state (e.g. live somewhere for ten years) then we use the present perfect simple.

> We**'ve known** each other since we were children.
> She**'s worked** there since she left university.

Notice the difference in meaning between these sentences.

> They**'ve been raising** money for a new children's hospital.
> (= how they've spent their time)
> They**'ve raised** over £100,000 so far. (= the present result of their actions)

Recent time and the news

The present perfect is often used:

- in situations where we want to talk about recent events and their impact on the present
  I**'ve lost** my keys. (= I lost them recently and haven't found them yet.)
- for news
  Police **have arrested** three men in connection with the Hatton Garden jewel robbery last month.

Notice how we use the past simple and past continuous to give further details (e.g. of time and place).

> I thought I **put** my keys down on the kitchen table.
> Police **arrested** the suspects as they **were checking** in for a flight to Spain.

Time phrases

Often a specific time phrase will indicate which tense it is appropriate to use.
Present perfect simple and continuous:

- before, yet, already and ever refer to an indefinite time
  Have you **ever** seen such a blue sky?
- just, recently and lately refer to recent time
  He's **recently** been appointed as chairman.
- in the last ten years, this week, since Tuesday, all my life, for the last two months, etc. indicate unfinished time
  She's been working from home **this week**.
  In the last ten years, the way we shop has completely changed.

Past simple or continuous:

- last week, three days ago, in the past indicate a past time
  We weren't so bothered by health and safety issues **in the past**.

▶ Exercises 1–4

EXPRESSIONS WITH STATISTICS

Describing quantity and number

We can use nouns describing quantity and number:

- to describe countable things, e.g. *a number of, a majority of, a minority of, a handful of*
  The majority of the respondents disagreed.
  There are **a small number of** facts which are very pertinent.

- to describe uncountable things, e.g. *an amount of, a quantity of, a good deal of*
  A good deal of the information is irrelevant to our study.

Some words (that describe parts of a whole) are used with both countable and uncountable nouns (e.g. *a proportion of, a percentage of, a fraction of*).
  Only **a small fraction** of people agreed.

We use percentages with countable and uncountable nouns, e.g. *ninety per cent of the cars, thirty per cent of the time*. We use phrases such as *one in four* and *four out of every five* with countable nouns.
  One in four students owns a car.
  Four out of every five home owners have insurance.

Collocations

There are many collocations to describe quantity and number.

- adjective + noun collocations
  A significant number of students got four A grades.

Other adjective + noun collocations include: *a significant/ substantial number; the vast majority; a large/enormous quantity; a good/small/sizeable/significant proportion; a negligible/significant/small/maximum amount; a small/tiny minority; a tiny fraction*.

- adverb + adjective collocations include: *relatively/very few; surprisingly/very little*

▶ Exercise 5

NOMINALIZATION

The transformation of a verb into a noun is known as nominalization. This is often used in formal writing.
  One person at the meeting **suggested** asking what employees **thought** of the idea.
  → One **suggestion** (made) at the meeting was to ask employees for their **opinion**.

Sometimes nominalization requires using a new verb (and changing other words in the sentence).
  He **suggested** that → He **made the suggestion** that.
  They **don't intend** to participate. → They **have no intention of** participating.
  She **checked** the timetable **quickly**.
  She did **a quick check** of the timetable.

▶ Exercises 6 and 7

EXERCISES

1 Complete the sentences with the present perfect simple, present perfect continuous, past simple and past continuous form of the verbs.

1 I _____ (play) a lot of sport in my younger days, but now I just don't seem to find the time.
2 I _____ (listen) to him speak on the radio as I _____ (drive) here earlier.
3 She _____ (have) a lot of trouble with her car ever since she _____ (buy) it.
4 He _____ (live) in Paris most of his life, but he _____ (never / go) up the Eiffel Tower because he's terrified of heights.
5 I remember the last time he _____ (give) a concert in London. He _____ (tour) with his original band.
6 She _____ (have) an extraordinary career, appearing in over 100 films, and she shows no sign of slowing down.
7 Are you leaving already? Well, thanks for coming. I hope you _____ (enjoy) yourself.
8 I _____ (try) to contact him all morning. I'm giving up now and going for lunch.

2 Choose the correct options to complete the conversations.

Conversation 1
A: Sorry. [1] *Have you been waiting / Have you waited* long?
B: No, not long. [2] *I've just been looking / I've just looked* at your new brochure. It looks great.
A: Yes, we're very pleased with it. [3] *Have you been seeing / Have you seen* the photo of me, though? It's terrible!

Conversation 2
A: [4] *I've been sorting / I've sorted* all the papers in the front office. What would you like me to do now?
B: Oh, that's great. [5] *I've been meaning / I've meant* to do that for ages. Well, if you're free, perhaps we could start on the schedule for next week. [6] *I haven't been having / I haven't had* a chance to look at it yet.

Conversation 3
A: [7] *I haven't been seeing / I haven't seen* that bicycle before. Is it new?
B: Actually, [8] *I've been owning / I've owned* it for about a year, but [9] *I haven't been riding / I haven't ridden* it often because [10] *it has been raining / it has rained* so much.

3 Complete the sentences with these time expressions. There are three extra expressions. Sometimes there is more than one possible answer.

before	ever	for months	in the last five years	just
lately	never	so far	this week	yet

1 Have you _____ heard such nonsense?
2 She hasn't won the race _____ , but she's currently in a very strong position.

3 My train has been delayed every day _____ . It's infuriating.

4 We've been talking to them _____ , but we haven't made much progress _____ .

5 It's _____ been announced that Ellen Reed is going to be the next CEO.

6 _____ the number of people taking holidays abroad has risen by 23 per cent.

4 Write the news headlines in full sentences using the correct form of the present perfect. Then write one more sentence in the past tense giving a detail of the story.

1 WOMAN FINDS ROMAN TREASURE BURIED ON LOCAL BEACH
A woman has found some Roman treasure buried on a local beach.
She *found the treasure while she was walking her dog.*

2 PATIENTS WAITING UP TO 14 WEEKS FOR HOSPITAL APPOINTMENT
_____
A spokesperson for the hospital _____ .
_____

3 MAN CROSSES ATLANTIC IN CANADIAN CANOE
_____
The journey _____ .

4 BUSINESSES TOLD TO BE MORE TRANSPARENT ABOUT SPECIAL OFFERS
_____
A report published yesterday _____ .
_____

5 MOBILE PHONE THIEVES TARGETING SCHOOLCHILDREN
_____
One victim _____ .

5 Complete the article about a survey of students' financial awareness with these words. There is one extra word.

amount	fraction	deal	few	hardly
proportion	substantial	tiny	vast	

Of the 4,000 students questioned, the [1] _____ majority (89%) had taken out loans to fund their studies. Of these, a significant [2] _____ (48%) had borrowed the maximum [3] _____ of money available to them. When asked about the terms of repayment, relatively [4] _____ students (8%) knew what these were. Even more alarmingly, a [5] _____ number of them (22%) thought that it was 'unlikely' that they would ever be forced to repay the loan. This should be of great concern to the government, who up to now have [6] _____ recouped any of the money that they have lent to students: £12.6 million, which is a tiny [7] _____ of the £930 million of total student loans. It seems that however good students may be at their individual subjects, there is a good [8] _____ of work to be done on their financial awareness.

6 Read the sentences. Then write sentences using the nominalized form of the verbs in bold. You may need to add verbs or change other words too.

1 Brazil has **confirmed** that it will **participate** in the talks.
Brazil has *given confirmation of its participation in the talks* .

2 Not everyone agreed with what the report **recommended**.
Not everyone agreed _____ .
_____

3 Researchers published what they had **found** after they had **analysed** the data carefully.
Researchers published _____ .

4 Environmentalists **oppose expanding** the UK's airport capacity.
There is _____ .
_____

5 Businesses have been **demanding** that corporation tax **be reduced**.
There has been a _____ .
_____

6 We **are committed** to improving working conditions in our factories.
We have made _____ .
_____

7 Correct the mistake in each sentence.

1 Thank you for inviting us to dinner last night – we have had a wonderful evening.

2 He's been owing me that money for weeks. Do you think he's forgotten?

3 You've just driven from Manchester? How long has it taken you?

4 I've been working here since three years, but it seems much less.

5 There is a large quantity of part-time workers in the company.

6 My work is so varied. With something new to think about virtually every day, there are very little opportunities to get bored.

FUTURE FORMS

There is no single tense for talking about the future in English. In many cases, the difference between the forms is very subtle, so it's often possible to use more than one form with very little difference in meaning.

will and *shall*

We use *will* + infinitive to talk about simple future facts.

>   The doors **will open** at seven o'clock.
>   It **will be** good to see him again.

We use *shall* (usually in the first person singular and plural) to make an offer or a suggestion, or express a determination to do something.

>   Don't worry – I **shall** definitely **be** there on time.
>   **Shall we** take a break for ten minutes?

Prediction

We use *will* + infinitive to make a general prediction about the future.

>   I think they **will** probably **win** their match.

We use *be going to* + infinitive to make a prediction when there is strong present evidence to show the event will happen or is imminent.

>   Hurry up. It**'s going to** rain any moment.

We use both *will* and *be going to* to talk about predictions and beliefs about future events or situations. The meaning is very similar, and when the prediction is based on the same information, either form can be used.

>   I think it **will be** difficult to persuade her.
>   I think it**'s going to be** difficult to persuade her.
>   You don't need to pick us up. We**'ll hire** a car at the airport.
>   You don't need to pick us up. We**'re going to hire** a car at the airport.

Intentions and arrangements

*   We use *will* + infinitive to describe a decision or offer made at the time we're speaking.
    I**'ll answer** that. I think it's a call for me.

*   We use *be going to* + infinitive to talk about a decision we have already made about a plan or an intention.
    I**'m going to discuss** it with my husband and then come to a decision.

*   We use the present continuous to talk about future fixed arrangements.
    We**'re flying** to Berlin on Saturday; then on Sunday we**'re taking** the train to Gdansk.

*   We use the present simple to describe scheduled events, often when they form part of a timetable.
    The meeting **starts** at 2.00 p.m.
    The flight from Amsterdam **arrives** at 10.45.

*   We use *be to* + infinitive (future infinitive) to talk about official events and formal arrangements.

>   The Queen **is to open** a new hospital in south London later today.
>   The sponsors **are to present** the team with the trophy.

*   We use *will* + infinitive for habits and typical behaviour.

>   He**'ll** often **read** the paper for half an hour before getting down to any serious work.

The future in clauses

After adverbs of future time (*when, as soon as, until,* etc.) we use the present simple or continuous (not *will* or *be going to*) even though the action is in the future.

>   I'm afraid it will be very noisy **when** we <u>are doing</u> the building work next week.
>   We won't begin **until** everyone <u>arrives</u>.

Sometimes we can use the present perfect simple after adverbs of future time.

>   We won't begin **until** everyone <u>has arrived</u>.

We use *be to* + infinitive in *if*-clauses to describe pre-conditions, but only when these can be controlled by people.

>   If we **are to win** the contract, we'll need to put together a good offer.
>   If you think the car **is going to break** down, then we should take the bus. (<u>not</u> ~~is to break down~~)

may and *might*

We can use *may* and *might* + infinitive to make predictions or state intentions when they are less certain.

>   It **may be** difficult to get tickets on the door.
>   She said she **might come** for a drink if she manages to leave work on time.

▶ Exercises 1 and 2

Future continuous and future perfect

We form the future continuous with *will* + *be* + *-ing* form of the verb (*will be doing*).

We use the future continuous to talk about:

*   an activity or event that will be in progress at a stated time in the future
    Today is my last day before my holiday. This time next week I**'ll be lying** on the beach.

*   a prediction about an activity that will be in progress at a certain time in the future
    In ten years' time, everyone **will be living** in high-rise flats in the city centre.

*   a prediction about what we think someone is doing now
    Now is not a good time to ring her. She**'ll be putting** the children to bed.

We often use time expressions with the future continuous to say when the activity will be in progress or the point when it will stop.

This time tomorrow, *you'll be flying to London.*
*I have to finish this report today, so I'll be working **until**
10.00 p.m. this evening.*

We form the future perfect with *will* + *have* + past participle
(*will have done*).

We use the future perfect to talk about:

*   actions and events that will be completed before a stated
    time in the future
    *They **will have moved** into their new house by the end of
    the month.*

We form the future perfect continuous with *will* + *have been* +
-ing form of the verb (*will have been doing*).

We use the future perfect continuous to talk about:

*   how long someone has been doing something, up to a
    certain point in the future
    *By the time he leaves school, he **will have been studying**
    English for twelve years.*

▶ Exercise 3

EXPRESSIONS OF CERTAINTY

We use various expressions (+ infinitive) to express degrees
of probability or certainty about the future.

be bound to	be certain to	be guaranteed to
be (very) likely to	be sure to	be (very) unlikely to

*You**'re bound to catch** a cold if you go out without a
coat. (= very probable)*
*We**'re unlikely to know** their answer before Wednesday.
(= not very probable)*

We use certain fixed expressions more often in conversation
e.g. *it's anyone's guess (whether), it's by no means certain
that, it's a forgone conclusion that.*

We can use *may/might/could* + *well* + infinitive to talk about
things which might happen in the future. The addition of *well*
gives the impression that the future event/action is more
likely to happen.
*I **may/might/could well** be late tomorrow. I have to go to
the dentist.*

Notice that we only use *can well* to talk about present
situations: *I can well understand your concerns.*

Immediate future

We use *be about to* (+ infinitive) and *be on the point/verge of*
(+ *-ing*) to talk about things that are going to happen in the
immediate future, or are on the point of happening.
*We**'re about to get** a new car.*
*She**'s on the verge of handing** in her notice.*

We often use *just* with *about to* to emphasize the closeness
of the event/action.
*I'm **just** about to finish work for the day.*

Notice that we cannot use a time expression with *about to*.
I'm about to leave in ten minutes.

▶ Exercise 4

FUTURE IN THE PAST

When we talk about the future from the perspective of the
past (i.e. an event or action which was in the future at a
particular point in the past), we use the 'future in the past'.
We use verbs or structures that we normally use to talk about
the future, but in the past tense form.

*   We use *was/were going to* + infinitive to talk about
    an intention which was then not fulfilled, or a plan or
    arrangement which then changed.
    *She **was going to buy** the dress but she decided it was too
    expensive.*

*   We use *was/were supposed to* or *was/were due to* to talk
    about a scheduled action or event which then didn't take
    place.
    *The plane **was supposed to land** at 8.00 p.m. but it didn't
    arrive until midnight.*

*   We use *was/were* + *to* + infinitive to talk about a plan or
    arrangement that did not happen. (The meaning is similar to
    be supposed to.)
    *Thursday **was to be** the day of our office party, but it has
    been postponed.*

*   We use *would* + infinitive to report ideas held in the past
    about the future.
    *Originally he said he **would help**, but in the end he was too
    busy.*
    *I thought I**'d be working** from home today, but they've
    called me in to the office for a meeting.*

▶ Exercises 5 and 6

EXERCISES

1 Complete the sentences with the correct future form of the verbs (*will*, *shall*, *be going to*, present continuous and present simple). Sometimes there is more than one possible answer.

1 A: Are you ready to order?
B: Yes, please. I [1] _____ (have) the steak, I think.
A: OK. How would you like it cooked?
B: I [2] _____ (have) it medium, please.

2 A: When [1] _____ (you / leave)?
B: We [2] _____ (fly) back to Munich tomorrow morning. Our daughter [3] _____ (meet) us at the airport.

3 A: Look out! That vase [1] _____ (fall) and break.
B: Oh, thanks. I [2] _____ (put) it on something more stable.

4 A: The conference [1] _____ (start) officially on Friday evening, but most of the delegates [2] _____ (not / arrive) until Saturday.
B: And when [3] _____ (you / get) there?
A: I [4] _____ (probably / be) there on Friday, because I'm on the executive committee.

5 A: I can see that the new tax laws [1] _____ (benefit) the middle classes but what about those people on low incomes?
B: The government has promised that it [2] _____ (help) poor people too.

2 Are the future forms correct or incorrect? If they are incorrect, rewrite them using a correct form.

1 I don't feel like cooking tonight. <u>Will we get</u> a takeaway?
_____

2 I'll look at your computer when I <u>have</u> a moment.
_____

3 If the film <u>is to start</u> at 8, we'd better get there by 7.30.
_____

4 From 3rd May, shops <u>are to be</u> able to open all day on Sundays, if they wish. _____

5 Things <u>might get</u> worse before they get better.
_____

6 Please don't touch anything until I <u>will have had</u> a chance to look at it. _____

7 I think you have to invite her. She <u>can be</u> offended otherwise. _____

8 Harry says he<u>'s going to look</u> for a new job.
_____

3 Choose the best option to complete the sentences.

1 I know it's very noisy with the builders here, but they *will be going / will have gone* by the end of the week.

2 I don't think he'll ever finish the book. By this summer, he *will be working / will have been working* on it for over ten years.

3 It's 7.00 a.m. in New York and people *will just be waking up / will just have been waking up* to the news.

4 Don't worry – in a few weeks' time, everyone *will be forgetting / will have forgotten* it ever happened.

5 You can give me Tania's phone, if you like. *I'll be seeing / I'll have seen* her later.

6 I think I'd better go now. My husband *will be wondering / will have been wondering* where I am.

4 Rewrite the sentences using the words in brackets.

1 I'm sure he will face some tough questions from reporters. (bound)
He _____ from reporters.

2 It's very probable that the government will lose the vote. (may well)
The government _____ .

3 I don't think they will have sold out of tickets yet. (unlikely)
I think they _____ .

4 I expect she'll be given a warm reception when she arrives. (likely)
I think she _____ when she arrives.

5 They will sign a new five-year contract in the next few days. (verge)
They _____ .

6 The 50-storey building will be demolished later today. (about)
The 50-storey building _____ .

5 Complete the sentences with the correct form of these verbs. Use the future in the past.

arrive	get married	make	not last	report	stay

1 I _____ at the party longer, but it was getting dark and I didn't have any lights on my bicycle.

2 We _____ at six o'clock, but our train broke down and we got in four hours late.

3 They _____ in June, but now Julia has to go abroad for her work for six months from May.

4 There were rumours that Elton John _____ an appearance at the concert, but these turned out to be false.

5 I knew that coffee machine _____ long. I said all along that it was cheap and poorly made.

6 I _____ my car stolen when my son phoned me and told me he had borrowed it to transport some musical equipment!

6 Correct the underlined mistake in each sentence.

1 Sorry, I can tell you're busy. I <u>call</u> you later.

2 OK. I<u>'m talking</u> about it with my wife this evening.

3 They plan to visit a lot of museums when they<u>'ll be staying</u> in Paris.

4 I think we should let them know we're delayed because <u>they're getting</u> worried.

5 I don't think anyone is likely <u>that they will notice</u> the difference.

6 I didn't realize you<u>'re going to perform</u> at the concert. I would have come.

Grammar summary | UNIT 3

STATIVE AND DYNAMIC VERBS

Dynamic verbs

Dynamic verbs describe an action (what we do) or an event (what happens), for example: *break, disappear, explode, lose, play, throw, walk, work.* They can be used in any tense and form (simple or continuous).

> She **broke** her leg when she was skiing.
> He **lost** the match.

Stative verbs

Stative (or state) verbs describe a state, usually one that continues for a period of time, rather than an action. We use stative verbs to describe thoughts, perceptions, feelings and possession (e.g. *believe, doubt, know, realize, seem, suppose, understand; smell, sound; deserve, hate, like, need, prefer, want, wish; belong, consist, contain, include, own.*) We do not use these verbs in the continuous form with their stative meanings.

> When he looks back on the experience, he **will realize** how lucky he is. (not *will be realizing*)
> They **own** two houses. (not *are owning*)
> How long **have you known** her? (not *have been knowing*)

Verbs that have two meanings

There are some verbs that can be used as both stative and dynamic verbs but with a difference in meaning. The main ones are: *be, have, mean, see, smell, think, taste.*

> He **is** a tall man. (= state)
> He **is** just **being** difficult. (= acting this way temporarily)
> That **tastes** good. (= state)
> I**'m tasting** the sauce. (= the action of testing the taste of)
> I **think** you're right (= believe)
> I**'ve been thinking** about what you said. (= reflecting on)
> They **have** two young children. (= possession)
> He**'s having** trouble finding a job. (= phrase with 'have')
> I **see** what you mean. (= understand)
> I**'m seeing** the doctor tomorrow. (= visiting)

Notice that we can use *be* in the continuous form to talk about behaviour and actions but not feelings.

> He feels sad about it. (not *He is being sad about it.*)

Stative verbs with dynamic usage

In some cases, with verbs that describe wants, needs and expectations, we can use a normally stative verb in a continuous tense to give it a dynamic sense.

> I **was** really **hoping** you would call.
> She**'s loving** her time at university.
> I**'ll be needing** some help with that.

We can use *always, forever* or *endlessly* with a continuous tense to describe a persistent (or irritating) habit.

> He**'s always forgetting** his books.

▶ Exercises 1–3

EMPHATIC STRUCTURES

Cleft sentences

We use cleft sentences to highlight an item or idea that we want to emphasize. We do this by introducing the item or idea with a phrase beginning *it's, what* or *the thing.*

Non-emphatic sentences:

> We are concerned by the high cost of the project.
> The high cost of the project concerns us.

Emphatic sentences:

> **It's** the high cost of the project **that** concerns us.
> The high cost of the project **is what** concerns us.
> **What** concerns us **is** the high cost of the project.
> **The thing that** concerns us is the high cost of the project.

Extra emphasis can be given to a cleft sentence by adding an adverb such as *really* or *particularly*.

> **It's** the high cost of the project **that really** concerns us.

Other emphatic structures

We can also add emphasis in the following ways:

- in a present or past simple sentence, we can use an auxiliary verb (*do, does, did*) + infinitive in place of the normal verb
  The high cost of the project **does concern** us.

Notice that with other tenses, we can emphasize something when speaking by placing added stress on the auxiliary.

> The high cost of the project <u>has</u> given us cause for concern.

▶ Exercise 4

DESCRIBING DIFFERENT PERSPECTIVES

We can describe the perspective from which we are viewing a particular situation or issue in various ways.

- adverb or adverb + *speaking*
  Personally (speaking), I don't like the on-screen keyboard.
  Statistically speaking, flying is much safer than driving.

- *from a(n)* + adjective + *perspective / point of view* or *from the point of view of* (+ noun)
  From an economic perspective, a break-up of the Union would not necessarily be a disaster.
  From the point of view of the economy, a break-up of the Union would not necessarily be a disaster.

- *as far as* + noun + *is concerned* or *in terms of* + noun
  As far as safety is concerned, we check all systems prior to departure.
  In terms of safety, we check all systems prior to departure.

In spoken English we can also add *-wise* to a noun.

> **Safety-wise**, there is no better car seat on the market.

▶ Exercises 5 and 6

EXERCISES

1 Complete the conversations with the simple or continuous form of the verbs in the correct tense.

1 A: I went for lunch at Kelly's restaurant yesterday. It gets two stars in the Good Food Guide, but it ¹ _____ (deserve) more than that.

   B: What ² _____ (you / have)?

   A: Soup and then some fish. I couldn't eat the dessert because it ³ _____ (contain) nuts. But you should go there. I ⁴ _____ (promise) you won't be disappointed.

2 A: I don't know why Kate ¹ _____ (not / want) to come with us to the party last night.

   B: I ² _____ (not / think) that she ³ _____ (be) unfriendly. She just ⁴ _____ (not / feel) in the mood.

3 A: ¹ _____ (you / enjoy) your new job?

   B: It's been great, so far. I ² _____ (learn) a lot, but it ³ _____ (involve) a lot of travelling at the moment – meeting all the customers, that kind of thing.

   A: ⁴ _____ (you / mind) that – the travelling, I ⁵ _____ (mean)?

   B: It ⁶ _____ (depend) on the distance.

4 A: Sorry, I missed your call. I ¹ _____ (have) lunch.

   B: Oh, I ² _____ (see). I ³ _____ (think) you must be out. I ⁴ _____ (just / call) about the project that we ⁵ _____ (discuss) the other day.

2 Cross out the verbs that cannot be used in the continuous form.

1 *I love / I'm loving* this chocolate cake you've made.
2 *I hoped / was hoping* that you could help me, actually.
3 *He owns / He's owning* a collection of vintage cars.
4 *She's promised / She's been promising* to lend her support to the campaign.
5 It *doesn't really matter / isn't really mattering* what I think.
6 It *doesn't surprise / isn't surprising* me in the least that they can't find anyone to do the job.
7 We *didn't believe / weren't believing* that it was right.
8 I *didn't imagine / wasn't imagining* that you'd contribute money – just some of your time.
9 I think everyone *deserves / is deserving* a second chance.

3 Complete the sentences with these verbs in the correct form.

feel	look	seem	sound	taste

1 A: What are you doing?

   B: I ¹ _____ this sauce to see if it needs more sugar. Actually, I think it ² _____ sweet enough.

2 A: You ¹ _____ very smart in your suit yesterday. Was there some special occasion?

   B: I had a job interview. I ² _____ pretty nervous about it, actually, but it ³ _____ to go OK.

3 A: Would you like to go for a drink this evening?

   B: Yes, that ¹ _____ great. It ² _____ ages since we had a chance to talk properly.

4 Rewrite the sentences to make them more emphatic using the words in brackets.

1 I find the relationship between spelling and pronunciation in English really difficult. (what)

_____

2 Planning the details of your trip in advance has its advantages, but it also has some drawbacks. (does)

_____

3 I liked that the documentary left you to make up your own mind about the rights and wrongs of the situation. (thing)

_____

4 Her answer didn't surprise me, but her violent reaction did. (it)

_____

5 Wherever you go in New Orleans, the quality of live music is impressive. (it's)

_____

6 People with that kind of selfless attitude and determination can change the world. (it)

_____

5 Complete the sentences about banning smoking in public bars and restaurants. Use one word (an adverb, adjective or noun) to describe perspective.

1 _____ , I think it's good idea.
2 _____ speaking, the idea should be relatively easy to implement.
3 _____ -wise, it should be beneficial for the population at large.
4 From a _____ perspective, the government feels this could be a vote-winner.
5 _____ , restaurant and bar owners fear it could damage business.
6 As far as _____ themselves are concerned, they feel that this is just another case of the government interfering in the choices of the individual.

6 Correct the mistake in each sentence.

1 It was his car, but it is belonging to me now.

_____

2 I am promising you that it won't take very long.

_____

3 I think she is just cautious on this occasion.

_____

4 I sent the chair back because it cost over $100 and it wasn't feeling comfortable.

_____

5 It is the tone of his letter what is so surprising.

_____

6 From an economically perspective, it doesn't make sense.

_____

PAST FORMS

Past simple

We use the past simple to talk about an event or action, or sequence of events / actions in the past. The past time is stated (*last week, five years ago*, etc.) or is clear from the context.

> I **moved** to Hong Kong two years ago.
> He **rushed** to the station, **bought** a ticket and **jumped** on the first available train.

Past continuous

We use the past continuous to talk about:

- activities or situations that were in progress in the past when another action took place
  We **were living** in New York when the financial crash happened in 2008. I **was working** for Lehman Brothers, the bank that famously went bankrupt.

- activities or states that describe the background to past actions
  My job **was going** well so I decided to stay in Chicago.

Remember that we do not use state verbs in the continuous form.

Past perfect simple

We use the past perfect simple to talk about an action that took place at an earlier time than the main event in a narrative, especially when the events are not mentioned in the sequence they happened.

> John was in a bad mood when I met him. His bank card **had been swallowed** by a cash machine and the bank **had refused** to let him withdraw any cash.

Past perfect continuous

We use the past perfect continuous to talk about an activity or state in progress before the main event took place.

> Laura wasn't happy. Her flight was overbooked and she **had been arguing** for nearly an hour with the check-in clerk before she managed to get a seat.

used to and would

- In most cases we use the past simple to talk about things that were done in the past. However, we use *used to* + infinitive to talk about habits and states when we want to emphasize the habitual nature of past actions. These forms also indicate that these actions do not happen or exist now.
  There **used to be** some beautiful old houses there, but they demolished them to make way for a shopping centre.
  I **used to play** tennis quite well when I was in my teens, but I haven't played for years.

- We use *would* + infinitive to talk about habits (not states) that took place in the past but do not happen now.
  In my first job, I **would** always **work** long hours, as I wanted to be promoted quickly.

When we are reminiscing about the past, if we are describing a sequence of habitual actions, we often use *used to* for the first verb and *would* for subsequent actions.

> We **used to go** down the lake in the afternoons. We **would swim** and play around. We **would** also **try** to catch fish, but we never caught anything much.

Notice that we don't use *would* + infinitive to talk about past states (i.e. with stative verbs).

> We **used to live** in the country until I was about nine years old. (not We ~~would live~~ in the country.)

▶ Exercises 1 and 2

could and was able to

We use *could* + infinitive or *was able to* + infinitive to talk about past abilities.

> I **was able to** / **could swim** when I was four years old.

If we are talking about an ability to do something on a specific (past) occasion or our ability to overcome a specific difficulty, we cannot use *could*. We must use *was able to* or *managed to* or *succeeded in* + -*ing*.

> The water was flowing fast and I was terrified. Luckily I **was able to grab** a branch and scramble to the bank.
> He took his driving test six times. On the seventh occasion he **succeeded in passing** it.

Notice that this rule does not apply to verbs of perception or in the negative.

> Once we reached the top of the building, we **could see** out over the entire city.
> I found an old radio in the attic but I **wasn't able to** / **couldn't** make it work.

Past modal verbs

Modal	Past form
must (obligation)	*had to* + infinitive
must (speculation)	*must have* + past participle
could / may / might (possibility)	*could have / may have / might have* + past participle
should (advice)	*should have* + past participle

- We use *had to* + infinitive to talk about the necessity to do something at a particular time in the past.
  We **had to drive** around the area for an hour before we found a parking space.

- We use *must have* + past participle to make a deduction about a past event or action.
  He **must have been** very unfit because he was breathing hard by the time we got to the top of the hill.

- We use *could have / may have / might have* + past participle to speculate on a past event or action.
  We realized that she **might have gone** to the wrong restaurant.

- We use should *have* + infinitive to talk about something that was done in the past, but would have been better not done. *They **shouldn't have invested** so much in one area of the business.*

▶ Exercise 3

INVERSION WITH ADVERBIAL PHRASES

We often use adverbial phrases in narratives. Sometimes, to give emphasis within a sentence, we use inversion after an adverbial phrase (e.g. *no sooner, not only, only when, never, little*) when it is placed at the beginning of the sentence.

> **Never** <u>had I seen</u> such a huge cake!
> **Little** <u>did I realize</u> how much work the job would entail.

With some adverbial phrases, other changes in the sentence are needed, for example, the addition of a word to connect the two clauses.

> *We set off and then there was a loud bang and the train came to a shuddering halt.*
> **No sooner** <u>had we set</u> off **than** there was a loud bang and the train came to a shuddering halt.

Examples of adverbial phrases which are used at the beginning of the sentence are:

> Only by (+ *-ing*) …
> No sooner … than …
> Not only … , (but) also …
> Not until …
> Such … that …
> So + adjective … that …
> Hardly … when …
> Only when (+ subject + verb) , (inverted verb form) …
> Only + clause

We were very captivated by the performance and entirely forgot the time.
→ **So captivated** <u>were we</u> by the performance **that** we entirely forgot the time.

When the smoke cleared, the extent of the damage became apparent.
→ **Only when** the smoke cleared <u>did</u> the extent of the damage <u>become</u> apparent.

Notice that many of these adverbial phrases using inversion are negative.

▶ Exercises 4 and 5

EXERCISES

1 Complete the conversations with the correct past tense of the verbs.

Conversation 1
A: What ¹ _____ (you / talk) to Philip about when I walked in a moment ago?
B: Oh he ² _____ (tell) me about his trip to America. He ³ _____ (go) to San Diego for a conference and then ⁴ _____ (stop) off in Las Vegas for three days on the way back home.
A: What ⁵ _____ (he / think) of Las Vegas?
B: He said you either love it or you hate it. Also he ⁶ _____ (not / appreciate) before what a cosmopolitan place it was. There were visitors from all over the world. He ⁷ _____ (meet) a Japanese couple who ⁸ _____ (go) there every year for the last forty years.

Conversation 2
A: How was your meeting yesterday?
B: It ¹ _____ (go) on far too long. Several people ² _____ (fall) asleep by the end!
A: Why ³ _____ (you / not / leave)?
B: I couldn't. I ⁴ _____ (be supposed) to be addressing the meeting, but I ⁵ _____ (not / get) a chance because Charles spoke for ages. By the time he ⁶ _____ (finish) speaking, everyone ⁷ _____ (be) desperate to get home.

Conversation 3
A: Oh, there you are. I ¹ _____ (get) worried.
B: Sorry, I ² _____ (get) held up in traffic. A lorry ³ _____ (overturn) on the A34 and spilled its load of live fish. A lot of other people ⁴ _____ (stop) and ⁵ _____ (try) to help pick them up.

2 Choose the correct option to complete the narrative. Sometimes both options are possible.

I ¹ *was loving / loved* the summer holidays when I was young. Some kids ² *used to say / would say* that they were too long, but it never seemed that way to me, because we ³ *were studying / had been studying* for months before they started. Not that we ⁴ *used to go / went* anywhere special for the holidays; we ⁵ *were living / lived* on a farm and there was always plenty to amuse us. I ⁶ *would often help / was often helping* Dad out with the jobs around the farm in the mornings and then when he ⁷ *used to finish / had finished* work for the day, he ⁸ *would take / took* us up to an area called the mounds, where you ⁹ *could see / were able to see* out over all the countryside. He ¹⁰ *built / had built* a small cabin for us there and we ¹¹ *would happily play / used to play happily* in it for hours or try to catch small animals like mice or rabbits. Once we even ¹² *could catch / managed to catch* a weasel.

3 Rewrite the sentences using an appropriate form of the modal verbs in brackets.

1 I don't think she went to the festival because she had to work that weekend. (could)
She _____,
because she had to work that weekend.

2 It was silly of her to leave her bags unattended. (should)
She _____.

3 We were obliged to take a taxi because the buses had stopped running for the night. (have)
We _____ because
the buses had stopped running for the night.

4 Perhaps I was mistaken, but I was sure that he winked at me as he said it. (could)
I _____ but I was sure that he winked
at me as he said it.

5 No one applies for a job to become a spy, so it's obvious to me that he was recruited by the secret service. (must)
No one applies for a job to become a spy, so he
_____.

6 I don't know how the window was broken, but perhaps a child threw a stone at it. (might)
I don't know how the window was broken, but a child
_____.

4 Put the words in order to make sentences using inversion with an adverbial phrase.

1 the food / it / was also burnt / was / cold / not only / but

2 the force of the blast / the windows in buildings three streets away / were / was / that / shattered / such

3 manage to stay awake / did / only / he / by / speaking to himself as he walked

4 had / when / opened his mouth to speak / she / interrupted / hardly / he

5 she / had / the room erupted into loud applause / finished speaking / than / no sooner

6 when / did / he / had / realize his mistake / opened the parcel / he / only

7 fatal / poisonous / just a small bite / so / that / was / the snake's venom / could have been

8 of giving up / he / only / had / ever thought / in moments of deep frustration

5 Correct the mistake in each sentence.

1 I used to owning a beautiful old Citroen DS, but I sold it.

2 It was a lucky escape. The car crashed right where the children had played a few minutes before.

3 I said it was going to rain. You should take your umbrella.

4 The concert was amazing. We could get seats right at the front.

5 Not only they stole my laptop, but they also stole my memory stick.

6 I couldn't find the tickets, so only by paying the entrance fee again we were able to get in.

PASSIVE FORMS

Form

We form the passive with the verb *be* + past participle. We can use the verb *be* in all tenses and with modal verbs, although the present perfect continuous and past perfect continuous forms are not used very often. The past participle of the main verb does not change form.

Active	Passive
They **are closing** the road for three weeks.	The road **is being closed** for three weeks.
They **opened** the new wing last year.	The new wing **was opened** last year.
People **have asked** that question many times before.	That question **has been asked** many times before.

For the passive form of modal verbs, we use modal + *be* + past participle.

We **can see** the coast of France from here.	The coast of France **can be seen** from here.
They **should have warned** us about the delays.	We **should have been warned** about the delays.

by + agent

If we want to say who or what performed the action (the agent), we introduce the agent with the preposition *by*.
*The building **was designed by** Zaha Hadid.*

We can give information about the purpose of the action or why it takes place using the preposition *for*.
*The tests **were carried out for** medical reasons.*

Verbs with two objects

Some verbs take two objects (e.g. *award, buy, book, find, give, offer, owe, pass, show, teach*). In these cases, there are two possibilities for forming a passive sentence.
My aunt gave me this watch when I was seven.
▶ *I was given **this watch** by my aunt when I was seven.*
▶ ***This watch** was given **to me** by my aunt when I was seven.*

Use

We use the passive to focus on what happens: the action or process which takes place. We often use the passive in (formal) writing contexts, for example news stories, technical descriptions, business reports and academic texts. We also use the passive for describing processes which consist of a series of stages.

We often use the passive:

• when the agent is unknown, obvious or not relevant
*The car **was stolen** some time during the night from in front of the house.* (= by some thieves, but we don't know who)

- in factual writing when we want to avoid using subjects like *they, we, you, people*
  *Further information **can be found** on our website.*
- when we want to describe a sequence of actions happening to one thing, i.e. a process
  *The gas **is cooled** until it becomes a liquid and **is** then **pumped** into tankers.*
- when we put new or interesting information later in the sentence ('the end-weight principle'). In the following example we know who *she* is (given information). The new information is who trained her.
  *Have you met my beauty therapist, Sonia? She **was trained** at Chanel.* (not *Chanel trained her.*)

We can only form the passive with transitive verbs (verbs that take a direct object). We don't form the passive with intransitive verbs (verbs without a direct object, e.g. *cry, disappear, laugh, rise, sleep*).
  *The musical **was** first **performed** in 1985.*
  *The book mysteriously **disappeared** from the library.* (not *The book was mysteriously disappeared from the library.*)

▶ Exercise 1

The passive infinitive and *-ing* form

We form the passive infinitive with *to be* + past participle.
  *I'm expecting the building work **to be finished** by December.*
  *It's embarrassing **to be told** off when you're an adult.*

We form the perfect passive infinitive with *to have been* + past participle. Often the perfect or the present passive infinitive can be used without a difference in meaning.
  *I expected the building work **to have been finished / to be finished** by now.*

We use *being* + past participle to form the passive *-ing* form.
  *I congratulated her on **being shortlisted** for a prize.*
  ***Being told off** when you're an adult is embarrassing.*

To form the negative, we put *not* before the passive infinitive or *-ing* form
  *We were surprised **not to be included** on the guest list.*
  *He was annoyed **not to have been asked** to the party.*
  *She resented **not being invited** to the press conference.*

▶ Exercise 2

NOMINALIZATION IN PASSIVE SENTENCES

When we form nouns from other parts of speech (e.g. verbs and adjectives), this is called 'nominalization'. We often use nominalization in formal writing and speech, for example to report on events. In these cases, we usually have to use another verb with the nominalized form. (For more information about nominalization, see page 75.) In formal writing, we can also make the added verb passive.

1 *They **announced** yesterday that they were selling the company.*
→ *They <u>made</u> **an announcement** yesterday that they were selling the company.*
Passive: ***An announcement** <u>was made</u> yesterday that they were selling the company.*

2 *We **prefer** candidates with an IT background.*
→ *We <u>give</u> **preference** <u>to</u> candidates with an IT background.*
Passive: ***Preference** <u>is given</u> to candidates with an IT background.*

Notice that in sentence 2, we have to add a preposition in the nominalized form.

▶ Exercise 3

PASSIVE REPORTING VERBS

We use passive reporting verbs to describe what people know, think or say about a particular event or situation – when we don't want to say something is an established fact. This structure is common in formal writing, e.g. newspaper articles, academic essays and business documents. We can report actions and events in two different ways.

- *It* + passive reporting verb + *that*-clause
  ***It is thought that** this is the first time that the drug has been used to treat cancer patients.*

Reporting verbs that commonly follow this pattern are: *agree, assume, allege, announce, believe, claim, consider, decide, hope, report, say, suggest, think, understand*.

- subject + passive reporting verb + *to* + infinitive
  ***This is thought to be** the first time that the drug has been used to treat cancer patients.*

Reporting verbs that commonly follow this pattern are: *allege, assume, believe, consider, know, report, say, think, understand*.

Passive reporting verbs are sometimes used with an agent, but often do not use an agent because the speaker is reporting what is generally believed or does not want to give the sources of the information.
  *In those days **it was believed that** the world was flat.*
  *In those days **the world was believed to be** flat.*

▶ Exercises 4 and 5

EXERCISES

1 Read the sentences. Then write sentences using the passive form of the verbs in bold. Include the agent where necessary.

1 The report **says** nothing about how they **are going to fund** these measures.

Nothing is said in the report about how these measures are going to be funded.

2 We **have carried out** numerous tests on the engine's reliability and we **will publish** the findings in due course.

_____

3 While a team of French engineers **was developing** the drone, several technical issues came to light.

_____

4 While some experts **claim** that global temperatures have risen by around 1.5 degrees, other experts **dispute** this fact.

_____

5 This is the actual spacesuit that Neil Armstrong **wore** when he took those first historic steps on the Moon.

_____

6 The travel agency **has just announced** that it **will not compensate** customers who cancelled their holidays because of the heatwave in Spain last month.

_____

7 They **would have added** extra concert dates to their tour, if demand had been stronger.

_____

8 They **should finish** the main building by the end of the year, but the ancillary buildings **will require** more time to complete.

_____

2 Complete the sentences with the passive infinitive or *-ing* form of the verbs.

1 Holidaymakers are advised to take extra precautions against _____ (bite) by mosquitoes.

2 I'd prefer _____ (tell) if I'm not doing the work in the way you like.

3 _____ (pressure) into doing something against your will is never a nice feeling.

4 She complained about _____ (treat) unfairly by her employer.

5 _____ (make) to work on a Sunday is illegal in some countries.

6 It was better _____ (call) for an interview and then rejected than _____ (not / call) at all.

7 Certain conditions need _____ (meet) before you can apply for citizenship.

8 I was disappointed _____ (not / ask) to join the team, but actually rather relieved _____ (not / involve) as it was a lot of work.

3 Complete the sentences using nominalization. Nominalize the verb in bold and use the verb in brackets in the correct passive form.

1 They **will announce** the winner tomorrow. (make)
The *announcement* of the winner *will be made* tomorrow.

2 **Has** anyone **attempted** to contact them? (make)
_____ any _____ to contact them?

3 We **thought** a lot about this before we came up with the proposal. (give)
A lot of _____ to this before we came up with the proposal.

4 They **concluded** that the project was not viable in the long-term. (reach)
The _____ that the project was not viable in the long-term.

5 The sales team **is meeting** in Geneva this year. (hold)
The sales team _____ in Geneva this year.

6 No one has **researched** this area thoroughly before. (do)
No thorough _____ in this area before.

7 I think we **must allow** for different age groups. (make)
I think _____ for different age groups.

8 We **need to consider** the opinions of everyone. (give)
_____ to the opinions of everyone.

4 Write follow-up sentences using a passive reporting verb structure. Use the words given.

1 There is great anticipation about the upcoming film. (It / say / feature / special effects not seen before)

2 Did you hear about the Van Gogh painting that someone found in the attic? (It / now / think / be / a fake)

3 The Queen will not be stopping off in Manchester as expected. (She / believe / go / straight to Scotland)

4 There was great excitement at Edinburgh Zoo yesterday. (The Giant Panda / report / give birth)

5 The CEO's announcement of his retirement came as a shock. (He / suppose / carry on / for another year)

6 News is just coming in about the Swarovski jewel thieves. (They / report / escape / from a high-security prison)

7 Police are warning people to stay indoors. (The escaped criminal / know / be / dangerous)

8 I wish I had seen the documentary on tigers last week. (It / suppose / be / fascinating)

5 Correct the mistake in each sentence.

1 The price of bread has been gone up by 200 per cent in the last eight months.

2 They are thought that they are hiding in the mountains.

3 The project was began in 2012 and it has been plagued with problems ever since.

4 I was surprised to not be invited for an interview.

5 No decision has taken yet, but I'm sure it won't be long.

6 I was doubted myself at times, but my friends encouraged me to persevere with the idea.

CAUSATIVES

have / get something done

We use *have / get* + object + past participle to mean that we arrange for another person to do something for us. We can use *by* + agent to mention the agent, but in many cases the agent is obvious and doesn't need to be mentioned.

> *I'm going to **get my eyes tested** next week.* (= by the optician)
> *I **had the parcel delivered** to my workplace.* (= by the courier)

Notice that we don't usually use *get something done* in the present perfect. (not *Have you got your hair cut?*)

We can also use *get* + object + past participle to say that the person did something themselves or something happened by accident.

> *I'll try to **get the report finished** today.* (= I'll do it myself)
> *She **got her fingers caught** in the elevator doors.* (= by accident)

I'll try to have the report finished today is also possible, but in this case it is unclear if the speaker or another agent will be involved.

We can use the verbs *want, would like, need* + object + past participle to talk about things we need or would like to be arranged to be done.

> *We **need (to get) the roof repaired**. It's leaking.*
> *I'd **like (to get) this suit cleaned** by next Thursday.*

▶ Exercise 1

have someone do / get someone to do

We can use *have* + person object + infinitive or *get* + person object + *to* + infinitive to describe that we are arranging for something to be done for us. We use these forms when we want to specify who the person doing the job is.

> *I **had an architect draw** up some plans.*
> *We need to **get a professional translator to do** this.*

get something to do / doing

We use *get* + object + *to* + infinitive to say that we managed or didn't manage to make something work.

> *She **got the phone to switch** on again.*
> *I couldn't **get the key to fit** in the lock.*

We sometimes use *get* + object + *-ing* to talk about things that we manage to set in motion.

> *I'd like to **get the discussion going** with a question about ...*
> *How did you manage to **get the washing machine working** again?*

▶ Exercises 2 and 3

EXPRESSIONS WITH *GO* AND *GET*

We use *go* or *get* + adjective like the verb *become*, to say that something has started to have that quality. Often it describes changes for the worse.

> *These oranges are **going bad**. We can't eat them.*
> *Sorry, I'm **getting confused**. Can you explain that again?*

Adjectives with *go* include: go bad, go bald, go bankrupt, go blind, go crazy, go deaf, go missing, go quiet, go red in the face, go rusty, go sour, go well/fine, go wrong

Adjectives with *get* include: get angry, get annoyed, get confused, get dark, get ill/sick, get involved, get lost, get married, get old, get pregnant, get ready, get started, get tired, get upset

With *somewhere, nowhere* and *anywhere*, *go* and *get* have a slightly different meaning.

> *He's **going nowhere**.* (= He is staying where he is.)
> *Are you **getting anywhere** in your discussions with John?* (= making any progress)

▶ Exercise 4

REPORTED SPEECH

We use reported speech to report someone's words or thoughts. When we report people's words, we put the verb we are reporting one step back in the past.

> *'I'm waiting for Jo.'* → *He said (that) he **was waiting** for Jo.*
> *'I'll think about it.'* → *She said (that) she **would think** about it.*

With the modal verbs *could, should, would, might, ought to* and with verbs in the past perfect, the verb remains the same.

> *'You **should see** them.'* → *He said (that) I **should see** them.*
> *'If I **had known**, I **would have left**.'* → *She claimed that if she **had known**, she **would have left**.*

If the situation you are reporting is still true when you report it (or true from your point of view at the time), the tense of the verb can stay the same.

> *'I **hate** eating fish.'* → *He said that he **hates / hated** eating fish.*
> *'I **didn't want** to go.'* → *She said that she **didn't want / hadn't wanted** to go.*

When we report questions, we don't use auxiliary verbs or question marks and the subject-verb order is affirmative.

- We use the same *wh*-question word to report questions.
  'When are you leaving?' → *He asked me **when I was leaving**.*

- For *yes/no* questions, the reported question is introduced with *if* or *whether*.
  'Have you heard of them?' → *She asked **if I'd heard** of them.*

When we report speech, we often need to change other words, such as time phrases or demonstrative pronouns.

> *'I like **these** games.'* → *He said (that) he liked **those** games.*
> *'I saw the film **yesterday**.'* → *She said (that) she had seen the film **the day before**.*

▶ Exercises 5 and 6

EXERCISES

1 Complete these conversations using *get* or *have* + object + past participle of the verbs given.

1

A: Your hair looks a different colour. Have you
¹ _____? (it / dye)

B: No, it's the same colour. I ² _____ last week, though. (cut)

2

A: Your finger looks very sore.

B: I know. I ³ _____ in a drawer at home. (it / stick)

A: You should ⁴ _____ by a doctor. (it / look at)

3

A: Our neighbours have an amazing house. They
⁵ _____ by a professional architect. (design)

B: When did they ⁶ _____ ? (do)

4

A: How's your book coming along? Have you written it?

B: No, I probably won't ⁷ _____ until the end of the year. (finish)

5

A: Is Sarah painting her bedroom?

B: Yes, but it's going very slowly. She's only managed to
⁸ _____ . (one wall / paint)

2 Choose the correct option to complete the sentences.

1 Can you have Francesca *call / to call* me as soon as she's free?
2 If you made a lot of mistakes, the teacher would get you *do / to do* the whole exercise again.
3 That documentary we saw last night got me *to think / thinking*. Why couldn't I do a cycle ride for charity?
4 It was so cold this morning that I couldn't get the car *started / starting*.
5 Because we didn't know much about Venezuela, we had a travel agent *organize / organized* the whole trip for us.
6 Can you help me get this window *to open / opening*? It seems to be stuck.
7 You'll never guess how much it cost me to get my suit *to dry clean / dry cleaned*.
8 Why did James have you *pick / to pick* him up at the airport? There's a bus that runs every fifteen minutes.

3 Put the words in order to make sentences.

1 your / need / tested / eyes / you / get / to
_____

2 at work / the flowers / to / get / I'll / delivered / her
_____

3 medium rare / would like / cooked / my steak / I
_____

4 never / me / to / get / you'll / go / on a motorbike
_____

5 the meeting / who / to / started / get / would like / ?
_____

4 Complete the text with the correct form of *go* or *get*.

The company ¹ _____ out of business last month. I don't know what ² _____ wrong exactly, but I think it was because Jenny, the manager ³ _____ ill earlier in the year and had to take several months off. So she left her deputy in charge, but then the deputy took time off to ⁴ _____ married. The guy who took over didn't really know what he was doing and the whole thing ⁵ _____ from bad to worse. So in the end, Jenny, who was ⁶ _____ crazy by this point, went back to try and rescue the situation, but by then things had ⁷ _____ out of control. A lot of their customers had ⁸ _____ frustrated with the situation and had found other companies to work with.

5 Read the statements. Then complete the reported statements.

1 'Have I seen that face somewhere before?'
I asked myself _____ .
2 'I will be here at the same time next week.'
He promised that _____ .
3 'I would like to come but I don't think I can.'
She said _____ .
4 'What would my father have done, if he were in this situation?'
I wondered _____ .
5 'Are you busy just now?'
She asked me _____ .
6 'You really ought to think hard before you make such a big decision.'
He advised me that _____ .
7 'Why didn't you ask for help two days ago?'
She questioned _____ .

6 Find and correct the mistake in each sentence.

1 What do I have to do to get you understanding?
_____
2 I like him as a teacher because he always gets you think.
_____
3 I need to have my passport to be renewed.
_____
4 I'm going to the hairdresser's to cut my hair.
_____
5 She told me yesterday that she is having a horrible day at work.
_____
6 I needed to know what time were they arriving.
_____

Communication activities

Unit 1.3 Exercise 8, page 14

1 make slippers? (this was the beginning of Clarks shoe company)
2 fruit in it. (Amazin' Raisin)
3 stay young.
4 worked in a London bank.
5 invented a system for each house to collect the water from its roof with pipes, filter it though an ordinary piece of mosquito net at the end of one pipe, and then transfer it to a large storage barrel.

Unit 1.4 Exercise 2, page 16

Statements of participants

1 Feeling part of a team: 'It's very democratic: office clerks and senior managers are operating on a level playing field in a way that they don't normally do in the workplace, so it breaks down barriers between people.'
2 Personal confidence: 'It's fantastic for building your self-confidence.'
3 Well-being: 'It just makes me feel good – I guess it's where I can release a lot of adrenaline.'
4 Sense of community and co-operation: 'We became so close working together as a choir – the support people gave each other was amazing.'
5 Positive attitude to work: 'What really struck me was how proud I felt to represent the company … in a totally different way than I normally do … but still I felt very proud.'

Unit 3.4 Exercise 7, page 39

Student A
Stress is bad for your health and productivity

Stress is not always bad for you. It does not increase your blood pressure. It gets your brain working faster. It stimulates the immune system and helps you to fight illness. Dealing with a stressful situation can help you the next time you face one. It drives you to succeed in stressful situations (e.g while playing a sport, giving a talk, etc.).

Unit 5.1 Exercise 13, page 55

Changes in global distribution of wealth

Percentage of people who can afford to fly abroad for a vacation:

1975: 70% were from the EU and North America; 30% were from the rest of the world

2014: 50% were from the EU and North America; 50% were from the rest of the world

2025: 37% will be from the EU and North America; 63% will be from the rest of the world

Unit 5.4 Exercise 2, page 60

1 True
2 Probably true: one prediction is that wild fish stocks will be so depleted by 2050 that we will have to stop fishing in the open seas.

3 True: half of the people in Africa live on less than one dollar a day; a cow in Europe receives two dollars a day in subsidies.
4 True: humans produce only four per cent of the world's CO_2 emissions; the other 96 per cent are natural. But the Earth's ability to absorb CO_2 is very finely balanced and human activity has upset this balance.
5 False: it produces twenty per cent of the world's oxygen.
6 False: deforestation is occurring at a rate of three football fields every minute.

Unit 5.4 Exercise 6, page 61

Student A

1 In the northern hemisphere, moss will grow most on the northern side of the tree where there is most shade. Also, if you find a tree that has been cut down and look at the rings, the bigger rings will be on the southern side, where the tree gets more sunlight. In the southern hemisphere it's the opposite.
2 It is known that loneliness increases blood pressure, accelerates dementia, and puts people at higher risk of developing a disability.

Unit 6.4 Exercise 3, page 70

1 Zappos preferred answers in the middle of the scale. They considered those who answered '1' to be too conservative and those who answered '10' to be too eccentric.
2 For the question 'If you were a cartoon character, which one would you be?', one candidate answered 'Yogi Bear' and got the job immediately!
3 You might say it depends how big the room is, but actually even a very small room should be able to do it. The Empire State Building has 102 floors. If the height of the room you're using is the same as the height of each floor of the Empire State Building, you will need 102 stacks of coins from floor to ceiling, plus maybe another 20 or so to account for the distance between each floor. These should fit into the room easily.
4 Tyma's mother's solution was to take each record off the top of the pile and look at the age. For each age, 21, 20, 19, 18, she made a separate stack. When she had finished, she put the stacks in order. This solution was quicker and more practical than many of the Google applicants' answers, who suggested complicated mathematical algorithms.

Unit 6.4 Exercise 13, page 71

Interview for a job with a charity

1 All candidates are put together in a big room to chat for twenty minutes (actually a test of your sociability)
2 Brainstorming session on ideas for fundraising
3 Presenting your ideas in pairs to the rest of the group (be enthusiastic)
4 Individual interviews: questions about experience and knowledge of the charity (read up about the charity before you go); ask questions yourself

Audioscripts

Unit 1

🎧 2

I don't mean to say that being wrong is the same thing as being creative. What we do know is, if you're not prepared to be wrong, you'll never come up with anything original.

🎧 3

A: What do you think of the choir idea, then?
B: I'm really in favour of it, actually. I can't sing to save my life, but it sounds like fun. What about you? You're into music, aren't you?
A: Well, yeah, in the sense that I really like listening to music, and going to gigs, but I'm not sure I want to sing that kind of music.
B: What kind of music?
A: You know, church choral music or, or music from a musical. That's not really my kind of thing.
B: What, so you aren't going to audition for it?
A: No, I think I will. I'm quite curious, but I'll be surprised if I get picked. I'm not great at singing either.
B: Oh, come on. I've heard you sing. You're a natural.
A: Er, I'd hardly say that, but it sounds fun. I have to say, I do like the idea of creating something from nothing – you know, the buzz you get from building something from scratch with other people. I reckon that aspect of it would be really rewarding.
B: Yes, that's exactly what appeals to me too. All right, well hope to see you there then.

Unit 2

🎧 5

I would be a beauty but my nose is slightly too big for my face
And I would be a dreamer but my dream is slightly too big for this space

🎧 6

These statistics are just a snapshot of how people feel at the moment. They show a group of newly industrialized countries like China, Brazil and India, where people feel things are going to get better, and a group of post-industrial countries – countries which no longer rely on heavy industry, like the US, Spain and France – where people think that in thirty years, things will have got considerably worse. In this way, they just reflect the current economic climate in these countries: the first group has growing economies, the second group is going through more challenging times.

But the situation is very likely to change. Don't get me wrong, I'm not saying that things are about to change. I'm saying that in thirty years or so, Western economies certainly won't be doing the same things they are doing now, relying on service sector industries like banking and insurance. If we are to progress, the post-industrial economy will have to evolve. And I think that will happen. We will use creative thinking and technology to overcome the problems that we are all bound to face in the future: problems of overpopulation, scarcity of resources, environmental change. A better standard of living in the post-industrialized nations may or may not come out of that, but I believe that a better quality of life, for all nations, almost certainly will. If you're interested in hearing more about this, follow the Future Optimist conference which takes place next week. It's online and I'm speaking on Tuesday. There are plenty of other speakers too who …

🎧 7

Scenario 1

Here's a worst-case scenario. You're on business in another country and you need to get back for the weekend because it's your sister's wedding. But there's a terrible snowstorm during the night and your flight home is cancelled. What should you do?

OK. The first thing is prevention. Always be aware of the weather conditions where you're going and, for your own peace of mind, check the weather reports before you travel in case there are any bad forecasts. Checking that your flight operator or travel insurance company covers you for such eventualities is also a good idea. Any reputable company should be obliged to look after you in these circumstances, although I'd say generally, avoid using low-cost operators, because asserting your rights can be more difficult with them.

What to do about it is more tricky. I'd strongly advise against finding alternative routes home. The chances are that everyone else is thinking the same thing and that boats, buses and trains will also be affected by the weather conditions. So the best thing is to sit tight and wait it out. Try to make friends with someone else in the same situation. It may be helpful if you're having to spend hours waiting at an airport and will keep you in a better mood when you go to speak to the harassed ground staff. Lastly, if it's going to be a lengthy wait at an airport, consider finding an executive airport lounge and paying the €30 or whatever they ask for non-members.

Scenario 2

How do you protect yourself against the possibility of leaving all your valuables in a local taxi? OK. The first thing I would say is: always take your time when getting out of a taxi. Check you have everything, then get out and pay the driver. Secondly, opt for official taxis over less regulated operators – and ask for their business card so you have the taxi operator's number. That way, your driver will be easier to track down. And always label all your belongings. That will ensure that should an honest person find them, they can return them. Lastly, tip your driver well – one good turn deserves another. And if you do find you've left something, call the company immediately and explain what's happened.

Unit 3

🎧 9

Over the next five minutes, my intention is to transform your relationship with sound. Let me start with the observation that most of the sound around us is accidental, and much of it is unpleasant. (*Traffic noise*) We stand on street corners, shouting over noise like this, and pretending that it doesn't exist. Well this habit of suppressing sound has meant that our relationship with sound has become largely unconscious.

There are four major ways sound is affecting you all the time, and I'd like to raise them in your consciousness today.

🎧 10

A: You'd imagine that peace and quiet was the best thing for concentrating and getting your work done, wouldn't you? But that's simply not the case for many people, especially younger people who've been brought up on a diet of background music and YouTube videos. I was chatting to a friend the other day who works from home and she said that, in point of fact, she finds it really difficult to work at her computer with no noise around her.
B: Really? So, what does she do – listen to music?

A: No, she finds that too distracting. She listens to a recording of background office noise. It's a kind of low-level noise of people typing and chatting on the phone, as if she were in an open-plan office.

B: That's really odd – 'cos I've read studies about this and the popular belief now is that open-plan offices don't work precisely because people find all the surrounding noise too invasive. But if it works for her, I guess you can't argue with that.

A: Yes, she claims it does. It's a bit like our neighbours too, actually. They turn on the vacuum cleaner to get their baby to sleep.

B: What?

A: Yes, apparently, according to them, it's the only thing that works. I have to say when they first did it, we wondered what on earth was going on. We thought they'd decided to start doing the housework at eleven o'clock at night.

Unit 4

🎧 **13**

4 So I want you to pay attention to what you're doing right now.

5 We're going to come back to that in a few minutes.

🎧 **14**

The earliest form of non-spoken communication – humans are believed to have started speaking to each other about 100,000 years ago – is the use of drawing. Around 40,000 years ago, people in Spain and Indonesia were making paintings on the walls of caves, showing aspects of their daily lives. This is important because it indicates growing human intelligence. The representation of words using pictograms naturally followed on from this, which was an important step in the development of the kinds of alphabet we know today. Writing using pictograms or early alphabets was first done on stone and then on papyrus in Ancient Egypt. The use of papyrus meant that messages could be transported from one place to another. By 780 BC, the Greeks were sending short handwritten messages by carrier pigeon. In this way, they conveyed messages far more quickly than people had been able to do before. The first proper postal service was created by the Persians in the sixth century BC. Horse riders used to carry documents from one posting station to another. Together they would cover distances of 2,000 kilometres or more in a matter of days. But the real revolution in written communication came with the invention of the printing press in 1440 AD. Up until then, people had been reading handwritten documents. That must have been an extraordinary time in history – a bit like the introduction of the Internet thirty years ago – because almost immediately, many more people had access to books and to ideas.

🎧 **15**

1 **A:** Here – let me give you a hand with that suitcase.
   B: Thanks, that's very good of you, but I can manage.
   A: Are you sure?
   B: Yes, but thanks for offering all the same.

2 **A:** Hello, Frank Haskins speaking.
   B: Hi, Frank. It's me, Megan. Could I possibly have a quick word with Sarah, if she's free?
   A: Sorry, she's busy just now.
   B: OK. I'll give her a ring later.

3 **A:** Hi, I'd like to speak to the bank manager.
   B: I'm sorry. She's not available at the moment. Perhaps I can help you?
   A: Thank you, but I really need to speak to her in person.

4 **A:** Do you fancy popping round for a drink later? Or shall I come to you?
   B: I don't mind really. Up to you.
   A: OK. I'll come to you, then. Say 7.30?
   B: Yup, that'd be perfect.

5 **A:** Hello, Sir, can I help you at all?
   B: Yes, I'd like to pay for the room now.
   A: One second. I'll get your bill.

6 **A:** When shall we meet?
   B: Let's say eight o'clock outside the cinema.
   A: Great. Eight o'clock suits me perfectly.

7 **A:** Thanks for the use of the car. By the way, I filled it up.
   B: Oh, thank you for doing that. You shouldn't have.
   A: No – thank you. I couldn't have got to my friends' house without it. It's a really out-of-the-way place.

8 **A:** Can I get you anything from the shops?
   B: That's kind of you, but I don't want to put you out.
   A: It's no trouble – I'm going anyway.

9 **A:** Bad news. My brother lost his job yesterday. The car factory is going to close down.
   B: Oh, I'm really sorry to hear that. I hope he can find another job.
   A: Yes, I know – it's terrible. He doesn't seem too down though, given the circumstances.

10 **A:** OK, I need to be off now. I've got a train to catch.
   B: Can I drop you off at the station?
   A: If it's on your way, that'd be great, thanks.
   B: Not at all.

Review 2 (Units 3 and 4)

🎧 **16**

I = Interviewer, J = Journalist

I: So, Blindekuh – it's a very interesting concept. Can you just tell me how it came about?

J: Yes, it was a project that was set up by four people who were working as guides at a design exhibition in Zurich in 1998 called 'Dialogue in the Dark'. They themselves were visually impaired. The point of the exhibition was to let fully-sighted people understand the experience of being blind. So visitors were given canes and were then guided through a series of everyday scenarios – a public park, a busy street, a food market. The four guides wanted to take this idea further so they set up a charitable foundation called the Blind-Leicht or 'blind light' foundation and the restaurant idea came out of that.

I: And what exactly are the benefits – for customers and employees?

J: Well, for employees, that's clear: they get to work in an environment which is usually not open to them. Actually, that they get to work at all is an important step – about seventy per cent of people of working age in Europe who have a severe sight impairment are unemployed. For the customers, the benefits are interesting. Generally when you go and eat in a restaurant or listen to a band play as you eat, you're taking in a lot with your eyes as well as with your taste buds and ears. But in this case, the experience of eating or listening is greatly intensified because one of your senses has effectively been shut off. This not only changes your experience, it also makes you aware of what it's like to have impaired vision.

I: And do some people feel uncomfortable with that – the fear that they might spill something, or eat something they don't like?

J: I think a lot of people feel very uneasy and even a bit scared at first, but they generally relax into it. After all, they know it's only temporary and that's the comment I hear most often – 'What must it be like to be in the dark all the time?'

I: So how does it work practically? Can you just take me through what happens when you arrive at the restaurant?

J: Yes, you're met by a waiter or waitress who guides you into the darkened restaurant area – you put your hand on their shoulder; when you're seated, they explain what's on the menu and take your order. Then you sit there and eat as you would normally. Actually, you eat much more slowly than you would normally, and you probably end up talking to your fellow guests much more than you would normally, because there's no visual distraction. It's actually quite an eye-opener, if you'll forgive the expression.

I: No, I can see that – it sounds amazing.

Unit 5

🎧 17

I was only four years old when I saw my mother load a washing machine for the very first time in her life. That was a great day for my mother. My mother and father had been saving money for years to be able to buy that machine, and the first day it was going to be used, even Grandma was invited to see the machine. And Grandma was even more excited. Throughout her life she had been heating water with firewood, and she had handwashed laundry for seven children. And now she was going to watch electricity do that work.

🎧 18

The disparity in energy use between different countries is linked of course to their level of economic development, but that's not the only factor. Both Germany and the USA are highly industrialized nations, but in the United States, much more energy is being consumed by each person. In part that's because it's a bigger country, so people travel more, but it's also down to attitudes.

American energy consumption could easily be reduced if greater priority was given to energy efficiency. Actually, I'm confident that efforts will be made in this direction, particularly by industry – cleaner fuels, cleaner industrial processes and so on – because the evidence for climate change is now so strong.

The big question is: will developing countries do the same? Transport's a big issue – air travel in particular. People in developing countries have been restricted by the cost up to now, but as they get richer and air travel becomes cheaper, its impact on energy consumption is bound to grow.

The statistics for energy use in the home show that the main area which needs to be addressed is heating and cooling. The solution is relatively cheap and simple. It just means homes being insulated properly. People complain about their energy bills, but it's pretty clear, to me at any rate, that energy is still too cheap, otherwise people would do something about reducing them – instead of leaving lights on at home and driving gas-guzzling cars.

🎧 19

A: Did you know that most of the carbon dioxide in the world is not produced by man-made activity?

B: No. I thought that industrial activity was the main cause of rising CO_2.

A: No, that's a common misconception. Most of the CO_2 is produced by the oceans. The human contribution is only about four per cent.

B: So why are people always saying that we need to reduce emissions from factories and power plants?

A: Because that's what the environmental lobby would have you believe, 'cos it fits with their general view that people shouldn't tamper with nature. But actually people are not the problem when it comes to climate change.

B: Hmm. Well, I don't know where you read that, but I'd take it with a big pinch of salt, if I were you. Ninety-nine per cent of scientists agree that human activity is the cause of climate change.

A: It's fact. Look on the Internet. You can see the statistics for yourself.

Unit 6

🎧 22

So there are lots of things that we're still working on, but one thing I have learned is that bamboo will treat you well if you use it right.

🎧 23

A: Did you know that a lot of people get injured doing DIY?

B: No, but it doesn't surprise me. My brother-in-law got his fingers caught in an attic trap door the other day and then he fell off the ladder he was standing on.

A: Ouch. Was he OK?

B: No, he had to get my sister to drive him to the hospital so he could have his fingers stitched.

A: What was he trying to do?

B: Yeah, good question. Actually, he couldn't get the light in the attic to work, so he went up to fit a new light bulb. Not the sort of job that you would get an electrician in for.

A: Well, that's the problem, isn't it? There are always so many little things in the house that go wrong or need doing that just aren't worth paying someone else to do. Like I wanted to get our bathroom repainted, but it's such a small room that it seems crazy to have a professional decorator do it.

B: No, that's right. There are some jobs you can easily do yourself, but there are others you really need to get a professional to do. I wouldn't know where to start changing the brake pads on my car. I get confused when I have to put air in the tyres.

A: Well, that's partly because you need specialist tools for things like that. If you try to do them without the right tools, you'll probably mess it up, or worse hurt yourself. I mean, I'm happy doing a bit of gardening, but there's no way I'd get up a tree and start sawing branches off! What I find surprising is that so many people – often men, actually – think they're good at DIY when they're not.

B: Yeah, I think my brother-in-law is one of them! He's terribly proud. Still, he managed to get the light fixed, even if it did cost him some crushed fingers.

24

Interview 1

I = Interviewer, C = Candidate 1

I: So you're currently self-employed.

C: Yes, that's right. I do translation work for various clients. I work from home.

I: I imagine that takes quite a lot of self-discipline. Do you find it difficult to keep to a strict work schedule?

C: Umm, no, not too hard. I try to start early and then basically I work through till I've got the job finished. Usually I'm working to very tight deadlines.

I: I see. And what's your best time of day? When are you most productive, would you say?

C: I couldn't tell you really. It usually depends on how much sleep I've had.

Interview 2

I = Interviewer, C = Candidate

I: OK. I want you to imagine this scenario. You've pushed a cork into a bottle and you want to get it out. How would you go about it?

C: Ooh, that's a tricky question. Hang on, is the bottle full?

I: Let's imagine it's half full.

C: OK. I guess the first thing I'd do is to empty out the liquid into another container so that I didn't make a mess. Then I suppose I'd try and find something long and sharp to spear the cork with, and I'd move the bottle around until the cork was sitting at the bottom in an upright position so that when I'd speared it, I could withdraw it more easily. But then it still might get stuck, mightn't it? Let me have a think. Hmm, actually, I don't see how this is going to work without breaking the bottle, because it's the nature of corks that they expand once they are out of the neck of the bottle.

Communication activities

Unit 3.4 Exercise 7, page 39

Student B

Listening to sad music makes you sad

Why is it that we often listen to sad music when we feel sad?
You would think it would make us sadder. But research shows
that listening to sad music when we are feeling sad:

- provides us with consolation, especially if we are relating to
  someone else's similar experience through a song
- makes us feel more peaceful and calm
- helps us to be more imaginative and find solutions to a
  particular problem

Unit 5.4 Exercise 6, page 61

Student B

1 Using an automatic dishwasher saves on average
  2,000 gallons of water a year. It uses electricity of course,
  but far less energy than is used to process that amount
  of water.
2 One medium carrot contains 200 per cent of your daily
  recommended vitamin A intake. This vitamin, also known
  as retinol, is responsible for maintaining the health of your
  eyes. Vitamin A helps your eyes retain their ability to adjust to
  changes in light and maintains the necessary moisture and
  mucus levels of your eyes.

TED Talk Transcripts

The transcripts use British English for all the talks, irrespective of the nationality of the speaker. Any grammatical inaccuracies in the talks have been left uncorrected in the transcripts.

Unit 1 Do schools kill creativity?

0.12 So I want to talk about education and I want to talk about creativity. My contention is that creativity now is as important in education as literacy, and we should treat it with the same status. Thank you. (*Applause*) That was it, by the way. Thank you very much. So, fifteen minutes left. (*Laughter*) Well, I was born … no. (*Laughter*)

0.46 I heard a great story recently – I love telling it – of a little girl who was in a drawing lesson. She was six, and she was at the back, drawing, and the teacher said this little girl hardly ever paid attention, and in this drawing lesson, she did. The teacher was fascinated. She went over to her, and she said, 'What are you drawing?' And the girl said, 'I'm drawing a picture of God.' And the teacher said, 'But nobody knows what God looks like.' And the girl said, 'They will, in a minute.' (*Laughter*)

1.22 When my son was four in England – actually, he was four everywhere, to be honest. (*Laughter*) If we're being strict about it, wherever he went, he was four that year. He was in the Nativity play. Do you remember the story? (*Laughter*) He didn't have to speak, but you know the bit where the three kings come in? They come in bearing gifts, and they bring gold, frankincense and myrrh. This really happened. We were sitting there and they I think just went out of sequence, because we talked to the little boy afterwards and said, 'You OK with that?' And he said, 'Yeah, why? Was that wrong?' They just switched. I think that was it. Anyway, the three boys came in, little four-year-olds with tea towels on their heads, and they put these boxes down, and the first boy said, 'I bring you gold.' And the second boy said, 'I bring you myrrh.' And the third boy said, 'Frank sent this.' (*Laughter*)

2.20 What these things have in common, you see, is that kids will take a chance. If they don't know, they'll have a go. Am I right? They're not frightened of being wrong. Now I don't mean to say that being wrong is the same thing as being creative. What we do know is, if you're not prepared to be wrong, you'll never come up with anything original – if you're not prepared to be wrong. And by the time they get to be adults, most kids have lost that capacity. They have become frightened of being wrong. And we run our companies like this, by the way. We stigmatize mistakes. And we're now running national education systems where mistakes are the worst thing you can make. And the result is that we are educating people out of their creative capacities. Picasso once said this, he said that all children are born artists. The problem is to remain an artist as we grow up. I believe this passionately, that we don't grow into creativity, we grow out of it. Or rather, we get educated out of it. So why is this?

3.21 I lived in Stratford-on-Avon until about five years ago. In fact, we moved from Stratford to Los Angeles. So you can imagine what a seamless transition this was. (*Laughter*) Actually, we lived in a place called Snitterfield, just outside Stratford, which is where Shakespeare's father was born. Are you struck by a new thought? I was. You don't think of Shakespeare having a father, do you? Do you? Because you don't think of Shakespeare being a child, do you? Shakespeare being seven? I never thought of it. I mean, he was seven at some point. He was in somebody's English class, wasn't he? Do you know what I mean? (*Laughter*) How annoying would that be? (*Laughter*) 'Must try harder.' (*Laughter*) Being sent to bed by his dad, you know, to Shakespeare, 'Go to bed, now!' – you know, to William Shakespeare – 'And put the pencil down.' (*Laughter*) 'And stop speaking like that.' (*Laughter*) 'It's confusing everybody.' (*Laughter*)

4.33 Anyway, we moved from Stratford to Los Angeles, and I just want to say a word about the transition, actually. My son didn't want to come. I've got two kids; he's 21 now and my daughter's sixteen. He didn't want to come to Los Angeles. He loved it, but he had a girlfriend in England. This was the love of his life, Sarah. He'd known her for a month. (*Laughter*) Mind you, they'd had their fourth anniversary by then, because it's a long time when you're sixteen. Anyway, he was really upset on the plane, he said, 'I'll never find another girl like Sarah.' And we were rather pleased about that, frankly – (*Laughter*) because she was the main reason we were leaving the country. (*Laughter*)

5.25 But something strikes you when you move to America and when you travel around the world. Every education system on Earth has the same hierarchy of subjects. Every one. Doesn't matter where you go. You'd think it would be otherwise, but it isn't. At the top are mathematics and languages, then the humanities, and at the bottom are the arts. Everywhere on Earth. And in pretty much every system too, there's a hierarchy within the arts. Art and music are normally given a higher status in schools than drama and dance. There isn't an education system on the planet that teaches dance everyday to children the way we teach them mathematics. Why? Why not? I think this is rather important. I think maths is very important, but so is dance. Children dance all the time if they're allowed to, we all do. We all have bodies, don't we? Did I miss a meeting? I mean, I think … (*Laughter*) Truthfully, what happens is, as children grow up, we start to educate them progressively from the waist up. And then we focus on their heads. And slightly to one side.

6.21 If you were to visit education, as an alien, and say 'What's it for, public education?' I think you'd have to conclude, if you look at the output, who really succeeds by this, who does everything that they should, who gets all the brownie points, you know, who are the winners – I think you'd have to conclude the whole purpose of public education throughout the world is to produce university professors. Isn't it? They're the people who come out the top. And I used to be one, so there. (*Laughter*) And I like university professors, but you know, we shouldn't hold them up as the high-water mark of all human achievement. They're just a form of life, another form of life. But they're rather curious, and I say this out of affection for them. There's something curious about professors. In my experience – not all of them, but typically – they live in their heads. They live up there, and slightly to one side. They're disembodied, you know, in a kind of literal way. You know, they look upon their body as a form of transport for their heads. (*Laughter*) Don't they? It's a way of getting their head to meetings. (*Laughter*)

7.31 Our education system is predicated on the idea of academic ability. And there's a reason. The whole system was invented, around the world, there were no public systems of education, really, before the nineteenth century. They all came into being to meet the needs of industrialism. So the hierarchy is rooted on two ideas. Number one, that the most useful subjects for work are at the top. So you were probably steered benignly away from things at school when you were a kid, things you liked, on the grounds you would never get a job doing that. Is that right? Don't do music, you're not going to be a musician; don't do art, you won't be an artist. Benign advice – now, profoundly mistaken. The whole world is engulfed in a revolution. And the second is academic ability, which has really come to dominate our view of intelligence, because the universities designed the system in their image. If you think of it, the whole system of public education around the world is a protracted process of university entrance. And the consequence is that many highly talented, brilliant, creative people think they're not, because the thing they were good at at school wasn't valued, or was actually stigmatized. And I think we can't afford to go on that way.

8.36 In the next thirty years, according to UNESCO, more people worldwide will be graduating through education than since the beginning of history. Suddenly, degrees aren't worth anything. Isn't that true? When I was a student, if you had a degree, you had a job. If you didn't have a job, it's because you didn't want one. And I didn't want one, frankly, so … (*Laughter*) But now kids with degrees are often heading home to carry on playing video games, because you need an MA where the previous job required a BA, and now you need a PhD for the other. It's a process of academic inflation. And it indicates the whole structure of education is shifting beneath our feet. We need to radically rethink our view of intelligence.

9.18 We know three things about intelligence. One, it's diverse. We think about the world in all the ways that we experience it. We think visually, we think in sound, we think kinaesthetically. We think in abstract terms, we think in movement. Secondly, intelligence is dynamic. If you look at the interactions of a human brain, as we heard yesterday from a number of presentations, intelligence is wonderfully interactive. The brain isn't divided into compartments. In fact, creativity – which I define as the process of having original ideas that have value – more often than not comes about through the interaction of different disciplinary ways of seeing things. And the third thing about intelligence is, it's distinct.

10.00 I'm doing a new book at the moment called *Epiphany*, which is based on a series of interviews with people about how they discovered their talent. I'm fascinated by how people got to be there. It's really prompted by a conversation I had with a wonderful woman who maybe most people have never heard of, she's called Gillian Lynne. Have you heard of her? Some have. She's a choreographer, and everybody knows her work. She did *Cats* and *Phantom of the Opera*. She's wonderful. I used to be on the board of The Royal Ballet in England, as you can see. Anyway, Gillian and I had lunch one day and I said, 'How did you get to be a dancer?' And she said it was interesting. When she was at school, she was really hopeless. And the school, in the '30s, wrote to her parents and said, 'We think Gillian has a learning disorder.' She couldn't concentrate; she was fidgeting. I think now they'd say she had ADHD. Wouldn't you? But this was the 1930s, and ADHD hadn't been invented at this point. It wasn't an available condition. (*Laughter*) People weren't aware they could have that. (*Laughter*) Anyway, she went to see this specialist.

11.03 So, this oak-panelled room, and she was there with her mother, and she was led and sat on this chair at the end, and she sat on her hands for twenty minutes while this man talked to her mother about all the problems Gillian was having at school. And at the end of it, because she was disturbing people; her homework was always late; and so on, little kid of eight. In the end, the doctor went and sat next to Gillian, and said, 'Gillian, I've listened to all these things that your mother's told me, I need to speak to her privately.' So he said, 'Wait here. We'll be back; we won't be very long,' and they went and left her. But as they went out of the room, he turned on the radio that was sitting on his desk. And when they got out the room, he said to her mother, 'Just stand and watch her.' And the minute they left the room, she said she was on her feet, moving to the music. And they watched for a few minutes and he turned to her mother and he said, 'You know, Mrs Lynne, Gillian isn't sick; she's a dancer. Take her to a dance school.'

11.56 I said, 'What happened?' She said, 'She did. I can't tell you how wonderful it was. We walked in this room and it was full of people like me. People who couldn't sit still. People who had to move to think.' Who had to move to think. They did ballet, they did tap, they did jazz, they did modern, they did contemporary. She was eventually auditioned for the Royal Ballet School; she became a soloist; she had a wonderful career at the Royal Ballet. She eventually graduated from the Royal Ballet School, founded her own company, the Gillian Lynne Dance Company, met Andrew Lloyd Webber. She's been responsible for some of the most successful musical theatre productions in history, she's given pleasure to millions, and she's a multi-millionaire. Somebody else might have put her on medication and told her to calm down.

12.38 What TED celebrates is the gift of the human imagination. We have to be careful now that we use this gift wisely and that we avert some of the scenarios that we've talked about. And the only way we'll do it is by seeing our creative capacities for the richness they are and seeing our children for the hope that they are. And our task is to educate their whole being, so they can face this future. By the way – we may not see this future, but they will. And our job is to help them make something of it. Thank you very much. (*Applause*)

Unit 2 Why I live in mortal dread of public speaking

0.12 I didn't know when I agreed to do this whether I was expected to talk or to sing. But when I was told that the topic was language, I felt that I had to speak about something for a moment.

0.32 I have a problem. It's not the worst thing in the world. I'm fine. I'm not on fire. I know that other people in the world have far worse things to deal with, but for me, language and music are inextricably linked through this one thing.

0.58 And the thing is that I have a stutter. It might seem curious given that I spend a lot of my life on the stage. One would assume that I'm comfortable in the public sphere and comfortable here, speaking to you guys. But the truth is that I've spent my life up unto this point and including this point, living in mortal dread of public speaking. Public singing, whole different thing. (*Laughter*) But we'll get to that in a moment. I've never really talked about it before so explicitly. I think that that's because I've always lived in hope that when I was a grown-up, I wouldn't have one. I sort of lived with this idea that when I'm grown, I'll have learned to speak French, and when I'm grown, I'll learn how to manage my money, and when I'm grown, I won't have a stutter, and then I'll be able to public speak and maybe be the prime minister and anything's possible and, you know. (*Laughter*) So, I can talk about it now because I've reached this point, where – I mean, I'm 28. I'm pretty sure that I'm grown now. (*Laughter*) And I'm an adult woman who spends her life as a performer, with a speech impediment. So, I may as well come clean about it.

2.47 There are some interesting angles to having a stutter. For me, the worst thing that can happen is meeting another stutterer. (*Laughter*) This happened to me in Hamburg, when this guy, we met and he said, 'Hello, m-m-m-my name is Joe,' and I said, 'Oh, hello, m-m-m-m-my name is Meg.' Imagine my horror when I realized he thought I was making fun of him. (*Laughter*)

3.23 People think I'm drunk all the time. (*Laughter*) People think that I've forgotten their name when I hesitate before saying it. And it is a very weird thing, because proper nouns are the worst. If I'm going to use the word 'Wednesday' in a sentence, and I'm coming up to the word, and I can feel that I'm going to stutter or something, I can change the word to 'tomorrow' or 'the day after Tuesday', or something else. You know, it's clunky, but you can get away with it, because over time I've developed this loophole method of using speech where right at the last minute you change the thing and you trick your brain. But with people's names, you can't change them. (*Laughter*) When I was singing a lot of jazz, I worked a lot with a pianist whose name was Steve. As you can probably gather, 'S's and 'T's, together or independently, are my kryptonite. But I would have to introduce the band over this rolling vamp, you know, and when I got around to Steve, I'd often find myself stuck on the 'St'. And it was a bit awkward and uncomfortable and it totally kills the vibe, you know. So after a few instances of this, Steve happily became 'Seve', and we got through it that way. (*Laughter*)

5.22 I've had a lot of therapy, and a common form of treatment is to use this technique that's called smooth speech, which is where you almost sing everything that you say. You kind of join everything together in this very singsong, kindergarten teacher way, and it makes you sound very serene, like you've had lots of Valium, and everything is fine. (*Laughter*) That's not actually me. And I do use that. I do. I use it when I have to be on panel shows, or when I have to do radio interviews, when the economy of airtime is paramount. (*Laughter*) I get through it that way for my job. But as an artist who feels that their work is based solely on a platform of honesty and being real, that feels often like cheating.

6.36 Which is why before I sing, I wanted to tell you what singing means to me. It's more than making nice sounds, and it's more than making nice songs. It's more than feeling known, or understood. It's more than making you feel the things that I feel. It's not about mythology, or mythologizing myself to you. Somehow, through some miraculous synaptic function of the human brain, it's impossible to stutter when you sing. And when I was younger, that was a method of treatment that worked very well for me, singing, so I did it a lot. And that's why I'm here today. (*Applause*)

7.54 Singing for me is sweet relief. It is the only time when I feel fluent. It is the only time when what comes out of my mouth is comprehensively exactly what I intended. (*Laughter*) So I know that this is a TED Talk, but now I'm going to TED sing. This is a song that I wrote last year. Thank you very much. Thank you. (*Applause*)

8.36 (*Piano*) I would be a beauty but my nose is slightly too big for my face / And I would be a dreamer but my dream is slightly too big for this space / And I would be an angel but my halo it pales in the glow of your grace / And I would be a joker but that card looks silly when you play your ace

10.07 I'd like to know / Are there stars in hell? And I'd like to know know if you can tell / That you make me lose everything I know / That I cannot choose to or not let go

10.50 And I'd stay forever but my home is slightly too far from this place / And I swear I try to slow it down when I am walking at your pace / But all I could think idling through the cities / Do I look pretty in the rain? / And I don't know how someone quite so lovely makes me feel ugly / So much shame

11.55 And I'd like to know / Are there stars in hell? And I'd like to know know if you can tell / That you make me lose everything I know / That I cannot choose to or not let go

12.52 Thank you very much. (*Applause*)

Unit 3 The 4 ways sound affects us

0.12 Over the next five minutes, my intention is to transform your relationship with sound. Let me start with the observation that most of the sound around us is accidental, and much of it is unpleasant. (*Traffic noise*) We stand on street corners, shouting over noise like this, and pretending that it doesn't exist. Well, this habit of suppressing sound has meant that our relationship with sound has become largely unconscious.

0.33 There are four major ways sound is affecting you all the time, and I'd like to raise them in your consciousness today. First is physiological. (*Loud alarm clocks*) Sorry about that. I've just given you a shot of cortisol, your fight/flight hormone. Sound's affecting your hormone secretions all the time, but also your breathing, your heart rate – which I just also did – and your brainwaves.

0.55 It's not just unpleasant sounds like that that do it. This is surf. (*Ocean waves*) It has a frequency of roughly twelve cycles per minute. Most people find that very soothing, and interestingly, twelve cycles per minute is roughly the frequency of the breathing of a sleeping human. So there is a deep resonance with being at rest. We also associate it with being stress-free and on holiday.

1.14 The second way in which sound affects you is psychological. Music is the most powerful form of sound that we know that affects our emotional state. (*Albinoni's Adagio*) This is guaranteed to make most of you feel pretty sad if I leave it on. Music is not the only kind of sound, however, which affects your emotions. Natural sound can do that too. Birdsong, for example, is a sound which most people find reassuring. (*Birds chirping*) There is a reason for that. Over hundreds of thousands of years we've learned that when the birds are singing, things are safe. It's when they stop you need to be worried.

1.42 The third way in which sound affects you is cognitively. You can't understand two people talking at once ('If you're listening to this version of me, you're on the wrong track') or in this case one person talking twice. ('Try to listen to the other one') You have to choose which me you're going to listen to.

1.52 We have a very small amount of bandwidth for processing auditory input, which is why noise like this – (*Office noise*) – is extremely damaging for productivity. If you have to work in an open-plan office like this, your productivity is greatly reduced. And whatever number you're thinking of, it probably isn't as

bad as this. (*Ominous music*) You are one third as productive in open-plan offices as in quiet rooms. And I have a tip for you. If you have to work in spaces like that, carry headphones with you, with a soothing sound like birdsong. Put them on and your productivity goes back up to triple what it would be.

2.25 The fourth way in which sound affects us is behaviourally. With all that other stuff going on, it would be amazing if our behaviour didn't change. (*Techno music inside a car*) So, ask yourself: Is this person ever going to drive at a steady 28 miles per hour? I don't think so. At the simplest, you move away from unpleasant sound and towards pleasant sound. So if I were to play this – (*Jackhammer*) – for more than a few seconds, you'd feel uncomfortable; for more than a few minutes, you'd be leaving the room in droves. For people who can't get away from noise like that, it's extremely damaging for their health.

2.55 And that's not the only thing that bad sound damages. Most retail sound is inappropriate and accidental, and even hostile, and it has a dramatic effect on sales. For those of you who are retailers, you may want to look away before I show this slide. They are losing up to thirty per cent of their business with people leaving shops faster, or just turning around on the door. We all have done it, and leaving the area because the sound in there is so dreadful.

3.18 I want to spend just a moment talking about the model that we've developed, which allows us to start at the top and look at the drivers of sound, analyse the soundscape and then predict the four outcomes I've just talked about. Or start at the bottom, and say what outcomes do we want, and then design a soundscape to have a desired effect. At last we've got some science we can apply. And we're in the business of designing soundscapes.

3.38 Just a word on music. Music is the most powerful sound there is, often inappropriately deployed. It's powerful for two reasons. You recognize it fast, and you associate it very powerfully. I'll give you two examples. (*First chord of The Beatles' 'A Hard Day's Night'*) Most of you recognize that immediately. The younger, maybe not. (*Laughter*) (*First two notes of 'Jaws' theme*) And most of you associate that with something! Now, those are one-second samples of music. Music is very powerful. And unfortunately it's veneering commercial spaces, often inappropriately. I hope that's going to change over the next few years.

4.10 Let me just talk about brands for a moment, because some of you run brands. Every brand is out there making sound right now. There are eight expressions of a brand in sound. They are all important. And every brand needs to have guidelines at the centre. I'm glad to say that is starting to happen now. (*Intel ad jingle*) You all recognize that one. (*Nokia ringtone*) This is the most-played tune in the world today. 1.8 billion times a day, that tune is played. And it cost Nokia absolutely nothing.

4.36 Just leave you with four golden rules, for those of you who run businesses, for commercial sound. First, make it congruent, pointing in the same direction as your visual communication. That increases impact by over 1,100 per cent. If your sound is pointing in the opposite direction, incongruent, you reduce impact by 86 per cent. That's an order of magnitude, up or down. This is important. Secondly, make it appropriate to the situation. Thirdly, make it valuable. Give people something with the sound. Don't just bombard them with stuff. And finally, test it and test it again. Sound is complex. There are many countervailing influences. It can be a bit like a bowl of spaghetti: sometimes you have to just eat it and see what happens.

5.14 So I hope this talk has raised sound in your consciousness. If you are listening consciously, you can take control of the sound around you. It's good for your health. It's good for your productivity. If we all do that, we move to a state that I like to think will be sound living in the world. I'm going to leave you with a little bit more birdsong. (*Birds chirping*) I recommend at least five minutes a day, but there is no maximum dose. Thank you for lending me your ears today. (*Applause*)

Unit 4 Your body language shapes who you are

0.12 So I want to start by offering you a free no-tech life hack, and all it requires of you is this: that you change your posture for two minutes. But before I give it away, I want to ask you to right now do a little audit of your body and what you're doing with your body. So how many of you are sort of making yourselves smaller? Maybe you're hunching, crossing your legs, maybe wrapping your ankles. Sometimes we hold onto our arms like this. Sometimes we spread out. (*Laughter*) I see you. So I want you to pay attention to what you're doing right now. We're going to come back to that in a few minutes, and I'm hoping that if you learn to tweak this a little bit, it could significantly change the way your life unfolds.

1.00   So, we're really fascinated with body language, and we're particularly interested in other people's body language. You know, we're interested in, like, you know – (*Laughter*) – an awkward interaction, or a smile, or a contemptuous glance, or maybe a very awkward wink, or maybe even something like a handshake.

1.24   Narrator: Here they are arriving at Number 10, and look at this lucky policeman gets to shake hands with the President of the United States. Oh, and here comes the Prime Minister of the – ? No. (*Laughter*) (*Applause*)

1.39   Amy Cuddy: So, a handshake, or the lack of a handshake, can have us talking for weeks and weeks and weeks. Even the BBC and *The New York Times*. So obviously when we think about nonverbal behaviour, or body language – but we call it nonverbals as social scientists – it's language, so we think about communication. When we think about communication, we think about interactions. So what is your body language communicating to me? What's mine communicating to you?

2.05   And there's a lot of reason to believe that this is a valid way to look at this. So social scientists have spent a lot of time looking at the effects of our body language, or other people's body language, on judgements. And we make sweeping judgements and inferences from body language. And those judgements can predict really meaningful life outcomes like who we hire or promote, who we ask out on a date. So, when we think of nonverbals, we think of how we judge others, how they judge us and what the outcomes are. We tend to forget, though, the other audience that's influenced by our nonverbals, and that's ourselves.

2.42   We are also influenced by our nonverbals, our thoughts and our feelings and our physiology. So what nonverbals am I talking about? I'm a social psychologist. I study prejudice, and I teach at a competitive business school, so it was inevitable that I would become interested in power dynamics. I became especially interested in nonverbal expressions of power and dominance.

3.06   And what are nonverbal expressions of power and dominance? Well, this is what they are. So in the animal kingdom, they are about expanding. So you make yourself big, you stretch out, you take up space, you're basically opening up. It's about opening up. And this is true across the animal kingdom. It's not just limited to primates. And humans do the same thing. (*Laughter*) So they do this both when they have power sort of chronically, and also when they're feeling powerful in the moment. And this one is especially interesting because it really shows us how universal and old these expressions of power are. This expression, which is known as pride, Jessica Tracy has studied. She shows that people who are born with sight and people who are congenitally blind do this when they win at a physical competition. So when they cross the finish line and they've won, it doesn't matter if they've never seen anyone do it. They do this. So the arms up in the V, the chin is slightly lifted. What do we do when we feel powerless? We do exactly the opposite. We close up. We wrap ourselves up. We make ourselves small. We don't want to bump into the person next to us. So again, both animals and humans do the same thing. And this is what happens when you put together high and low power. So what we tend to do when it comes to power is that we complement the other's nonverbals. So if someone is being really powerful with us, we tend to make ourselves smaller. We don't mirror them. We do the opposite of them.

4.35   So I'm watching this behaviour in the classroom, and what do I notice? I notice that MBA students really exhibit the full range of power nonverbals. So you have people who are like caricatures of alphas, like really coming into the room, they get right into the middle of the room before class even starts, like they really want to occupy space. When they sit down, they're sort of spread out. They raise their hands like this. You have other people who

are virtually collapsing when they come in. As soon they come in, you see it. You see it on their faces and their bodies, and they sit in their chair and they make themselves tiny, and they go like this when they raise their hand.

5.14   I notice a couple of things about this. One, you're not going to be surprised, it seems to be related to gender. So women are much more likely to do this kind of thing than men. Women feel chronically less powerful than men, so this is not surprising. But the other thing I noticed is that it also seemed to be related to the extent to which the students were participating, and how well they were participating. And this is really important in the MBA classroom, because participation counts for half the grade.

5.44   So, business schools have been struggling with this gender grade gap. You get these equally qualified women and men coming in and then you get these differences in grades, and it seems to be partly attributable to participation. So I started to wonder, you know, OK, so you have these people coming in like this, and they're participating. Is it possible that we could get people to fake it and would it lead them to participate more?

6.08   So my main collaborator Dana Carney, who's at Berkeley, and I really wanted to know, can you fake it till you make it? Like, can you do this just for a little while and actually experience a behavioural outcome that makes you seem more powerful? So we know that our nonverbals govern how other people think and feel about us. There's a lot of evidence. But our question really was, do our nonverbals govern how we think and feel about ourselves?

6.34   There's some evidence that they do. So, for example, we smile when we feel happy, but also, when we're forced to smile by holding a pen in our teeth like this, it makes us feel happy. So it goes both ways. When it comes to power, it also goes both ways. So when you feel powerful, you're more likely to do this, but it's also possible that when you pretend to be powerful, you are more likely to actually feel powerful.

7.08   So the second question really was, you know, so we know that our minds change our bodies, but is it also true that our bodies change our minds? And when I say minds, in the case of the powerful, what am I talking about? So I'm talking about thoughts and feelings and the sort of physiological things that make up our thoughts and feelings, and in my case, that's hormones. I look at hormones. So what do the minds of the powerful versus the powerless look like?

7.36   So this is what we did. We decided to bring people into the lab and run a little experiment, and these people adopted, for two minutes, either high-power poses or low-power poses, and I'm just going to show you five of the poses, although they took on only two. So here's one. A couple more. This one has been dubbed the 'Wonder Woman' by the media. Here are a couple more. So you can be standing or you can be sitting. And here are the low-power poses. So you're folding up, you're making yourself small. This one is very low-power. When you're touching your neck, you're really protecting yourself. So this is what happens. They come in, they spit into a vial, we for two minutes say, 'You need to do this or this.' They don't look at pictures of the poses. We don't want to prime them with a concept of power. We want them to be feeling power, right? So two minutes they do this. We then ask them, 'How powerful do you feel?' on a series of items, and then we give them an opportunity to gamble, and then we take another saliva sample. That's it. That's the whole experiment.

8.45   So this is what we find. Risk tolerance, which is the gambling, what we find is that when you're in the high-power pose condition, 86 per cent of you will gamble. When you're in the low-power pose condition, only sixty per cent, and that's a pretty whopping significant difference. Here's what we find on testosterone. From their baseline when they come in, high-power people experience about a twenty per cent increase, and low-power people experience about a ten per cent decrease. So again, two minutes, and you get these changes. Here's what you get on cortisol. High-power people experience about a 25 per cent decrease, and the low-power people experience about a fifteen per cent increase. So two minutes lead to these hormonal changes that configure your brain to basically be either assertive, confident and comfortable, or really stress-reactive, and, you know, feeling sort of shut down. And we've all had that feeling, right? So it seems that our nonverbals do govern how we think and feel about ourselves, so it's not just others, but it's also ourselves. Also, our bodies change our minds.

9.54　But the next question, of course, is can power posing for a few minutes really change your life in meaningful ways? So this is in the lab. It's this little task, you know, it's just a couple of minutes. Where can you actually apply this? We decided that the one that most people could relate to because most people had been through was the job interview. So we published these findings, and the media are all over it, and they say, OK, so this is what you do when you go in for the job interview, right? (*Laughter*) You know, so we were of course horrified, and said, Oh my God, no, no, no, that's not what we meant at all. For numerous reasons, no, no, no, don't do that. Again, this is not about you talking to other people. It's you talking to yourself. What do you do before you go into a job interview? You do this. Right? You're sitting down. You're looking at your iPhone – or your Android, not trying to leave anyone out. You are, you know, you're looking at your notes, you're hunching up, making yourself small, when really what you should be doing maybe is this, like, in the bathroom, right? Do that. Find two minutes. So that's what we want to test. OK? So we bring people into a lab, and they do either high or low-power poses again, they go through a very stressful job interview. It's five minutes long. They are being recorded. They're being judged also, and the judges are trained to give no nonverbal feedback, so they look like this. Like, imagine this is the person interviewing you. So for five minutes, nothing, and this is worse than being heckled. People hate this. It's what Marianne LaFrance calls 'standing in social quicksand'. So this really spikes your cortisol. So this is the job interview we put them through, because we really wanted to see what happened. We then have these coders look at these tapes, four of them. They're blind to the hypothesis. They're blind to the conditions. They have no idea who's been posing in what pose, and they end up looking at these sets of tapes, and they say, 'Oh, we want to hire these people,' – all the high-power posers – 'we don't want to hire these people.'

11.51　When I tell people about this, that our bodies change our minds and our minds can change our behaviour, and our behaviour can change our outcomes, they say to me, 'I don't – it feels fake.' Right? So I said, fake it till you make it. I don't – it's not me. I don't want to get there and then still feel like a fraud. I don't want to feel like an impostor. I don't want to get there only to feel like I'm not supposed to be here. And that really resonated with me, because I want to tell you a little story about being an impostor and feeling like I'm not supposed to be here.

12.21　When I was nineteen, I was in a really bad car accident. I was thrown out of a car, rolled several times. I was thrown from the car. And I woke up in a head injury rehab ward, and I had been withdrawn from college, and I learned that my IQ had dropped by two standard deviations, which was very traumatic. I knew my IQ because I had identified with being smart, and I had been called gifted as a child. So I'm taken out of college, I keep trying to go back. They say, 'You're not going to finish college. Just, you know, there are other things for you to do, but that's not going to work out for you.' So I really struggled with this, and I have to say, having your identity taken from you, your core identity, and for me it was being smart, having that taken from you, there's nothing that leaves you feeling more powerless than that. So I felt entirely powerless. I worked and worked and worked, and I got lucky, and worked, and got lucky, and worked.

13.16　Eventually I graduated from college. It took me four years longer than my peers, and I convinced someone, my angel advisor, Susan Fiske, to take me on, and so I ended up at Princeton, and I was like, I am not supposed to be here. I am an impostor. And the night before my first-year talk, and the first-year talk at Princeton is a twenty-minute talk to twenty people. That's it. I was so afraid of being found out the next day that I called her and said, 'I'm quitting.' She was like, 'You are not quitting, because I took a gamble on you, and you're staying. You're going to stay, and this is what you're going to do. You are

going to fake it. You're going to do every talk that you ever get asked to do. You're just going to do it and do it and do it, even if you're terrified and just paralyzed and having an out-of-body experience, until you have this moment where you say, "Oh my gosh, I'm doing it. Like, I have become this. I am actually doing this."' So that's what I did. Five years in grad school, a few years, you know, I'm at Northwestern, I moved to Harvard, I'm at Harvard, I'm not really thinking about it anymore, but for a long time I had been thinking, 'Not supposed to be here. Not supposed to be here.'

14.22　So at the end of my first year at Harvard, a student who had not talked in class the entire semester, who I had said, 'Look, you've gotta participate or else you're going to fail,' came into my office. I really didn't know her at all. And she said, she came in totally defeated, and she said, 'I'm not supposed to be here.' And that was the moment for me. Because two things happened. One was that I realized, oh my gosh, I don't feel like that anymore. You know. I don't feel that anymore, but she does, and I get that feeling. And the second was, she is supposed to be here! Like, she can fake it, she can become it. So I was like, 'Yes, you are! You are supposed to be here! And tomorrow you're going to fake it, you're going to make yourself powerful, and, you know, you're gonna – (*Applause*) And you're going to go into the classroom, and you are going to give the best comment ever.' You know? And she gave the best comment ever, and people turned around and they were like, oh my God, I didn't even notice her sitting there, you know?

15.28　She comes back to me months later, and I realized that she had not just faked it till she made it, she had actually faked it till she became it. So she had changed. And so I want to say to you, don't fake it till you make it. Fake it till you become it. You know? It's not – do it enough until you actually become it and internalize.

15.50　The last thing I'm going to leave you with is this. Tiny tweaks can lead to big changes.

Unit 5　The magic washing machine

0.12　I was only four years old when I saw my mother load a washing machine for the very first time in her life. That was a great day for my mother. My mother and father had been saving money for years to be able to buy that machine, and the first day it was going to be used, even Grandma was invited to see the machine. And Grandma was even more excited. Throughout her life she had been heating water with firewood, and she had hand washed laundry for seven children. And now she was going to watch electricity do that work.

0.50　My mother carefully opened the door, and she loaded the laundry into the machine, like this. And then, when she closed the door, Grandma said, 'No, no, no, no. Let me, let me push the button.' And Grandma pushed the button, and she said, 'Oh, fantastic! I want to see this! Give me a chair! Give me a chair! I want to see it,' and she sat down in front of the machine, and she watched the entire washing programme. She was mesmerized. To my grandmother, the washing machine was a miracle.

1.32　Today, in Sweden and other rich countries, people are using so many different machines. Look, the homes are full of machines. I can't even name them all. And they also, when they want to travel, they use flying machines that can take them to remote destinations. And yet, in the world, there are so many people who still heat the water on fire, and they cook their food on fire. Sometimes they don't even have enough food, and they live below the poverty line. There are two billion fellow human beings who live on less than two dollars a day. And the richest people over there – there's one billion people – and they live above what I call the 'air line', because they spend more than $80 a day on their consumption.

2.22　But this is just one, two, three billion people, and obviously there are seven billion people in the world, so there must be one, two, three, four billion people more who live in between the poverty line and the air line. They have electricity, but the question is, how many have washing machines? I've done the scrutiny on market data, and I've found that, indeed, the washing machine has penetrated below the air line, and today there's an additional one billion people out there who live above the 'wash line'. (*Laughter*) They consume more than $40 per day. So two billion have access to washing machines.

3.02 And the remaining five billion, how do they wash? Or, to be more precise, how do most of the women in the world wash? Because it remains hard work for women to wash. They wash like this: by hand. It's a hard, time-consuming labour, which they have to do for hours every week. And sometimes they also have to bring water from far away to do the laundry at home, or they have to bring the laundry away to a stream far off. And they want the washing machine. They don't want to spend such a large part of their life doing this hard work with so relatively low productivity. And there's nothing different in their wish than it was for my grandma. Look here, two generations ago in Sweden – picking water from the stream, heating with firewood and washing like that. They want the washing machine in exactly the same way.

3.59 But when I lecture to environmentally-concerned students, they tell me, 'No, everybody in the world cannot have cars and washing machines.' How can we tell this woman that she ain't going to have a washing machine? And then I ask my students, I've asked them – over the last two years I've asked, 'How many of you doesn't use a car?' And some of them proudly raise their hand and say, 'I don't use a car.' And then I put the really tough question: 'How many of you handwash your jeans and your bed sheets?' And no one raised their hand. Even the hardcore in the green movement use washing machines. (*Laughter*)

4.38 So how come [this is] something that everyone uses and they think others will not stop it? What is special with this? I had to do an analysis about the energy used in the world. Here we are. Look here, you see the seven billion people up there: the air people, the wash people, the bulb people and the fire people. One unit like this is an energy unit of fossil fuel – oil, coal or gas. That's what most of the electricity and the energy in the world is. And it's twelve units used in the entire world, and the richest one billion, they use six of them. Half of the energy is used by one seventh of the world's population. And these ones who have washing machines, but not a house full of other machines, they use two. This group use three, one each. And they also have electricity. And over there they don't even use one each. That makes twelve of them.

5.32 But the main concern for the environmentally-interested students – and they are right – is about the future. What are the trends? If we just prolong the trends, without any real advanced analysis, to 2050, there are two things that can increase the energy use. First, population growth. Second, economic growth. Population growth will mainly occur among the poorest people here because they have high child mortality and they have many children per woman. And that you will get two extra, but that won't change the energy use very much.

6.03 What will happen is economic growth. The best of here in the emerging economies – I call them the New East – they will jump the air line. 'Wopp!' they will say. And they will start to use as much as the Old West are doing already. And these people, they want the washing machine. I told you. They'll go there. And they will double their energy use. And we hope that the poor people will get into the electric light. And they will get a two-child family without a stop in population growth. But the total energy consumption will increase to 22 units. And these 22 units – still the richest people use most of them.

6.40 So what's needed to be done? Because the risk, the high probability of climate change is real. It's real. Of course they must be more energy-efficient. They must change behaviour in some way. They must also start to produce green energy, much more green energy. But until they have the same energy consumption per person, they shouldn't give advice to others – what to do and what not to do. (*Applause*) Here we can get more green energy all over.

7.12 This is what we hope may happen. It's a real challenge in the future. But I can assure you that this woman in the favela in Rio, she wants a washing machine. She's very happy about her minister of energy that provided electricity to everyone – so happy that she even voted for her, you know. And she became Dilma Rousseff, the president-elect of one of the biggest democracies in the world, you know – moving from minister of energy to president. If you have democracy, people will vote for washing machines. They love them.

7.45 And what's the magic with them? My mother explained the magic with this machine the very, very first day. She said, 'Now Hans, we have loaded the laundry. The machine will make the work. And now we can go to the library.' Because this is the magic: you load the laundry, and what do you get out of the machine? You get books out of the machines, children's books. And mother got time to read for me. She loved this. I got the 'ABC' – this is where I started my career as a professor, when my mother had time to read for me. And she also got books for herself. She managed to study English and learn that as a foreign language. And she read so many novels, so many different novels here, you know. And we really, we really loved this machine.

8.36 And what we said, my mother and me, 'Thank you, industrialization. Thank you, steel mill. Thank you, power station. And thank you, chemical processing industry that gave us time to read books.' Thank you very much. (*Applause*)

Unit 6 Magical houses, made of bamboo

0.13 When I was nine years old, my mom asked me what I would want my house to look like, and I drew this fairy mushroom. And then she actually built it. (*Laughter*)

0.26 I don't think I realized this was so unusual at the time, and maybe I still haven't, because I'm still designing houses. This is a six-storey bespoke home on the island of Bali. It's built almost entirely from bamboo. The living room overlooks the valley from the fourth floor. You enter the house by a bridge. It can get hot in the tropics, so we make big curving roofs to catch the breezes. But some rooms have tall windows to keep the air conditioning in and the bugs out. This room we left open. We made an air-conditioned, tented bed. And one client wanted a TV room in the corner of her living room. Boxing off an area with tall walls just didn't feel right, so instead, we made this giant woven pod.

1.25 Now, we do have all the necessary luxuries, like bathrooms. This one is a basket in the corner of the living room. And I've got tell you, some people actually hesitate to use it. We have not quite figured out our acoustic insulation. (*Laughter*) So there are lots of things that we're still working on, but one thing I have learned is that bamboo will treat you well if you use it right.

1.51 It's actually a wild grass. It grows on otherwise unproductive land – deep ravines, mountainsides. It lives off of rainwater, spring water, sunlight, and of the 1,450 species of bamboo that grow across the world, we use just seven of them.

2.11 That's my dad. He's the one who got me building with bamboo, and he is standing in a clump of *Dendrocalamus asper niger* that he planted just seven years ago. Each year, it sends up a new generation of shoots. That shoot, we watched it grow a metre in three days just last week, so we're talking about sustainable timber in three years.

2.35 Now, we harvest from hundreds of family-owned clumps. Betung, as we call it, it's really long, up to eighteen metres of usable length. Try getting that truck down the mountain. And it's strong: it has the tensile strength of steel, the compressive strength of concrete. Slam four tons straight down on a pole, and it can take it. Because it's hollow, it's lightweight, light enough to be lifted by just a few men, or, apparently, one woman. (*Laughter*)

3.14 And when my father built Green School in Bali, he chose bamboo for all of the buildings on campus, because he saw it as a promise. It's a promise to the kids. It's one sustainable material that they will not run out of. And when I first saw these structures under construction about six years ago, I just thought, this makes perfect sense. It is growing all around us. It's strong. It's elegant. It's earthquake-resistant. Why hasn't this happened sooner, and what can we do with it next?

3.50 So along with some of the original builders of Green School, I founded Ibuku. *Ibu* means 'mother', and *ku* means 'mine', so it represents my Mother Earth, and at Ibuku, we are a team of artisans, architects and designers, and what we're doing together is creating a new way of building. Over the past five years together, we have built over fifty unique structures, most of them in Bali. Nine of them are at Green Village – you've just seen inside some of these homes – and we fill them with bespoke furniture, we surround them with veggie gardens, we would love to invite you all to come visit someday. And while you're there, you can also see Green School – we keep building classrooms there each year – as well as an updated fairy mushroom house.

4.46 We're also working on a little house for export. This is a traditional Sumbanese home that we replicated, right down to the details and textiles. A restaurant with an open-air kitchen. It looks a lot like a kitchen, right? And a bridge that spans 22 metres across a river.

5.09 Now, what we're doing, it's not entirely new. From little huts to elaborate bridges like this one in Java, bamboo has been in use across the tropical regions of the world for literally tens of thousands of years. There are islands and even continents that were first reached by bamboo rafts. But until recently, it was almost impossible to reliably protect bamboo from insects, and so, just about everything that was ever built out of bamboo is gone. Unprotected bamboo weathers. Untreated bamboo gets eaten to dust. And so that's why most people, especially in Asia, think that you couldn't be poor enough or rural enough to actually want to live in a bamboo house. And so we thought, what will it take to change their minds, to convince people that bamboo is worth building with, much less worth aspiring to? First, we needed safe treatment solutions. Borax is a natural salt. It turns bamboo into a viable building material. Treat it properly, design it carefully, and a bamboo structure can last a lifetime.

6.22 Second, build something extraordinary out of it. Inspire people. Fortunately, Balinese culture fosters craftsmanship. It values the artisan. So combine those with the adventurous outliers from new generations of locally trained architects and designers and engineers, and always remember that you are designing for curving, tapering, hollow poles. No two poles alike, no straight lines, no two-by-fours here. The tried-and-true, well-crafted formulas and vocabulary of architecture do not apply here. We have had to invent our own rules. We ask the bamboo what it's good at, what it wants to become, and what it says is: respect it, design for its strengths, protect it from water, and to make the most of its curves.

7.17 So we design in real 3D, making scale structural models out of the same material that we'll later use to build the house. And bamboo model-making, it's an art, as well as some hardcore engineering.

7.34 So that's the blueprint of the house. (Laughter) And we bring it to site, and with tiny rulers, we measure each pole, and consider each curve, and we choose a piece of bamboo from the pile to replicate that house on site.

7.52 When it comes down to the details, we consider everything. Why are doors so often rectangular? Why not round? How could you make a door better? Well, its hinges battle with gravity, and gravity will always win in the end, so why not have it pivot on the centre where it can stay balanced? And while you're at it, why not doors shaped like teardrops?

8.14 To reap the selective benefits and work within the constraints of this material, we have really had to push ourselves, and within that constraint, we have found space for something new. It's a challenge: how do you make a ceiling if you don't have any flat boards to work with? Let me tell you, sometimes I dream of sheet rock and plywood. (Laughter) But if what you've got is skilled craftsmen and itsy bitsy little splits, weave that ceiling together, stretch a canvas over it, lacquer it. How do you design durable kitchen countertops that do justice to this curving structure you've just built? Slice up a boulder like a loaf of bread, hand-carve each to fit the other, leave the crusts on, and what we're doing, it is almost entirely handmade. The structural connections of our buildings are reinforced by steel joints, but we use a lot of hand-whittled bamboo pins. There are thousands of pins in each floor. This floor is made of glossy and durable bamboo skin. You can feel the texture under bare feet.

9.29 And can the floor that you walk on, can it affect the way that you walk? Can it change the footprint that you'll ultimately leave on the world? I remember being nine years old and feeling wonder, and possibility, and a little bit of idealism. And we've got a really long way to go, there's a lot left to learn, but one thing I know is that with creativity and commitment, you can create beauty and comfort and safety and even luxury out of a material that will grow back. Thank you. (Applause)

**Word lists can be downloaded from the Keynote website:
ngl.cengage.com/keynote**

TED TALKS

Keynote

PROFICIENT
Workbook

Contents Split A

1 Creativity   **104**

2 Hopes and fears   **114**

3 Perception   **124**

4 Human interaction   **134**

5 Economic resources   **144**

6 Practical design   **154**

Answer key   **164**
Audioscripts   **176**

Jon Hird
Paul Dummett
Mike Harrison
Sandy Millin

NGL.Cengage.com/Keynote

PASSWORD keynoteStdt#

1 Creativity

1.1 Do schools kill creativity?

TEDTALKS

Sir **KEN ROBINSON** was born in Liverpool, UK, in 1950. He was educated in and around Liverpool and then studied for a BEd (Bachelor of Education) in English and drama at Bretton Hall College of Education, graduating in 1972. He then worked as a teacher and, in 1981, he completed a PhD at the University of London, researching the role of drama and theatre in education. From 1985 to 1988, he was the Director of the Arts in Schools Project, an initiative to develop arts education throughout England and Wales. He then became Professor of Education at the University of Warwick in the UK, where he is now professor emeritus.

Sir Ken works with governments, education systems, businesses and other agencies and organizations across the world, advising on the development of creativity, innovation and human resources in education and in business, an area in which he is recognized as one of the world's leading authorities. He is also recognized as one of the world's leading speakers on these topics and videos of his famous TED Talks have been seen by a record estimated 250 million people in over 150 countries. In fact, his 2006 talk *Do schools kill creativity?* became the most viewed in TED's history. He has also written a number of best-selling books, some of which have been translated into over 20 languages.

Sir Ken has received many prestigious awards and accolades. In 2011, *Fast Company Magazine* listed him as 'one of the world's elite thinkers on creativity and innovation'. He has also been named as one of *TIME/Fortune/*CNN's 'Principal Voices' and has been ranked among the Thinkers50 list of the 'world's top business thought leaders'. He has received a number of honorary degrees from UK and US universities in recognition of his work in the arts and education, the Benjamin Franklin Medal for outstanding contributions to cultural relations between the United Kingdom and the United States and has been knighted by Queen Elizabeth II for his services to the arts.

Sir Ken Robinson

CAREER PATHWAYS

1 Read the text. Answer the questions.

   1 In terms of academic background, what were Sir Ken Robinson's two main fields of study?

   2 What is Sir Ken Robinson a global expert in?

   3 What TED Talk records did Sir Ken achieve?

   4 In which areas has Sir Ken's work been recognized?

   5 For what did he become 'Sir' Ken Robinson?

TED PLAYLIST

2 Other TED speakers are interested in topics similar to Sir Ken Robinson's TED Talk. Read the descriptions of four TED Talks at the top of page 105. In your opinion, which is the best title for this playlist, a, b or c?

   a Celebrating the individual in learning
   b Unlocking the doors to learning
   c Leaving the textbook at the classroom door

3 Read the TED playlist again. Find a speaker who …

   1 realized their method of teaching was ineffective.
   2 wants a switch of focus from academic to practical learning.
   3 is making an appeal specifically to other teachers.
   4 wants education to be adapted to individual learning styles.

▶ **Sir Ken Robinson: Bring on the learning revolution**

In this poignant, funny follow-up to his fabled 2006 talk, Sir Ken Robinson makes the case for a radical shift from standardized schools to personalized learning – creating conditions where kids' natural talents can flourish.

▶ **Ramsey Musallam: 3 rules to spark learning**

It took a life-threatening condition to jolt chemistry teacher Ramsey Musallam out of ten years of 'pseudo-teaching' to understand the true role of the educator: to cultivate curiosity. In a fun and personal talk, Musallam gives three rules to spark imagination and learning, and get students excited about how the world works.

▶ **Rita F. Pierson: Every kid needs a champion**

Rita Pierson, a teacher for 40 years, once heard a colleague say, 'They don't pay me to like the kids.' Her response: 'Kids don't learn from people they don't like.' A rousing call to educators to believe in their students and actually connect with them on a real, human, personal level.

▶ **Geoff Mulgan: Intro to the Studio School**

Some kids learn by listening; others learn by doing. Geoff Mulgan gives a succinct introduction to the *Studio School*, a new kind of school in the UK where small teams of kids learn by working on projects that are, as Mulgan puts it, 'for real'.

4 Find adjectives in the TED playlist that describe the talks as …

a inspiring   b touching   c legendary
d entertaining   e concise

5 Which talk would you most like to see? Why? Watch the talk at TED.com.

AUTHENTIC LISTENING SKILLS
Rhythm and stress

6 🎧 **1 01** You are going to hear a podcast in which a member of the *Keynote* team talks about Rita F. Pierson's TED Talk, *Every kid needs a champion*. Circle the content words in the sentence below. Then listen and underline the stressed words and syllables. Were they the same?

I've seen this talk quite a few times and I still get really emotional watching it.

7 🎧 **1 02** Now listen to the next sentence and write in the missing content words. Then underline all the stressed words.

I _____ it has _____ to do with the kind of _____ _____ – _____ even – that Rita F. Pierson _____ her students.

LISTENING

8 🎧 **1 03** Listen to the full podcast. Choose the correct words to make true sentences.

1 Paul is a teacher and *lecturer / teacher trainer*.
2 Paul admires Rita F. Pierson as a teacher because of the emphasis she puts on human *dignity / connections*.

9 🎧 **1 03** Listen again. Complete the reasons.

1 Why Paul gets emotional watching this TED Talk:
a) Rita F. Pierson's kindness to her pupils b) the _____ of her pupils c) Pierson's power as a(n) _____ .
2 Why Paul says some teachers emphasize discipline: they've failed to _____ their students.
3 Why kids underperform at school: they're born into a) _____ b) the wrong _____ .
4 Why Paul thinks the talk should be renamed: so that _____ _____ sees it.

VOCABULARY IN CONTEXT

10 Read the extracts from the podcast. Choose the correct meaning of the words in bold.

1 … they're from disadvantaged backgrounds and that sort of **tugs at the heartstrings** too.
Makes you feel: **a** sympathetic ☐   **b** upset ☐
c hurt ☐
2 I've had kids so educationally **deficient** I could have cried.
a unintelligent ☐   **b** lacking ☐   **c** uninterested ☐
3 The best teachers are the ones who seem to befriend their pupils and **win them over** …
Get someone to: **a** obey you ☐
b agree with you ☐   **c** admit they are wrong ☐
4 She put a smiley face on his paper and told him he was **on a roll**.
a not being serious ☐   **b** making good progress ☐
c falling behind ☐
5 Kids have to feel that you're on their side and **rooting for** them.
a supporting ☐   **b** working for ☐
c explaining things for ☐

1.2 What've you been up to?

GRAMMAR Definite and indefinite time

1 Read the text about creativity in the professions. Match the events or situations (1–10) with what they are expressing (a–c).

a finished event or situation in a finished time ☐ ☐ ☐ ☐ ☐
b finished event or situation in an unfinished time ☐ ☐
c event or situation that continues to the present ☐ ☐ ☐

Creativity ¹ *has for a long time been seen* as important in a number of professions. But until recently, only a limited number of fields ² *were considered* to be primarily creatively driven: the arts, product design and marketing. Architecture is also an area which ³ *has always been* associated with creativity. By contrast, fields such as science and engineering ⁴ *have traditionally experienced* a less explicit relation to creativity. However, a number of studies in recent years ⁵ *have shown* how some of the major scientific and industrial advances of the 20th century ⁶ *came about* as a direct result of the creativity of individuals. And a 2010 study, which ⁷ *interviewed* around 1,500 company CEOs, ⁸ *showed* that the leadership trait, that today is considered to be most crucial for success, is creativity. This suggests that the world of business ⁹ *has begun* to accept that creativity is of value in a range of industries, rather than being simply the preserve of the more traditional creative industries. But this is not such a new concept. In the early part of the 20ᵗʰ century, many economists ¹⁰ *considered* creativity to be the key factor in economic growth.

2 Choose the correct words or phrases to complete the quotations.

I think the human race ¹ *made/has made* a big mistake at the beginning of the industrial revolution, we ² *leaped/have leaped* for the mechanical things; people need the use of their hands to feel creative.

Andre Norton, writer

I think it's fair to say that personal computers ³ *became/ have become* the most empowering tool we ⁴ *ever created/ have ever created*. They're tools of communication, they're tools of creativity, and they can be shaped by their user.

Bill Gates, businessman and co-founder of Microsoft

Without this playing with fantasy, no creative work ⁵ *ever yet came/has ever yet come* to birth. The debt we owe to the play of the imagination is incalculable.

Carl Jung, psychiatrist

I ⁶ *didn't see/haven't seen* it then, but it ⁷ *turned out/has turned out* that getting fired from Apple was the best thing that could have ever happened to me. The heaviness of being successful ⁸ *was replaced/has been replaced* by the lightness of being a beginner again, less sure about everything. It ⁹ *freed/has freed* me to enter one of the most creative periods of my life.

Steve Jobs, businessman and co-founder of Apple

3 🎧 **1 04** Read the extract from an interview with a psychologist, who is talking about creativity and the brain. Complete the interview using the correct verb form: present perfect simple, present perfect continuous, past simple or past continuous. Then listen and check your answers.

Interviewer: Is it true that to be creative you need to be right-brained?

Psychologist: This idea that right-brained people are more creative and imaginative and that left-brained equals logical and analytical ¹ _____ (be) around for a long time. But it's an oversimplification and possibly simply untrue. We ² _____ (know) since the 19ᵗʰ century that the two hemispheres of the brain function differently, but most functions in fact involve the two sides working together. Furthermore, a recent study, which ³ _____ (involve) scanning the brains of over 1,000 people, ⁴ _____ (find) no evidence for people being predominantly either right-brained or left-brained. So, even though we ⁵ _____ (talk) about this distinction for a long time, it seems we may ⁶ _____ (be) misguided all along.

Interviewer: What about the idea that the most creative people are loners and eccentric geniuses?

Psychologist: Yes, this stereotype of a highly creative person as a lonely, perhaps eccentric, artist or poet ⁷ _____ (be) around for a long time. Indeed, recent research suggests that people tend to consider work to be of higher quality and have greater value if they ⁸ _____ (be told) that the person who ⁹ _____ (produce) it was eccentric. The reality, however, is that creativity is, more often than not, a result of collaboration. For example, Thomas Edison, who is often considered as a lone genius, ¹⁰ _____ (have) a great deal of input and support from a large group of scientists and engineers. Similarly, Michelangelo, when he ¹¹ _____ (paint) the Sistine Chapel, ¹² _____ (work) in collaboration with a creative team of artists.

4 Complete the sentences using the verb given in: the present perfect simple, the present perfect continuous, the past simple and the past continuous.

1 *work*

a She _____ on a couple of similar projects already.

b She _____ on this project for over six months now.

c She _____ on her new project when I last spoke to her.

d She _____ on a similar project in her old company.

2 *finalize*

a They _____ the schedule for a few days now.

b I think they _____ the schedule a few days ago.

c _____ they _____ the schedule yet?

d They _____ the schedule this morning. I'm not sure if it's ready yet.

3 *wait*

a I saw you earlier. You _____ for a bus outside the university.

b We _____ and _____ , but he didn't turn up. So, we went without him.

c We _____ only _____ for a few minutes so far. Let's give him a little longer.

d Come on, let's go. We _____ long enough.

4 *go*

a Sorry I couldn't stop for a chat. I _____ to my creative writing class.

b I _____ to my creative writing class last night.

c I _____ to creative writing classes for about a year now.

d I _____ to my creative writing class only once this term.

LANGUAGE FOCUS Expressions with statistics

5 Complete the sentences. Use the words in the box.

almost	significant	small	vast
good	relatively	sizeable	tiny

1 Only a _____ handful of startups go on to become successful businesses.

2 The _____ majority of people, around 90%, are right-handed.

3 Research suggests that the effect of environmental factors on children's creativity is _____ negligible.

4 A _____ number of people with dyslexia work in creative fields such as graphic design.

5 Only a _____ fraction of new patents go on to become successfully commercial products.

6 In many countries, a _____ proportion of students leave school with no qualifications.

7 _____ few people consider themselves to be creative.

8 A _____ deal of research suggests that creativity can be as valuable as intelligence in terms of employability.

6 Find and correct the mistakes in each sentence.

1 Globally, about one of eight males have some form of colour blindness, whereas only about one from 200 women is colour blind.

2 About one in each sixteen Americans plays a musical instrument.

3 In most of countries, over 99 per cents of all students graduating in medicine find jobs or enter further study within six months of graduating.

4 Geography is the worst degree for gaining employment in a number countries, with only around three out from every ten graduates in subject-related employment six months after graduating.

5 Research suggests that only one from four employees believe they are allowed to fulfil their creative potential at work.

6 According to a study, about four in of every ten people consider themselves to be in some way artistic.

DICTATION

7 🎧 **1 05** Listen to someone talking about the Italian architect Renzo Piano. Complete the sentences.

Renzo Piano is an Italian architect and engineer, born in Genoa in 1937, who is known for his ground-breaking and creative designs. He [1] _____ . In 2006, *TIME Magazine* [2] _____ in the world and as the tenth most influential person in the Arts and Entertainment category. In 2013, [3] _____ in the Italian Senate.

Over his career, Piano [4] _____ , including Louis Kahn, Richard Rogers and Gianfranco Franchini. With Franchini he [5] _____ Centre Georges Pompidou in Paris, which [6] _____ 'turned the architecture world upside down'.

Since 1981, Piano [7] _____ Renzo Piano Building Workshop and, since 2004, he [8] _____ for the Renzo Piano Foundation. This [9] _____ to promote the architectural profession through education.

Recently, a number of Piano's [10] _____ _____ . These include the Shard in London, at the time Europe's tallest skyscraper, and The New York Times Building in Manhattan.

1.3 How talent thrives

READING

1 Read the first paragraph of the text. What kind of text is it?

  a an academic essay ☐
  b a text book extract ☐
  c a book review ☐

2 Read the whole text. Which is the best summary?

  a An account of how certain working practices tend to be associated with certain fields of creativity. ☐
  b A description and analysis of how different people prefer different working practices. ☐
  c An explanation of how changes in working practice can negatively affect the creative process. ☐

3 Read the text again and answer the questions.

  1 Which of the paragraphs (1–4) has each purpose (a–d)?
    a Summarizes what the book gives the reader. ☐
    b Describes the broad concept of the book. ☐
    c Gives examples of working practices. ☐
    d Explains the origins of the book. ☐

  2 What is Mason Currey's main source of information?
    a The individuals themselves and their associates.
    b The work of other writers and academics.
    c A combination of the above.

  3 Which of the people mentioned in the text:
    a had a strict quota of work to be done each day?
    b worked in short bursts?
    c had a novel way of refocussing the mind?

Working habits of creative minds

When aspiring to complete a particular project or task, we may look to the example set by former greats for inspiration about how best to organize our time and optimize creativity and productivity. This is exactly what author Mason Currey did and, after discovering that great minds don't think so alike after all, he set about writing a book on the subject. *Daily Rituals: How artists work* describes the habits and routines of some of history's most creative minds, breaking their days down into where and when they ate, slept, attended work, exercised and dedicated time to their crafts.

Based on each individual's letters, diaries and interviews, and drawing on some secondary sources, the book summarizes and analyzes the daily rituals of over 160 world famous novelists, poets, musicians, playwrights, painters, philosophers, scientists and mathematicians. The poet W. H. Auden, for example, who once said that 'routine is a sign of ambition', set himself an exacting timetable, in which eating, drinking, writing, shopping, and even doing crossword puzzles, were all timed to the minute. The writer Thomas Wolfe only wrote standing up in his kitchen, using the top of the refrigerator as a desk. Novelist Anthony Trollope forced himself to write 3,000 words (250 words every fifteen minutes for three hours) every morning before going off to his job at the postal service, which he kept for 33 years during the writing of more than two dozen books. In contrast, novelist and poet Gertrude Stein could never sustain writing for more than half an hour at a time. The choreographer George Balanchine did his ironing while working, while Igor Stravinsky had to be absolutely sure he was out of earshot in order to compose. Additionally, when suffering from creative block, he stood on his head to 'clear the brain'. Charles Darwin started the day by doing exercise.

Charles Dickens did several hours' exercise in the afternoon. And while the writer Mary Flannery O'Connor worked only in the morning, Franz Kafka generally only wrote at night, often until dawn, and then slept for most of the afternoon.

Bizarrely, Currey's own book was a product of procrastination while trying to write a story for an architecture magazine. As he did everything but write the article – reading *The New York Times* online, tidying his desk, making endless cups of coffee – he decided to search the Internet for information about how other writers managed to focus. Finding the results highly entertaining, he started to collect them. These soon became a blog, and later evolved into the book.

By writing about the mundane details of artists' daily schedules, Currey initially hoped to shine new light on their personalities and careers. But what the reader gains insight into is how grand creative visions are often the product of efforts made in small daily increments and how working habits themselves strongly influence the end product. *Daily Rituals* is a fascinating book about the raw mechanics of genius and eccentricities of the personalities behind it.

4 What initial event led to the publication of the book?
   a Currey was looking for ideas to help him concentrate on his work more.
   b Currey wanted to find out how to efficiently combine work and leisure.
   c Currey felt being entertained would help him and others work better.

5 What was Currey's original aim for the book?
   a To write a novel based on the entertaining personalities he had researched.
   b To relate an individual's working practice to their character and personality.
   c To show how creativity and working practices are dependent on each other.

4 Complete definitions (a–f) with words or phrases from the text.

   a _____ = separating into parts (paragraph 1)
   b _____ = using something that is available to you (paragraph 2)
   c _____ = needing a lot of effort and care (paragraph 2)
   d _____ = the act of delaying something that you should do (paragraph 3)
   e _____ = not interesting or exciting (paragraph 4)
   f _____ = a small section or part of something (paragraph 4)

VOCABULARY Creativity collocations

5 Complete the sentences with a word from each box.

broke	build	came	came	devoted
~~express~~	follow	had	take	

angle	convention	experience	~~freely~~	hobby
idea	inspiration	path	work	

1 The creative arts, be it painting, music, dance or writing, allow you to _express_ yourself _freely_ with few constraints.

2 Chester Greenwood always claimed that the idea for the earmuff, which he invented in 1873 at the age of 15, came to him after he _____ a flash of _____ while ice skating.

3 People had been using the wheel on its side to make pottery for hundreds of years before someone _____ up with the _____ of putting it upright and using it for transport.

4 Talking about his debut album *In The Lonely Hour*, singer Sam Smith said he wanted to write an album about love that _____ from a different _____ .

5 Studies suggest that if you really want to stay sharp in old age you need to _____ up a new _____ to boost your memory.

6 After the death of her husband Pierre in a road accident in 1906, Marie Curie _____ herself to her _____ on radioactivity.

7 Romanticist landscape artists such as Constable _____ with _____ to change the way we see the world.

8 Most creative geniuses first _____ on the _____ of others before they _____ their own _____ and start to create a niche of their own.

WORD FOCUS *create*

6 Complete the words with the correct endings.

1 It is thought that the Ancient Greeks are responsible for the **creat**_____ of the first true alphabet.

2 Brazilian footballer Pelé is widely regarded as one of the most **creat**_____ players of all time.

3 Tim Berners-Lee is best known as the **creat**_____ of the World Wide Web.

4 **Creat**_____ is increasingly recognized as an essential higher-order skill for learning.

5 Studies indicate that teachers who teach **creat**_____ and enthusiastically tend to be more popular with their students.

6 The temple, one of the oldest in Asia, is a truly impressive **creat**_____ .

7 A recent online trend is to make short films **recreat**_____ famous movie scenes.

8 **Creat**_____ is the belief that the universe and life originated from acts of divine creation. Those who believe in this are known as **creat**_____ .

7 Complete the sentences. Use the words in the box.

demonstrate	force	foster	highly
impression	stifling	streak	thinking

1 For a student to get high marks, he or she needs to clearly _____ creativity and originality in academic thinking and writing, whatever the discipline.

2 Creative _____ requires a very different set of skills to critical thinking.

3 Most of us have a creative _____ hiding somewhere inside us, be it for music, art, dancing, writing poetry or just having a vivid imagination.

4 Steven Spielberg was for many years the biggest creative _____ in the world of cinema.

5 Because of her flamboyant style, the singer tended to create an _____ wherever she went.

6 Research suggests that _____ creative children often require more individualized attention at school.

7 Many would say that having too much objective assessment and testing in schools is _____ creativity or even inhibiting it completely.

8 The course aims to encourage and _____ creativity in a number of ways, from course design to lesson planning.

1.4 It's not really my thing

DESCRIBING LIKES AND DISLIKES

1 🎧 **1 06** Listen to two people talking about likes and dislikes. Tick (✓) what they like and cross (✗) what they don't like.

Conversation 1:
1 films in general ☐
2 psychological thrillers ☐
3 more lightweight films ☐

Conversation 2:
4 rugby ☐
5 football ☐
6 live sport ☐

Conversation 3:
7 Van Gogh ☐
8 contemporary art ☐
9 Turner ☐

2 🎧 **1 06** Complete the sentences. Then listen and check your answers.

1 Well, yeah, **I'm not that** _____ films to be honest. **It's** _____ **really my** _____ .
2 I _____ **like** a good psychological thriller, though ... But **I'm** _____ **so** _____ **on** the more lightweight stuff.
3 What sports **are you** _____ ?
4 **I'm** _____ **huge** rugby _____ . My favourite sport by a mile. **I'm** _____ **really** _____ football. It's OK, but **I can** _____ **it or** _____ **it.**
5 **I'm** _____ **big** _____ **of** Van Gogh.
6 I _____ **really get** _____ **about** much contemporary art, to be honest. **It just doesn't** _____ **to me** at all.

DESCRIBING TALENTS AND ABILITIES

3 🎧 **1 07** Listen to four people talking about what they are good at and not good at. Tick (✓) what they are good at and cross (✗) what they are not good at.

1 playing the piano ☐   singing ☐
2 teaching ☐   administrative tasks ☐
3 making tea ☐   cooking ☐
4 shopping ☐   saving money ☐

4 🎧 **1 07** Put the words into the correct order to make sentences. Then listen again and check your answers.

1 Well, I play the piano, so I guess *quite / one / at / I'm / thing / that's / good* _____

2 *great / I'm / singing / not / at* _____

3 *I'm / a / teaching / think / I / quite / at / natural* _____

4 *a / not / when it comes to / most definitely / I'm / natural* all the admin side of it. _____

5 *my / can't / a cup of tea / I / to / make / life / save* _____

6 *a / I / for / talent / do / cooking / have* _____

7 *it / I'm / at / saving / hopeless / pretty* _____

8 *born / I'm / a / spendaholic* _____

5 Use the words to write full sentences.

1 I / not / fan / rock music
_____

2 Football / OK / but / I / take / leave
_____

3 I / can't / excited / modern art / just / not / appeal
_____

4 Anna / natural / when / comes / learning languages
_____

5 I / cook / save / life
_____

6 He / born / leader
_____

PRONUNCIATION
Emphasis and de-emphasis

6 🎧 **1 08** Underline the words you think will be stressed. Then listen and check your answers.

1 I do like watching a good film.
2 I really want to learn the piano one day.
3 The lecture was quite good, but I thought it was a bit slow in places.
4 Modern art's really not my thing, I'm afraid.
5 I quite like modern art, actually. Especially earlier modern art.
6 Sam does tell a good story.
7 I did enjoy that film last night.
8 I know it's quite expensive, but I really do think it's worth it.

WRITING SKILL Nominalization

7 Complete the sentences so the meaning is similar. Use a noun and any other words necessary.

1 We intend to submit the proposal later this week.
   Our _____ to submit the proposal later this week.
2 It has been decided that we will extend the trial period by a further two weeks.
   The _____ to extend the trial period by a further two weeks.
3 It is vital that departments communicate clearly and openly with each other at all times.
   _____ departments is vital at all times.
4 Satisfaction levels have increased significantly since the new system was implemented.
   There _____ satisfaction levels since _____ the new system.
5 Not many people responded to the survey and a number of people complained about its length.
   There _____ to the survey and _____ about its length.
6 We need to further consult about distributing the new product.
   We need _____ about _____ the new product.

8 Rewrite the sentences using noun phrases in place of the phrases or clauses in bold. Make any other changes necessary.

1 **When it was published, it** caused a sensation.
   Its publication caused a sensation.
2 **If you don't get sufficient sleep it** can affect your concentration.
   _____
3 **They have changed a number of things in** the proposal.
   _____

4 Technology is advancing alarmingly.
   _____

5 I think **what the marketing department is proposing** is too technical and **unnecessarily complicates things**.
   _____

6 Thanks for your email. I'm just about to go away on a work trip, but I'll have a think about **what you suggest** and get back to you **when I get back** in a couple of weeks.
   _____
   _____
   _____

9 Rewrite the short progress report using nouns in place of the words in bold. Make any other changes necessary.

Online marketing: A progress report

We **attempted** on two separate occasions to market the product online, but neither **succeeded** very well. In hindsight, the way we **developed** the two sites was not based on any kind of comprehensive e-commerce strategy. We didn't think enough about the way we **designed** them and the way they **functioned**. In addition, we didn't properly **implement** how to **process** credit card transactions and the way we **fulfilled** orders was inefficient. Looking forward, we have been **consulting** with a specialist e-commerce firm and we are currently **discussing** with the board about additional financial and human resources **being available**.

There were two separate attempts to market the product online, but neither was very successful. In hindsight, ...

_____
_____
_____
_____
_____
_____
_____
_____
_____
_____

YOUR IDEA

1 Read what each person says about discovering their talent and answer the questions a–f.

1 Joel: I have a very analytical mind. I was good at school, doing well in subjects like maths and science. That's not very cool, though, is it? Being good with numbers has served me well in my career – I'm an accountant – but I never thought it could lead to anything very exciting. Then I read something about how mathematical patterns and classical music might be related. I did a lot of reading around the subject and decided I wanted to learn a musical instrument to find out if there really was a link between maths and music. I took up violin classes at a local music school and just loved it. It hasn't always been easy and it takes me a long time to pick up different tunes. My teacher is great though, and she's always pushing me to do better. In fact she entered me for a talent show.

2 Tammy: When I was younger, I didn't take part in school sports activities. I was excluded from most activities for health and safety reasons – being in my wheelchair, I could watch and cheer on my classmates, but I couldn't get involved. I didn't think that you could be an athlete and be in a wheelchair. That all changed when I went to see a wheelchair marathon. I was so interested that I bugged my parents to find out how I could train to be like the marathon competitors. I ended up going to a try-out at a local sports club and raced for the first time in an upright chair. Luckily my time was good enough to join the team and since then I've trained and raced in a proper racing wheelchair. I'm looking forward to my next track meet – I've got a great chance of winning a medal.

3 Claudia: I think I was quite misunderstood as a child. My mum always told me that I seemed to have unlimited energy – I'd never sit still and always fidgeted. I think the teachers at school agreed, and there was some talk of taking me to see a doctor. Not all of them though, thankfully. One of my teachers, Mrs Giles, suggested something different to my parents. She was really passionate about dance and theatre and gave my mum and dad the idea of taking me along to dance classes. To be honest, I've never really looked back – now I run my own dance school and our students compete all over the world. I sometimes wonder what would have happened if Mrs Giles hadn't been there to give me the push I needed. I might never have discovered that I had a real knack for dancing.

a Who wasn't fully involved in sporting activities at school? _____

b Who experienced difficulty at school? _____

c Who did well academically at school? _____

d Who received encouragement from a teacher? (2 people) _____

e Who is confident they will succeed because of their talent? _____

f Who sometimes thinks about what their life would have been like without their talent? _____

2 Write notes about a talent you have or would like to have.

3 Answer the following questions about your talent or a talent you would like to have.

If you have a talent …

1 How did you discover your talent? How do you think you could develop it?

_____

2 Who helped you develop your talent? Who could help you?

_____

3 What opportunities does having this talent give you?

_____

If you would like to have a talent …

1 How do you think you could develop this talent?

_____

2 Who could help you develop this talent?

_____

3 What opportunities would having this talent give you?

_____

4 Practise describing your talent out loud. Remember to practise using humour in your presentation, but remember …

- its purpose is to relax people.
- it should illustrate the point you are making and not distract from it.
- it should not offend any group or individual.
- it helps if the humour is based on an anecdote about you or your experience, which others can easily relate to.
- it's essential to test any jokes on friends or colleagues before your presentation.

ORGANIZING YOUR PRESENTATION

5 Match the five steps of a presentation (1–5) with the examples of useful language (a–e).

1 Introduce yourself and your topic ☐
2 Say what talent you're talking about ☐
3 Say who or what helped you develop this talent ☐
4 Say what opportunities this talent would give you ☐
5 Finish ☐

a I left my office job and I've opened my own art gallery to showcase my and my friends' work.

b Hello everyone. Welcome to my presentation today. I'm going to talk about a talent I am lucky to have.

c I'm very fortunate to have had the support of my partner while I attended evening classes.

d I wasn't very artistic as a child, but I've been able to develop my skills as a painter.

e That brings us to the end of my presentation. If you have any questions, please feel free to ask them.

YOUR PRESENTATION

6 Read the useful language on the left and make notes for your presentation.

1 Introduce yourself and your topic Hello everyone. Welcome … The purpose of the presentation is to …	
2 Say what talent you're talking about I've been able to … Something I'm good at is … Something I'd like to do is …	
3 Say who or what helped you develop this talent … has/have been so helpful to me. I couldn't have done this without … I would need … to help me … They could help me by …	
4 Say what opportunities this talent would give you Now I've … I'd be able to …	
5 Finish That brings us to the end of … If you have any questions, please …	

7 Film yourself giving your presentation or practise in front of a mirror.
Give yourself marks out of ten for …

- using humour in your presentation.　☐ /10
- acting naturally as you talk.　☐ /10
- following the five steps in Exercise 6.　☐ /10
- using correct grammar.　☐ /10

2 Hopes and fears

2.1 Why I live in mortal dread of public speaking

TEDTALKS

Australian singer/songwriter, **MEGAN WASHINGTON**, was born in Papua New Guinea in 1986 and lived there until she was ten years old, when the family moved to Brisbane, Australia. During her teenage years she developed a love of music and, after finishing school, studied for a Bachelor of Music degree at the Queensland University of Technology and then studied jazz voice at the Queensland Conservatorium of Music. Early in her career, she played jazz piano with a number of acts and, before going solo, founded a band called *Washington*. Her style has evolved from jazz via blues and roots to indie pop and alternative rock, and today she sings and plays piano and guitar. On her Facebook page, she describes herself as a chanteuse.

Washington has won a number of awards, including Australia's 'Best Female Artist' and 'Breakthrough Artist', following the release of her platinum-selling debut album in 2010. She has since released a number of other best-selling albums, including *Insomnia* and *There There*. Washington tends to sing about issues such as heartbreak, insecurity and rage, and the lyrics to her songs have been described as having a beautiful and confessional tone.

Since her breakthrough solo album, which reached number three in the Australian charts, she has attracted the attention of a wider audience by appearing on a number of Australian TV music shows. A number of her songs have also appeared on other kinds of high-profile TV shows.

Washington developed a stutter early in her life, but avoided sharing this publicly until her talk at the TEDxSydney event in 2014. She explained that while it can hamper her during conversations, it disappears when she sings. This has helped her to develop a number of strategies for coping with her speech impediment, which include avoiding certain letter combinations where possible and by 'singing' the things she has to say rather than speaking them.

Megan Washington

CAREER PATHWAYS

1 Read the text. Are these statements true (T) or false (F)?

1 The first group she played with was called *Washington*. ☐
2 Washington's voice has been described as beautiful. ☐
3 She first came to fame when she appeared on TV. ☐
4 The public didn't know about her stutter until her 2014 TED Talk. ☐
5 Singing has helped Washington to cope with her stutter. ☐

TED PLAYLIST

2 Other TED speakers are interested in topics similar to Megan Washington's TED Talk. Read the descriptions of four TED Talks at the top of page 115. In your opinion, which is the best title for this playlist, a, b or c?

a Music is a medicine
b There's a song inside all of us
c The power of music

3 Read the TED playlist again. Find a speaker who ...

1 re-found their voice.
2 told their story through music.
3 overcame a physical setback.
4 uses music to help others.

▶ **Robert Gupta: Between music and medicine**

When Robert Gupta was caught between a career as a doctor and as a violinist, he realized his place was in the middle. He tells a moving story of society's marginalized and the power of music therapy, which can succeed where conventional medicine fails.

▶ **The Lady Lifers: A moving song from women in prison for life**

The ten women prisoners in this chorus share a moving song about their experiences: their hopes, regrets and fears. 'I'm not an angel,' sings one, 'but I'm not the devil.' Filmed inside Muncy State Prison, it's a rare and poignant look inside the world of people imprisoned with no hope of parole.

▶ **Sting: How I started writing songs again**

Sting's early life was dominated by a shipyard – and he dreamed of escaping its industrial drudgery. But after a nasty bout of writer's block that stretched on for years, Sting found inspiration in the stories of the shipyard workers from his youth. In a lyrical, confessional talk, Sting treats us to songs from his musical based on this theme.

▶ **Charity Tillemann-Dick: Singing after a double lung transplant**

You'll never sing again, said her doctor. But in a story from the very edge of medical possibility, operatic soprano Charity Tillemann-Dick tells a double story of survival – of her body, from a double lung transplant, and of her spirit, fuelled by an unwavering will to sing.

4 Find words in the TED playlist that mean the same as the words and phrases a–d.

  a traditional   **c** unpleasant

  b emotional   **d** strong and determined

5 Which talk would you most like to see? Why? Watch the talk at TED.com.

AUTHENTIC LISTENING SKILLS
Listening to songs

6 🎧 **1 09** You are going to hear a podcast in which a member of the *Keynote* team talks about Robert Gupta's TED Talk, *Between music and medicine*. Look at the lyrics in the song extract that the podcaster plays at the end. Complete the lines. Then listen and check your answers.

I see the sun in your smile
Watching it rise in your _____
See the dusty road ahead
Stretching out for miles and miles
Sick and tired of skipping the _____
Dodging the holes in the road
I need a helping hand
To help me shoulder this _____
Do, do you, well, wouldn't you
Do the same in my _____ ?
I wouldn't do, just couldn't _____
Another mile without you
Another mile without you

LISTENING

7 🎧 **1 10** Listen to the full podcast. Answer the questions.

  1 Who does Robert Gupta aim his music therapy at?

  2 In what way does Mike Harrison think that Gupta's presentation is different to a lecture?

8 🎧 **1 10** Listen again. Complete the facts using one word in each space.

  1 Robert Gupta's profession is _____ ; his hobby is playing the _____ .

  2 Gupta uses music to give _____ to people in distress.

  3 Mike Harrison has tried using music in his _____ .

  4 Mike Harrison is not really a _____ , but he believes in the _____ of music.

VOCABULARY IN CONTEXT

9 Read the extracts from the podcast. Choose the correct meaning of the words in bold.

  1 I was interested to watch this TED Talk exploring how medicine **intersects with** another creative pursuit.
    a connects with ☐   **b** changes ☐
    c enhances ☐

  2 ... about music is about its potential to help people in really **dire** circumstances.
    a frightening ☐   **b** unusual ☐   **c** desperate ☐

  3 Gupta shows us how music can give society's most **marginalized** some sort of hope.
    Treated as: **a** unteachable ☐   **b** disregarded ☐
    c unintelligent ☐

  4 I think it's sad that most of the time we **take** music and other sounds **for granted**.
    a neglect ☐   **b** undervalue ☐   **c** ignore ☐

  5 .... particularly when it can be so effective at **articulating** our emotions.
    a stimulating ☐   **b** expressing ☐   **c** mirroring ☐

GRAMMAR Future forms

1 Read the sentences below. Do the phrases in bold refer to present (P), general (G) or future (F) time?

1 Give him a call. His meeting **will have finished**. ☐
2 **I'll watch** a couple of hours TV before bed most evenings. ☐
3 I'm a bit busy now. **I'll call** you back. ☐
4 We**'re about to leave**. Are you ready? ☐
5 They've been driving all day. They**'ll be** exhausted. ☐
6 Get a move on! The taxi **will be waiting**. ☐
7 The exhibition **starts** on Friday. ☐
8 He **will insist** on singing that awful song. ☐

2 Choose the best words or phrases to complete the news article.

New population growth forecast

A recent analysis shows that the Earth's population ¹*will continue / will be continuing* to rise from around 7bn today and ²*will be reaching / will have reached* 11bn by 2100. This means that by the end of the century, the world population ³*is likely to be / is likely to have been* between 50% and 75% larger than today and ⁴*is still going to grow / will still be growing*.

The study overturns the long-standing theory that the global population ⁵*is peaking / is going to peak* in around 2050 at about 9bn people and then possibly even decline. Experts now believe that population growth should return to the top of the international agenda. James Oliver, of the international think tank Population Awareness who ⁶ *hold / are holding* a conference in London next month, said 'This new projected population growth, unless it ⁷ *is slowed / will be slowed*, ⁸ *is going to cause / is going to have caused* all kinds of challenges.' He went on to say that if we ⁹ *don't take / won't take* action very soon, in 50 or so years we ¹⁰ *are very likely facing / will very likely be facing* a number of issues which are all linked to rapid population growth, such as insufficient healthcare, increasing poverty and rising social unrest and crime.

3 Complete the news items using the correct future form of the verbs in italics.

not / be able	may / double	likely / have

1 By the end of the decade, demographers say China _____ a surplus of around 25 million men who, because of China's gender imbalance, _____ to find a wife. It is thought that by the middle of the century, this figure _____ .

live	continue

2 If the current rate of increasing longevity _____ , it is likely that some people born today _____ to be 130.

focus	meet

3 The United Nations Expert Group on Population Change _____ in New York next month to discuss 'changing population trends and development'. The meeting _____ particularly on fertility issues.

prove	only / be	soon / be able
may / eventually / follow		

4 Medical scientists predict that we _____ to regrow damaged body parts. At first it _____ possible to regrow fingers and toes, but if this _____ successful, the regeneration of whole limbs and even internal organs _____ .

travel	start

5 It is predicted that by the end of the century, humans _____ to colonize Mars and it is possible that we _____ between the two planets on a regular basis.

4 🎧 1 11 Complete the dialogues with the correct future form of the verbs in the box. Then listen and check your answers.

be	call back	do	finish	have
have	make	say	start	tell

1 A: Have you booked the meeting room yet?
   B: I'm just about _____ it.

2 A: I can't speak. I'm in a meeting right now.
   B: OK, I _____ later this afternoon.

3 A: Did you get an invite to Jenny's do next week?
   B: Oh, she _____ a party, is she?

4 A: See you at six, then.
   B: Well, as long as the traffic _____ OK.

5 A: Term _____ on the 15th, right?
   B: The 22nd, I think.

6 A: Where are they? The gate's about to close.
   B: Yep, doesn't look like they _____ it, does it?

7 A: I'll pop round at 7.30ish.
   B: We _____ dinner then. Can you make it nearer nine? We _____ eating by then.

8 A: _____ you _____ anything to him?
   B: Yep, I _____ him exactly what I think!

LANGUAGE FOCUS Expressions of certainty

5 Put the words in the correct order to make sentences.

1 all / will reach / likelihood, / the population / in / by the year 2100 / eleven million

_____

2 to / a cure / we / sooner or later / bound / find / 're / for cancer

_____

3 well / may / one day / very / a third world war / happen

_____

4 colonize / foregone / a / that / it's / we'll / conclusion / one day / Mars

_____

5 likely / is / remain / the / for a long time / to / the US / world's / economy / biggest

_____

6 certain that / it's / means / by / on another planet / no / there / is / life

_____

6 Rewrite the sentences using the word or words given so the meaning is the same.

1 I'm sure she'll know what to do.   *bound*

_____

2 It's very possible that they won't agree.   *no means*

_____

3 It's possible it was my fault.   *may well*

_____

4 I'm pretty sure it won't be here.   *highly unlikely*

_____

5 I suspect we'll never hear from them again.   *likelihood*

_____

7 Complete the responses.

1 A: Do you think we'll get there in time?
   B: Unless the traffic improves, it's _____ unlikely.

2 A: How many people do you think will turn up?
   B: No idea. _____ anyone's _____ .

3 A: Do you think we've done the right thing?
   B: I think it _____ well turn _____ to be a bad move, actually.

4 A: How come you're so sure about it?
   B: Oh, it's a _____ conclusion.

5 A: Are they going to be there?
   B: I think so, but it's _____ no means _____ .

DICTATION

8 🎧 1 12 Listen to part of a lecture about population growth in China. Complete the sentences.

China has one of the lowest birth rates in the world. At about 1.26 children per female, it is currently less than half of the world's average and below the fertility replacement rate of 2.2, which a country needs to maintain its current population. This means that if
[1] _____ , China's population [2] _____ .
It has been suggested that by the end of the century, China's population [3] _____ 30 per cent. And if this prediction [4] _____ , then China [5] _____ demographic crises in the world. The sharply declining birth rate means that by 2050, between a quarter and a third of China's population [6] _____ age. They, of course, [7] _____ to the economy while at the same time government expenditure on the elderly [8] _____ .

2.3 Expanding your horizons

READING

1 Look at the opening sentence of each paragraph (1–5) of the blog. Say which one(s) you think give:

a advice ☐☐☐

b a word of caution ☐

c a definition ☐

2 Read the whole text. Find examples of types of adversity that people face in paragraphs 1–5.

1 *poverty, lack of education and discrimination, illness, personal loss*

2 _____

_____

3 _____

_____

4 _____

_____

5 _____

3 Read the text again. Choose the best option to complete the sentences.

1 It's *illogical / natural* to feel depressed in the face of adversity.

2 Not getting a promotion at work *is / isn't* an example of facing adversity.

3 Negative events *generally have / don't necessarily have* a negative effect.

4 Dealing with adversity *makes us better able / doesn't actually help us* to deal with it when it arises again.

5 We can *specifically relate to / generally learn from* the stories of others who have triumphed over adversity.

6 Talking about your problems always helps to *find solutions / relieve the tension*.

7 Facing adversity has a positive outcome for a *majority / minority* of people.

8 Many people *are overwhelmed / simply give up* in the face of adversity.

Five things you should know about adversity

1 Adversity is not just an occasional setback. It usually refers to a chronic situation or condition that seriously hampers your ability to achieve your ambitions or to find security and happiness. Adversity may come from your social situation – poverty or lack of education or discrimination – or it may come in the form of a personal tragedy, like illness or loss of a loved one. In fact, most of us face adversity at some point in our lives and will, quite understandably, feel depressed and hopeless as a result. The first thing to do is not to allow a series of seemingly minor setbacks (not getting a promotion at work, a big repair bill on your car, etc.) to snowball into a feeling that you're facing overwhelming adversity.

2 What doesn't kill you, makes you stronger. Scientific studies have shown that those who have experienced adversity in their lives are better equipped to deal with fresh difficulties or challenges when they arise. That is not to say that negative events don't have negative effects; simply that if we're able to work our way through traumas and setbacks, we come out the other side more resilient. One study showed that among people who suffered serious back pain, those who had experience of some other adversity in life were more mobile and better able to cope than those who had no such experience.

3 Stories can inspire. The pages of magazines – business magazines in particular – are full of stories of people who have triumphed over adversity. Richard Branson, CEO of Virgin Group, has struggled with dyslexia all his life. Jim Carrey, the comic actor, was the son of an unemployed musician and dropped out of school at 15 to support the rest of his family. The film *The Theory of Everything* celebrates the life of the famous physicist Stephen Hawking who has survived motor neurone disease against all the odds. All these stories serve as a useful metaphor for our own struggles against adversity, whatever they might be.

4 A problem shared is a problem halved. As I said, we all face adversity at some point in our lives so you can almost always find a sympathetic ear in a friend or colleague. Talking about your financial problems, for example, will automatically make you feel less burdened; you might even feel able to share a joke about it. Additionally, as you talk through what's happened and what you're feeling, solutions that had half-formed in your mind, but not yet been articulated, may begin to appear.

5 Adversity can be crushing too. For every one person that has achieved success in the face of adversity there are nine people who feel crushed by it. Recognize that there are situations – notably chronic poverty and social discrimination – that many people cannot escape from, however valiantly they try. So it's incumbent on all of us either to give a helping hand directly to such groups in society or to encourage our governments to do so.

4 Choose the correct word to complete the definitions.

1 **hampers** your ability to = makes it more *difficult / impossible* for you to ...

2 allow [something] to **snowball** = to allow something to become *bigger / smaller*.

3 we become more **resilient** = we become more able to *ignore / resist* shocks or stresses

4 survived against **all the odds** = survived in spite of a *high / low* probability of not surviving

5 talking will make you feel less **burdened** = talking will lift a *weight / pain* from your shoulders

6 not yet been **articulated** = not yet been *explained / expressed* clearly

7 **chronic** poverty = being poor for a *short / long* period of time

8 it's **incumbent** on all of us to = it is our *choice / duty* to ...

5 🎧 **1 13** Listen to someone talking about adversity in their life. Which of the points about adversity in the article do they talk about?

6 🎧 **1 13** Listen again and answer the questions.

1 What was the main adversity the speaker faced in their life?

2 What was the main adversity J.K. Rowling faced?

3 Where did J.K. Rowling usually do her writing?

4 What was the lesson the speaker took from J.K. Rowling's life?

VOCABULARY Idioms: hopes and fears

7 Complete the idioms in the extracts with the correct words.

1 Some people feel they are facing adversity when their expectations are not met. They ¹p_____ their hopes on getting something – like a new job or a flat they have been looking for – and then their hopes are ²d_____ when they don't get it. But that isn't really adversity. It's just an ordinary setback. Real adversity is about facing conditions which are extremely tough and not ³g_____ up hope.

2 Did you see the story of the girl who stood up to other girls who were bullying her at school? I was really moved by it. She had been getting bullied for three years and had thought several times about going to the head of the school, but she got ⁴c_____ feet. Then one day she ⁵p_____ up the courage to speak about it in a school assembly – in front of all the teachers and pupils. At first she was a bundle of ⁶n_____ , but once she got started she spoke very articulately and with real passion. At the end everyone got to their feet and applauded her.

3 Her parents were very poor and she was sent away at sixteen to earn money in a laundry in the city. I think that's what made her the person she is. She set up her own laundry company at 23 – it was a complete ⁷l_____ in the dark – and made a success of it. Now the sky's the ⁸l_____ for her.

WORD FOCUS Courage, guts and bravery

8 Choose the correct word to complete these expressions about bravery and courage.

1 It *needs / takes* **guts** to stand up and disagree with a course of action you think is wrong when everyone else is in favour of it.

2 She took a risk investing all her savings in her new venture, but it turned out to be a huge success. **Fortune *assists / favours* the brave**.

3 He was very disappointed not to be chosen for the team, but he **put a *brave / courageous* face on** it.

4 The ruling party lost the election by 45% to 55%. They **put *on / up* a brave fight**, but people wanted a change.

5 The best advice my father ever gave me was 'Lead your own life, in spite of what others may say or think and **have the courage of your *convictions / beliefs***'.

6 You'll get soaked if you cycle to work now. I admire the fact that you're prepared to ***brave / gut* the elements**, but why don't you just take the car instead?

7 She **took her courage in both *arms / hands*** and jumped into the cold water.

8 Only Dan would ***have / feel* the guts to** speak to the boss like that.

9 Complete these sentences with the correct form of the expressions in Exercise 8.

1 The open-air concert turned out to be on one of the wettest weekends on record, but still, over 10,000 people _____ to come and see their heroes play.

2 Our manager says that he is going to support us and argue against the new working contract. I just hope he _____ .

3 You shouldn't be disheartened. You _____ , but you just came up against someone who was exceptionally talented.

4 _____ to admit that you've been wrong all along.

5 It's no good carrying on and _____ . If you're feeling that stressed, you've got to do something about it or you'll end up having a breakdown.

6 I admit it: I'm a coward. I don't _____ to confront her about it.

2.4 Worst-case scenario

GIVING AND JUSTIFYING ADVICE

1 🎧 **1 14** Listen to a university tutor talking about plagiarism. According to the tutor, are these statements true (T) or false (F)?

1 The university routinely checks submitted work for evidence of plagiarism. ☐
2 It is OK to use open-source websites such as Wikipedia. ☐
3 Plagiarism may result in a student being thrown out of the university. ☐
4 Using synonyms and changing the word order is the best way to avoid plagiarism. ☐
5 Your tutors will help you to understand what is and isn't plagiarism. ☐

2 🎧 **1 14** Complete the extracts from Exercise 1. Then listen again and check your answers.

1 You need to be _____ that the university routinely checks submitted work for evidence of plagiarism.
2 And on that subject, we strongly _____ _____ using open-source websites such as Wikipedia that have unverifiable content.
3 In the _____ _____ plagiarism, you will be given a formal warning and have to rewrite your essay.
4 To avoid plagiarism, the _____ _____ is to become familiar with the principles of good academic practice as soon as you start your university studies.
5 That _____, you _____ more quickly develop an awareness of the requirements ...
6 ... although it is _____ _____ thoroughly check them through before you submit your work.

7 _____ simply using a few synonyms and changing the word order. The _____ are that you will be caught out.
8 Following his or her advice will _____ that your work is plagiarism-free.

3 Complete the responses using the words in brackets.

1 A: I just don't know what to do about it.
   B: I'd _____ (time / think) it through if I were you. _____ (talk / someone / also / good idea).
2 A: Work's really starting to get me down.
   B: Maybe it's time _____ (consider / look) something else?
3 A: This hotel is in a better location, but this one has better facilities.
   B: I'd _____ (opt / location / facilities) every time.
4 A: I just can't help wondering if he's OK.
   B: _____ , (own / peace / mind) why don't you give him a call?
5 A: Do you think I should ask for a meeting with them?
   B: I think for now _____ (best thing / say) nothing. _____ (way / not) pre-empt anything. I think things will probably sort themselves out.
6 A: What should I do about my new boss?
   B: Well, I _____ (advise / against / do) anything too rash and _____ (avoid / be) too confrontational. _____ (the chances) he's also a little uneasy about things.

PRONUNCIATION Consonant clusters

4 🔊 **1 15** The following words contain combinations (or clusters) of consonants that can be difficult to pronounce. Underline the consonant clusters and practise saying the words. Listen and check and then practise again.

1 sixth	**11** hundredth
2 through	**12** filmed
3 spring	**13** health
4 asked	**14** crisps
5 clothes	**15** helpful
6 length	**16** splendid
7 months	**17** explained
8 depth	**18** instincts
9 twelfth	**19** facts
10 breathes	**20** rejects

WRITING SKILL Future in the past

5 Complete the sentences with *was/were going to* and the words in the box.

originally/get	originally/hold	not/say
just/stay	tell	

1 We _____ for a few hours, but we ended up spending the whole weekend there.

2 I _____ anything to him, but I just felt it wasn't fair to keep him in the dark any longer.

3 I think they _____ married in June. I'm not sure why they changed it.

4 I'm really sorry you heard it from someone else. I _____ you myself, honestly.

5 They _____ the conference in Liverpool, but they went for Birmingham instead.

6 Put the words in order to complete the sentences.

1 _____ *she / as though / looked / was / she / going / something, / say / to* but she turned and walked out of the room.

2 _____ *to / tomorrow, / going / were / the two leaders / meet* but the meeting has been postponed.

3 _____ *Jones / yesterday, / originally / going / discharged / was / be / to* but doctors decided to keep him in for further observations.

4 _____ *wasn't / rain, / to / it / supposed* but the heavens opened and we got absolutely soaked.

5 _____ *resume / play / due / to / three, / was / at* but at quarter to it started raining again.

6 _____ *to / it / a working lunch, / was / meant / be* but we didn't get much work done at all.

7 _____ *would / I / was / us, / he / waiting / sure / for / be* but he must've got the times confused.

8 _____ *were / nine o'clock, / we / at / to / supposed / meet* but he didn't turn up.

7 Rewrite the sentences using the word given so the meaning is similar.

1 We had planned to leave at about six, but we were still there at seven. *going*
We _____

2 They didn't arrive on Tuesday as was scheduled. *supposed*
They _____

3 I expected them to leave early, but they stayed until the early hours. *would*
I _____

4 We hadn't planned to take a taxi, but it was raining. *going*
We _____

5 They said the flight would take off at 5.30, but it was delayed again until seven o'clock. *due*
The flight _____

6 We hadn't anticipated it taking so long. *would*
We _____

8 Complete the review from a travel forum using the words in the box.

due/move	going/have to/make	going/improve
originally/going/stay	supposed/meet	would/take
would/not/recognize		

Where do I begin? First, someone from the hotel [1]_____ us at the airport, but after waiting over an hour, it became clear we [2]_____ our own way there. As the airport was pretty well deserted, it took us another 30 minutes to find a taxi that [3]_____ us to the hotel. When we finally got to the hotel, it was terrible, nothing like its website and nothing at all like some of the reviews we'd read. The whole place was dark and tired and in general need of repair. The owner kept telling us how he [4]_____ things and that we [5]_____ the place if we came back in a few months. He insisted that no-one else had ever complained – yeah, right. Our room looked like it hadn't had a proper clean for weeks. We [6]_____ for three nights, but, after the first night, we couldn't stand it anymore. We [7]_____ up the coast a few miles and change hotels anyway, so we rang them and they had a room available that night.

Writing 1 | AN ARTICLE

IDEAS

You will read an article written to answer the question below.

> A business magazine is running a series of articles on attitudes to work and leisure time. The magazine has invited readers to send in articles briefly describing their work-life balance. The article should explain the importance of maintaining an appropriate work-life balance and consider what companies can do to help their employees achieve this.

Write your article in **280–320 words** in an appropriate style.

1 In the question, underline the three topics which need to be covered in the article.
What points could be included in each topic?

MODEL

2 Read the article. Which topic is dealt with in each paragraph? Are any of your ideas included?

A new lease of life

[1] Exhausted, depressed and coming down with a cold, I opened the door to my office and sat down at my desk. It was 8 a.m. and I'd already been up for three hours. Looking at the list of things that I needed to get through in the next twelve hours, I realized that if I didn't change something soon, I ran the risk of burning out and having to give up a career that I had dreamed of for years.

[2] My own experience illustrates why our current obsession with working as much as possible is unsustainable. It has been proved time and time again that employees who maintain a healthy work-life balance contribute much more to their companies than those who only live to work. Their stress levels are lower, they take fewer sick days and they are able to complete tasks more efficiently.

[3] Taking this into account, the way companies encourage employees to use their time at work is an important way to change their mindsets. This can be done by following the example of businesses that provide recreation areas in their offices. Not only does this allow their staff to switch off from the stresses of work, but it also gives them the chance to build stronger relationships. Another idea is to encourage staff to leave the office at break times or earlier in the evening to spend time enjoying the natural world.

[4] The decision I made that day was one of the hardest of my life: moving from the prestigious city law firm I'd been lucky to get a job at to a local one, closer to home and demanding much shorter working hours. Only by doing this did my quality of life drastically improve. I'm happier, healthier and have more of a social life than ever before. It's a choice I would make again in a heartbeat.

3 Read the article. Say which section (1–4) each of the following statements (a–d) matches.

a Businesses have a responsibility to encourage staff to use their time wisely.
b The author felt overwhelmed by all of the work they had to do, despite being in the career they wanted.
c By changing jobs, the author has seen huge positive changes in their life.
d It's healthier to have a good work-life balance than to work too much.

USEFUL LANGUAGE

4 Match the phrases (1–3) with three alternative ways of saying the same thing (a–i).

1 The author **realized** they needed a different job.
☐ ☐ ☐
2 Having a good work-life balance **is important to** stay healthy. ☐ ☐ ☐
3 Helping employees to reduce stress levels **can be done by** providing recreation areas at work. ☐ ☐ ☐

a The author **came to realize** a new job was necessary.
b **It suddenly occurred to** the author **that** they should change their job.
c **The essence of** being healthy **lies in** having an appropriate work-life balance.
d **A possible route to** reducing employees' stress levels **would be to** give them places to relax at work.
e **One way to approach** the reduction of employees' stress levels **is to** provide places to relax at work.
f **It dawned on** the author **that** it was time for a new job.
g **A key ingredient of** staying healthy **is** balancing work and relaxation.
h **A possible course of action for** helping employees to reduce stress levels **is to** give them somewhere to relax at work.
i Balancing your work and home lives **is vital to** remain healthy.

5 These sentences are taken from the article in Exercise 2. Rewrite the sentences using a–i. Each sentence can be rewritten in three different ways. Try to do it without looking at Exercise 4.

1 I realized that if I didn't change something soon, I ran the risk of burning out.
I came to realize that if I didn't change something soon, I ran the risk of burning out.

2 The way companies encourage employees to use their time at work is an important way to change their mindsets.

_____

_____

3 This can be done by following the example of businesses that provide recreation areas in their offices.

_____

_____

6 A stylistic device often used in articles is the 'rule of three'. This involves repeating a similar grammatical structure three times in the same section of the article. Sometimes a sound is also repeated to add to the effect. Find three examples of the rule of three in the model in Exercise 2.

Note: If one of the three points is longer than the others, it is usually the last of the three, e.g.

My job was too challenging, too stressful and taking up far too much of my time.

7 Match one phrase from each column to create five more 'threes' which could be used in an article about work-life balance.

over-worked, under-paid and under-valued

over-worked	encouraging job shares	or simply lunch at a local restaurant
by organizing a night out	more creative	and under-valued
by allowing flexi-time	under-paid	and breathing their jobs
having been awake since six	sleeping	and not likely to get home until seven
they are more productive	a weekend away	and their imaginations are given free rein
living	at my desk since eight	or letting staff leave early on Fridays

PLANNING

You will answer the following question.

> A technology magazine is inviting readers to contribute to a series of articles about our changing relationship with technology. You decide to submit an article about how one piece of technology has affected your life. You should briefly describe why the technology is important to you, explain what people would have done before this technology existed and assess whether these changes are positive or negative.

Write your article in **280–320 words** in an appropriate style.

8 Plan your article. Write notes to answer these questions. Don't write full sentences yet.

1 Which piece of technology will you write about?
2 Why is it important to you?
3 What did people do/use before this technology existed?
4 Has this technology had a positive or a negative effect on society?

WRITING

9 Write an article to reply to the question in Exercise 8. In your article you should:

- include a title and introduction which will attract the reader's attention and encourage them to read on
- describe how one piece of technology has affected your life
- explain what people did/used before this technology existed
- evaluate whether any changes in society have been positive or negative

Write **280–320 words**.

ANALYSIS

10 Check your article. Answer the questions.

Content: Does the article describe your personal experience? Is this contrasted to life before this technology existed? Are the effects of this technology on society clearly evaluated? Is it 280 to 320 words long?

Communicative achievement: Does the title attract the reader's attention? Is the article interesting to read?

Organization: Is the article logically organized? Are the links between paragraphs and ideas clear?

Language: Does it use correct grammar and vocabulary? Is there a good range of structures and stylistic devices, such as the 'rule of three'?

3 Perception

3.1 The 4 ways sound affects us

TEDTALKS

JULIAN TREASURE was born in London, UK. He was educated at the 600-year-old St Paul's School, one of the UK's original public schools, then at the University of Cambridge, where he studied economics. After university, he worked in advertising and then in magazine publishing. He started TPD Publishing in 1988, which produced magazines for brands like Apple, Lexus and Microsoft and which went on to become one of the UK's leading contract magazine publishing companies. Treasure sold the company in 2001, but stayed on working there for a further two years. Around this time, he also held a number of senior posts in various publishing associations and agencies and, in 2002, he received a Professional Publishers Association Award for services to the UK magazine publishing industry.

In 2003, Treasure had a change of direction, leaving TPD to pursue his passion for sound. As a drummer and musician – his band, *The Transmitters*, once played on live TV to an audience of 18 million – he had for a long time been interested in the noise of modern life, and in particular how businesses and other organizations were using sound in their work. As he researched this, he discovered that most sound in business environments was having a negative effect on people and he realized there was an opportunity for businesses to improve their results by becoming more sound-conscious. As a result, he started The Sound Agency, which advises organizations on all aspects of sound. Examples of this include the use of ambient sound to reduce crime in urban areas and the creation of in-store soundscapes that increase both sales and customer satisfaction. The company's motto is 'Good sound is good business'. Treasure has also written the best-selling book *Sound Business*, which was published in 2007.

Treasure is a sought-after international speaker and has given a number of TED Talks on various aspects of sound and communication.

Julian Treasure

CAREER PATHWAYS

1 Read the text. Answer the questions.

1 What three main areas does Treasure have a background in?
2 What particular successes in publishing did Treasure have?
3 What led to Treasure's interest in 'the noise of modern life'?
4 What prompted Treasure to start The Sound Agency?
5 How has The Sound Agency helped with (i) crime and (ii) customer behaviour?

TED PLAYLIST

2 Other TED speakers are interested in topics similar to Julian Treasure's TED Talk. Read the descriptions of four TED Talks at the top of page 125. In your opinion, which is the best title for this playlist, a, b or c?

a The importance of sound in our lives
b Designing for all the senses
c Raising awareness of our senses

3 Read the TED playlist again. Find a speaker who …

1 wants to create calmer environments.
2 is primarily interested in enhancing our sensory experiences.
3 is interested in the relationship between senses and feelings.

4 Find words or phrases in the TED playlist that mean the same as the words and phrases (a–e).

a slowly diminishing   b attack   c range   d pay attention to   e practical

5 Which talk would you most like to see? Why? Watch the talk at TED.com.

▶ **Julian Treasure: Shh! Sound health in 8 steps**

Julian Treasure says our increasingly noisy world is gnawing away at our mental health – even costing lives. He lays out an eight-step plan to soften this sonic assault (starting with those cheap earbuds) and restore our relationship with sound.

▶ **Jinsop Lee: Design for all 5 senses**

Good design looks great, yes – but why shouldn't it also feel great, smell great and sound great? Designer Jinsop Lee shares his theory of five-sense design, with a handy graph and a few examples. His hope: to inspire you to notice great multisensory experiences.

▶ **Mira Calix: Sound and sentiment**

What does happiness sound like? What about misery? Mira Calix explores the emotional qualities embedded in music and noise, and shares a sound-based spectrum of human sentiments that emerged from her recent work.

▶ **Julian Treasure: Why architects need to use their ears**

Because of poor acoustics, students in classrooms miss 50 per cent of what their teachers say and patients in hospitals have trouble sleeping because they continually feel stressed. Julian Treasure sounds a call to action for designers to heed the 'invisible architecture' of sound.

AUTHENTIC LISTENING SKILLS
Understanding fast speech

6 🎧 **1 16** You are going to hear a podcast in which a member of the *Keynote* team talks about Mira Calix's TED Talk, *Sound and sentiment*. Tick (✓) the things (1–4) she will talk about. Then listen to the opening sentences and check your answers.

1 the speaker's background ☐
2 whether the talk was enjoyable ☐
3 what she knows about the subject already ☐
4 what the talk is about ☐

7 🎧 **1 16** Listen to the extract again. What other details does she give about 1–4 in Exercise 6?

LISTENING

8 🎧 **1 17** Listen to the full podcast. Which words in italics are not true?

According to the podcaster, Mira Calix has very *fixed* ideas about the effects of *music* on our *emotions*.

9 🎧 **1 17** Listen again. Complete the summary.

Mira Calix worked on a project to transform an old railway ¹_____ into a walkway for ²_____ .

As people walk along, light and music ³_____ are switched on. The music makes people think of a particular ⁴_____. It reminded the speaker of when she was in ⁵_____ , listening to a Fado ⁶_____ and she could really feel the emotion in the music. The message is that the feelings that music provokes are often beyond ⁷_____ .

VOCABULARY IN CONTEXT

10 Read these sentences from the podcast. Tick (✓) the correct meaning of the words in bold.

1 Actually, I **put that badly**. It's not her intention to change their perceptions, but to …
   a expressed that negatively ☐
   b expressed that unkindly ☐
   c expressed that wrong ☐
2 As people pass along the tunnel, they **trigger** light and music installations …
   a are faced with ☐
   b cause to function ☐
   c are surprised by ☐
3 She just tries to **coax** a certain *kind* of emotion out of her audience.
   a gently persuade ☐
   b strongly provoke ☐
   c quickly generate ☐
4 *Fado* is a deeply **melancholic** genre of music.
   a sad ☐
   b serious ☐
   c confusing ☐
5 … it's about a **yearning** for things or people lost or things that have disappeared into the past.
   a longing ☐
   b search ☐
   c sadness ☐

3.2 Judging by appearances

GRAMMAR Stative and dynamic verbs

1 Read the article giving advice about how to create a good first impression. Are the verbs in bold stative (S) or dynamic (D)?

Whether at work or in your social life, first encounters [1] **matter**. You usually [2] **have** just a few seconds to make that all-important first impression, so it's important to get it right from the word go. Much of what you [3] **need** to do to make a good first impression is common sense, but here we [4] **provide** you with a few basic tips.

Be punctual: Whether they [5] **believe** you or not, a person you [6] **are meeting** for the first time [7] **has** no interest in your excuse for being late.

Be well-presented: Your appearance [8] **matters**. You [9] **are meeting** someone who [10] **does not know** you, and how you [11] **look** will have a lasting first impression. So, whatever image you [12] **are wanting** to present, make sure that's precisely what you present.

Be relaxed: If you [13] **are feeling** nervous, this can make the other person feel uncomfortable. If you [14] **are** calm and relaxed, the other person will [15] **feel** the same.

Be yourself: To make a good first impression you [16] **do need** [17] **to fit** in to a certain extent. But do not go out of your comfort zone in trying to give the right impression. Be true to yourself and the other person [18] **will see** that.

Be focussed: The person you [19] **are meeting** will [20] **be expecting** you to be focussed and attentive, so be just that. And he or she [21] **deserves** your undivided attention, so [22] **resist** reaching for your mobile phone.

1 ☐	5 ☐	9 ☐	13 ☐	17 ☐	21 ☐
2 ☐	6 ☐	10 ☐	14 ☐	18 ☐	22 ☐
3 ☐	7 ☐	11 ☐	15 ☐	19 ☐	
4 ☐	8 ☐	12 ☐	16 ☐	20 ☐	

2 Choose the correct words and phrases to complete the texts. More than one answer may sometimes be possible.

1 Do first impressions last? Well, it *depends / is depending* what you *mean / are meaning* by that. I *think / 'm thinking* it's the last impression of a first meeting that's important. It *seems / 's seeming* to me that it's the impression you leave someone with that really *counts / is counting*.

2 You *think / 're thinking* of going to Budapest? Well, my first impression was that it was quite like Prague, if you've ever been there. It sort of *looks / 's looking* quite similar, the old bridge and the view of the castle and church on the hill in front of you with the centre behind you. But after a while you *realize / 're realizing* that it's quite different. I *think / 'm thinking* people *seem / are seeming* to *prefer / be preferring* one or the other, and I *guess / 'm guessing* that might *depend / be depending* on which one you *see / are seeing* first.

3 Their apartment *is / is being* just amazing. Really nicely done, very tasteful and *must've cost / been costing* a fortune. Mind you, I think they *own / are owning* two or three flats that they *rent / 're renting* out so they can't be short of a few quid. Anyway, it's all very modern and minimalist, and you really *get / are getting* that 'wow factor' when you walk in.

3 🎧 **1 18** Complete the dialogues using the correct verb form: simple or continuous. Then listen and check your answers.

1 A: _____ (you / know) those people over there?
   B: No, they _____ (not / look) familiar. But then again, I _____ (not / know) many people here, anyway. As you _____ (know), I _____ (not / work) here long.
   A: No, I _____ (not / recognize) them either. I _____ (not / think) they _____ (work) here. Well, I _____ (not / see) them here before, at least.

2 A: Ah, David, I _____ (mean) to talk to you. I _____ (trust) you _____ (settle) in well in your new role.
   B: Yes, thanks. Everything _____ (seem) to _____ (go) fine. I _____ (really / enjoy) the challenge, actually.
   A: That's good to hear. And how _____ (you / get on) with everyone in the department? _____ (you / work) with any of them before?
   B: No, I haven't, actually. But everyone _____ (seem) really nice, very welcoming.
   A: Well, it _____ (sound) like everything _____ (go) fine. OK, I _____ (leave) you to it. And _____ (not / forget) my door _____ (be) always open if you _____ (need) anything.

3 A: _____ (you / know) who this bag
_____ (belong) to?

B: It _____ (look) like Tamara's.

A: Yes, I _____ (think) you might be right.
I _____ (imagine) she _____ (come
back) for it. I _____ (not / suppose) she
_____ (get) very far without it.

4 Complete these quotations about first impressions using the correct form of the verbs in the boxes. Then circle the stative verbs.

be	have	not/get

1 The strangest part about being famous _____
you _____ to give first impressions anymore.
Everyone already _____ an impression of you
before you meet them.
Kristen Stewart, actor

matter	say	size

2 First impressions _____ . Experts _____
we _____ up new people in somewhere
between 30 seconds and two minutes.
Elliott Abrams, diplomat

not/always/appreciate	come from	not/know	mean

3 We _____ where our first impressions
_____ or precisely what they _____ ,
so we _____ their fragility.
Malcolm Gladwell, journalist and author

LANGUAGE FOCUS Emphatic structures

5 Rewrite the sentences using the words given.

1 What impressed me was their attention to detail. *it*
It was their attention to detail that impressed me.

2 I don't understand how on earth this was allowed to happen. *what*
_____

3 I enjoyed that meal. *did*
_____

4 What worries me is not knowing the dangers. *it*
_____

5 I want to know where he got all his information from. *thing*
_____

6 It wasn't what he said, but the timing of it that surprised me. *what*
_____

6 Complete the responses with words or phrases to make them more emphatic.

1 A: The new marketing manager seems pretty good, don't you think?
B: Yes, his energy and drive struck me.
Yes, what _____ .

2 A: How's work?
B: Work's fine. But I'm not so keen on the commuting.
Work's fine. But it _____ .

3 A: There just seem to be more and more talent shows on TV these days.
B: Yeah. I can't understand why they are so popular.
Yeah. The thing _____ .

4 A: What a great place, hey?
B: Yes, I really like that you can get everywhere on foot.
Yes, what _____ .

5 A: Well, what did you think?
B: What really impressed me was their enthusiasm for the project.
Their _____ .

DICTATION

7 🎧 **1** **19** Listen to some advice about having a job interview. Complete the sentences.

1 _____
to start as you mean to go on. First, your interviewers will start to form an impression as soon as they see you, so
2 _____
you get your appearance right. 3 _____
_____
your body language, eye contact, smile and handshake, so make sure they are all positive. 4 _____
_____
can make all the difference; be as positive as you can and show interest in the interviewers' questions.
5 _____
to show that you want the job because it is a positive career move, not because you're not happy in your current or previous job. 6 _____
sets the tone for the interview and a positive attitude makes an invaluable first impression. Research suggests that
7 _____
determines whether or not they will be considered for the job.

3.3 Lights, music, action

READING

1 Look at the title of the article. What do you think the following colours, used in branding and web design, convey to the viewer or customer?

a red   **b** black   **c** green   **d** blue   **e** orange

2 Read the whole text. How does the article describe the symbolism of each colour in Exercise 1? Did they match your ideas?

3 Read the text again. Choose the best way to complete the statements.

1 The effect each colour has varies from person to person because …

  a colour has both natural and social/cultural associations.

  b when it comes to colour, people's individual tastes are different.

  c symbolism is related to different natural environments.

Colour in branding

Colour psychology is the study of how colours affect moods and behaviour. It is founded on the principle that each colour carries a different meaning for us: either an association with nature, such as the calming effect of the blue in the sky, or an association with social or cultural habits, like the happy yellow of the smiley face. This cultural aspect means that the same colour can have different significance for different people. White, for example, is a symbol of purity and cleanliness in western society, whereas in eastern culture, it more often has associations with unhappiness or mourning.

For marketers and advertisers, whose job is to get us to make the right associations (primarily through visual stimuli), appropriate use of colour has enormous significance, as colours convey emotions far more quickly and powerfully than words ever can. On average, people form an impression of a brand within 90 seconds and the most influential factor (70%) in that is colour.

While an agreed palette of colours and meanings exists – blue for calm and stability (e.g. Barclays Bank), red for passion and excitement (e.g. Ferrari), green for health and nature (e.g. Whole Foods Market), orange for friendliness and fun (e.g. Harley Davidson), and black for elegance and power (e.g. Chanel) – colour symbolism also has to do with context. Each colour has a whole host of cultural, linguistic, historical and political associations. In English-speaking countries, blue is associated with the cold and with sadness ('feeling blue'); in the United States blue is for the Democratic party, but in Britain is for the Conservative party. Colours are also subject to local changes in fashion – an avocado green bathroom suite was a must-have in British homes in the 1970s.

As cultures become closer through globalization and the Internet, companies can no longer be so certain about the associations that colours will provoke. Increasingly, they have to test their colour choices through market research and customer feedback. When Yahoo used its traditional logo purple as a background colour for its new weather app, the reaction (not to the app but the colour) was surprisingly negative – so much so that for a while they reverted to a blue background.

There is a tendency in web branding to opt for safety, using softer colours – blues, greens, greys, subtle shades of white – which convey simplicity and modernity and are unlikely to offend. The problem is that such colours are also unlikely to prompt action. Hubspot conducted an experiment to see if a button asking users to 'Get started now' would be more effective with a green or red background. They expected that the more friendly green and its association with 'go' (rather than red with its associations with warnings and 'stop') would yield higher action rates. In fact the eye-catching red gave 21% better results. Our emotional connection with colour is strong, but not entirely predictable. There is security in following traditional symbolism, but, as with other aspects of business, with colour it pays to experiment – with a little homework, of course.

2 It's very important to marketers and advertisers that people …

   a form a quick judgement about the meaning of a brand.

   b pay more attention to colour in brand design than to a verbal message.

   c interpret the brand's message correctly when they first see it.

3 The symbolism of each colour …

   a depends on many factors.

   b is more or less fixed.

   c is changing all the time.

4 The article implies that an avocado green suite in a bathroom …

   a is no longer fashionable in Britain.

   b was an unattractive colour.

   c was an unpopular choice of colour at the time.

5 Yahoo's new weather app is given as an example of …

   a how unpredictable the effects of a particular colour choice can be.

   b how companies are not prepared to admit they have made a mistake with colour choice.

   c how important it is not to ignore obvious colour associations such as blue with weather.

6 The author believes that experimenting with colour …

   a is a dangerous game for a company.

   b is the only way forward for companies.

   c is good for companies provided they test their ideas.

4 Complete the definitions with words from the text.

1 _____ = feeling or showing sorrow for the loss of a person

2 _____ = things which provoke a physical, mental or emotional reaction

3 _____ = a great number

4 _____ = returned to a previous state or condition

5 _____ = degrees of colour

6 _____ = attracting attention

VOCABULARY Feelings and emotions

5 Match the words (1–9) with their meanings (a–i).

1 off-putting   **a** soothing

2 stirring   **b** energizing

3 tempting   **c** distracting

4 disconcerting   **d** reassuring

5 infuriating   **e** compelling

6 relaxing   **f** rousing

7 stimulating   **g** enticing

8 comforting   **h** unsettling

9 irresistible   **i** maddening

WORD FOCUS *sense*

6 Add the correct word ending from the box to the word being defined.

-ation	-eless	-ibility	-ible	-itive
-itivity	-itize	-or	-ory	-uous

1 sens_____ adj. able to make or based on good judgements based on reason and experience

2 sens_____ adj. 1 aware of and able to understand something or someone's feelings, 2 easily offended or upset

3 sens_____ noun 1 the ability to understand something or someone's feelings, 2 easily offended

4 sens_____ adj. connected with your physical senses, e.g. sight

5 sens_____ noun a device that reacts to a stimulus such as light

6 sens_____ adj. giving pleasure to your senses

7 sens_____ adj. 1 having no meaning or purpose, 2 not using good judgement

8 sens_____ noun the ability to experience and understand deep feelings, especially in art and literature

9 sens_____ verb make someone more aware of something, negative is *de-*

10 sens_____ noun 1 a feeling when something affects your body, 2 a general feeling that is difficult to explain

7 Complete the sentences with the words (1–10) from Exercise 6.

1 The outside light has a _____ which is triggered by movement.

2 It wasn't very _____ to book the hotel without checking out the reviews first, was it?

3 Be careful what you say. He can be very _____ to criticism.

4 The eyes, ears and tongue are examples of an animal's _____ organs.

5 You need to show a bit more _____ towards people at times. What you said was quite hurtful.

6 I had a sort of _____ of falling, like in a dream, even though I was standing perfectly still.

7 The musical _____ of Stravinsky was influenced by jazz.

8 The demonstration was marred by what the police described as unprovoked and _____ violence.

9 Research suggests that, because of the Internet, people are becoming more _____ to seeing acts of violence.

10 I find some of Debussy's music to be very _____ .

3.4 Contrary to popular belief

DESCRIBING BELIEFS AND FACTS

1 🎧 **1 20** Listen to four short talk extracts. Are these statements true (T) or false (F)?

1 A computer monitor screen should ideally be 50–60 cm away from the eyes. ☐
2 We should ideally drink eight glasses of water a day. ☐
3 Einstein was good at maths and science as a child. ☐
4 Sherlock Holmes often used the phrase 'Elementary, my dear Watson'. ☐

2 🎧 **1 20** Complete the extracts. Then listen again and check your answers.

1 In the work place, the c_____ wisdom is that your computer monitor should be about 50–60 cm away. In a_____ fact, the best distance is as far away as possible while you are still able to read what's on the screen. The 50–60 cm recommendation is probably too near and could be damaging to the eyes over time.

2 S_____, we should be drinking eight glasses of water a day. But, in r_____, the amount we need depends on a number of factors ... It s_____ that this figure was thought up basically as part of an awareness-raising campaign ...

3 It has often been said that Albert Einstein failed mathematics at school. But this, however, is not the c_____. On the f_____ of it, Einstein was actually very good at maths as a child. He did, however, ap_____ fail the entrance exam into polytechnic school ... and he al_____ scored highly in the mathematics and science sections.

4 The popular b_____ is that Sherlock Holmes used to use the phrase 'Elementary, my dear Watson' ... The t_____ is, however, that the character never actually said those words ... The words 'my dear Watson' and 'elementary' did both appear a few lines apart in ... *The Crooked Man*, but they never in f_____ appeared together as in the famous misquote.

3 Put the words in the correct order to complete the sentences.

1 _____
think / you / that / would aging is the biggest cause of hearing loss. But _____
fact / actual / in the majority of cases of hearing loss are due to prolonged listening to excessive noise.

2 _____
of / face / the / on / it, the film was a success, but apparently it hardly made any money at all.

3 Ostensibly, the minister resigned.

matter / but / the / of / truth / the is that he was forced out. And _____
lies / the / surface / behind a rather intricate trail of evidence against him.

4 _____
is / belief / popular / the that career success is due primarily to hard work, belief and perseverance.

_____
truth, / however, / is / the that the biggest factor is luck.

_____
that / seems / it being in the right place at the right time can be the difference between success and failure.

5 In terms of financial investment, _____

the / wisdom / is / conventional that wide diversification is best. _____
case / but / not / always / that's / the. In reality, too much diversification can result in a trade-off between diversification and returns.

6 _____
the / of / outward / gives / he / appearance someone who is confident and in control. _____

_____
told / if / be / truth, however, he's not like that at all. In fact, he's rather shy and insecure.

PRONUNCIATION Stress in contrasts

4 🎧 **1 21** Read the sentences. Underline the word in the second sentences you think will be stressed. Then listen and check your answers.

1 In terms of light, mixing red and green makes yellow. But with paint it makes a sort of brown colour.
2 They say you can see the Great Wall of China from the moon. But, in fact, you can't.
3 Contrary to popular belief, Thomas Edison didn't invent the light bulb. He did, however, patent and improve an existing design.
4 Bats are not blind. All bat species have eyes and can see and, in fact, some have excellent vision.
5 Humans have more than the five commonly cited senses of sight, smell, taste, touch and hearing. Among other things, humans can sense balance, acceleration, pain and relative temperature.
6 Chameleons do not change colour to match their background. But they do change colour to communicate and as a response to mood, temperature and light conditions.

WRITING SKILL Describing different perspectives

5 Read the sentences. Correct the mistakes.

1 In term of communication and collaboration, an open-plan workspace may have positive results. However, research suggests that it may have an adverse effect when comes to concentration and productivity.

2 From point of view for office equipment, heating and electricity costs, an open-plan workspace can benefit economically a business.

3 The chairless office has a number of benefits for the employee, notably when coming to reported physical well-being.

4 Financial speaking, family-run businesses tend to have long-term rather than short-term goals.

5 From purely business perspective, the aim is simply to maximize the value of the organization.

6 Statistical, there are more billionaires in London than in any other city in the world, with over 80 claiming the city to be their home.

6 Complete the sentences using a word formed from the adjectives in brackets. Make any other changes necessary.

1 _____ perspective, it is likely that coins were first used as an expression of gratitude. (historic)

2 In _____ , the software delivers excellent performance. (flexible)

3 _____ , laser eye surgery is a relatively simple procedure. (technical)

4 _____ speaking, isn't using a tablet preferable to buying books? (environmental)

5 The film is _____ inaccurate in a number of instances. (factual)

6 _____ perspective, there needs to be a number of modifications to the device. (safe)

7 Complete the text using the words in the box.

commercially	historically	socially	in terms
of engineering	from a social science perspective		
from a business point of view			

¹ _____ , autonomous robots have been largely used for tasks requiring very little interaction with humans. Today, however, robotics is concerned more and more with the development of ² _____ interactive robots. And one of the main driving forces for this is the use of robots in the workplace. ³ _____ , there is an ever-increasing range of applications for robots that interact with humans, especially in the tourism and hospitality sector. In the US, one hotel has introduced a robot bellhop that accompanies guests to their rooms. Robotic tour guides are being developed that not only direct people around cities, but which respond to questions about the places being visited. Robot waiting staff have been used in restaurants for some time and a US hardware store is currently experimenting with a robot that welcomes customers and accompanies them to the correct aisle. ⁴ _____ , this makes sense. The novelty factor seems, at least for now, to be generating income while, in the long run, companies will benefit from reduced staffing overheads. Business and commerce aside, building robots that can interact with humans is benefitting us in a number of other ways. ⁵ _____ , we are learning a lot about ourselves from the process of building and programming socially intelligent robots. And ⁶ _____ , mimicking human movement, speech and expression is driving biomechanics technology forward at an unprecedented rate.

Presentation 2 | MY PIECE OF ADVICE

YOUR IDEA

1 Read three different pieces of advice. Match each piece of advice with a topic (a–c).

1 Pawel: It's not very exciting. Boring as managing your money might seem, there is no doubt that it is very important. But where do you begin? Some people find saving to be a real challenge. They might worry about not having enough cash for day-to-day purchases if they've committed to saving money. Sometimes it is better to set an overall saving goal. To stop yourself worrying about the money you have to set aside every month, it can help to have a target to focus on. The first target might just be to make sure you have a back-up fund in case of emergencies. But after that you can start saving for bigger things – a new computer, a car, maybe even a house? See, saving can be exciting! ☐

2 Simone: I'm sure I'm not the only person who has trouble when packing for a trip. I go away quite often for business and, as you can imagine, I always struggle with the weight limits that airlines have for passenger luggage. So here are my tips for business travellers. Try just taking hand luggage if you can. This might limit what you can take, but you'll be surprised how much you can fit into a carry-on case. Now, I recommend making a list of exactly what you need to take – just the bare essentials that you cannot do without. This makes it much easier to get organized and pack sensibly. Ever since I started making a packing list I've always managed to fit my things into a smaller suitcase. It makes my journeys abroad much more stress-free, and I'm sure it will for you too. ☐

3 Gastón: I used to get called terrible nicknames by my friends. They were only joking, but I knew the reason why – I'd turn up late again and again whenever we met up for a get-together. I knew I had to do something about this, so I took action. Whenever we planned an activity, I would save the date and time in my smartphone calendar. I'd also set reminders a week and a day before the actual event. It might not be for everyone, but if you're having trouble like this then I really recommend taking advantage of technology in this way. Now that my phone keeps track of my appointments, I never have to worry about being late again! ☐

a Timekeeping
b Finances
c Travelling

2 Write notes about a piece of advice you could give.

_____

_____

_____

_____

3 Organize the information from your notes. Write sentences on these areas.

1 The main focus of my advice _____

_____

2 Who this advice is aimed at _____

_____

3 How this advice could help someone do something

_____

_____

4 Practise your presentation out loud. Focus on the structure of your presentation. Try to …

- begin strong – think about how you will really grab the audience's attention and hold it.
- create a need to listen – explain why you're talking about this topic and why it's important to the audience.
- end powerfully – summarize your main message and emphasize your emotional attachment to it.

ORGANIZING YOUR PRESENTATION

5 Match the five steps of the presentation with the examples of useful language (a–e).

1 Introduce yourself and say why you're talking about this topic ☐
2 Set the scene and give your main piece of advice ☐
3 Explain the effects of this advice ☐
4 Summarize the main points from your presentation ☐
5 Thank the audience for listening ☐

a So, to sum up what I've said, you can solve this problem very simply. Just a small change can improve your shopping experience immensely.

b This practical tip should help you avoid hurting your hands when you have to carry a lot of shopping home. You do have to make an investment in buying the plastic ring, but you can use it time and time again.

c Thank you for your attention! We have a bit of time left. If you have any questions, I'll do my best to answer them.

d Hello. My name's Patricia, and I'm here today to offer you a piece of advice.

e Have you ever had trouble carrying your shopping home? All those bags can get pretty heavy. Well, the solution is to buy a special ring-shaped piece of plastic. Just loop all the bag handles onto the piece of plastic and you'll be able to carry them all easily.

YOUR PRESENTATION

6 Read the useful language on the left and make notes for your presentation.

1 Introduce yourself and say why you're talking about this topic What's one piece of advice that you always give? Well, I'm here today to suggest … This talk will …	
2 Give your main piece of advice Have you ever … ? The solution is … You can solve this by …	
3 Explain the effects of this advice This practical tip … You do have to … It should help you …	
4 Summarize the main points from your presentation My conclusion is that … So, to sum up what I've said, … Going over the main points again …	
5 Thank the audience for listening Thank you for … We have … If you have any questions, I'll …	

7 Film yourself giving your presentation or practise in front of a mirror. Give yourself marks out of ten for …

- using relaxed body language. ☐ /10
- including relevant stories about yourself or people you know. ☐ /10
- following the five steps in Exercise 6. ☐ /10
- using correct grammar. ☐ /10

4 Human interaction

4.1 Your body language shapes who you are

TEDTALKS

AMY CUDDY was born in 1972 and grew up in the small town of Robesonia in Pennsylvania, USA. She was a classically trained ballet dancer and, through high school and as an undergraduate at the University of Colorado, she continued to take her dancing seriously. While a student, she also worked as a roller-skating waitress at a local diner.

When she was in her second year of her university studies, Cuddy was involved in a road accident and suffered severe head trauma. She was told it was likely that she would not fully recover and that she might not be able to finish her undergraduate degree. Her IQ fell by about 30 points. Cuddy had to take time off from her studies and had to 'relearn how to learn'. She worked hard and 'studied circles around everyone'. After two years, her IQ had returned and she could dance again. By the time she returned to university, because of her experiences and her understanding of how the brain functions, she had developed a deep interest in social psychology.

Cuddy completed her studies and graduated from the University of Colorado in 1998. She then began a job as a research assistant at the University of Massachusetts. She completed an MA in social psychology and earned her PhD in the same subject from Princeton in 2005. Cuddy then held the position of Assistant Professor of Psychology at Rutgers University and Assistant Professor at the Kellogg School of Management at Northwestern University before joining the Business Administration faculty at Harvard Business School in 2008, where she teaches courses in negotiation and power and influence. Cuddy's main areas of research are the psychology of power, stereotyping and discrimination. She also specializes in nonverbal communication and how body posture can be empowering, known as 'power posing.' She believes this interest in nonverbal communication stems from her time as a ballet dancer.

Amy Cuddy

CAREER PATHWAYS

1 Read the text. Answer the questions.

1 Where does Cuddy's interest in social psychology stem from?
2 From how many universities did Cuddy obtain an academic qualification?
3 Which phrase in paragraph 2 means she studied harder than her fellow students?
4 How do you think Cuddy's current professional interests are related to her road accident experience?
5 How has Cuddy's interest in ballet influenced her career?

TED PLAYLIST

2 Other TED speakers are interested in topics similar to Amy Cuddy's TED Talk. Read the descriptions of four TED Talks at the top of page 135. In your opinion, which is the best title for this playlist, a, b or c?

a Problems of self-image
b Posture and gesture
c Body and mind

3 Read the TED playlist again. Find a speaker who ...

1 wants to help people deal with physical issues.
2 can give us more confidence in our abilities.
3 is interested in the effects of body language.

▶ **Ron Gutman: The hidden power of smiling**

Ron Gutman reviews a raft of studies about smiling, and reveals some surprising results. Did you know your smile can be a predictor of how long you'll live and has a measurable effect on your well-being? Flex a few facial muscles as you learn more about this contagious behaviour.

▶ **Meaghan Ramsey: Why thinking you're ugly is bad for you**

About 10,000 people a month Google the phrase, 'Am I ugly?' Meaghan Ramsey of the Dove Self-Esteem Project has a feeling many of them are young girls. In a deeply unsettling talk, she walks us through the surprising impacts of low body and image confidence, and then shares the key things we can do to disrupt this reality.

▶ **Emily Balcetis: Why some people find exercise harder than others**

Why do some people struggle more than others to keep off the pounds? Social psychologist Emily Balcetis shows research that addresses one of the many factors: vision – the fact that we all view the world differently. In an informative talk, she offers a surprisingly simple solution to overcome these differences.

▶ **Carol Dweck: The power of believing that you can improve**

Carol Dweck researches 'growth mindset' – the idea that we can grow our brain's capacity to learn and to solve problems. In this talk, she describes two ways to think about a problem that's slightly too hard for you to solve. A great introduction to this influential field.

4 Find verbs or phrasal verbs in the TED playlist that mean the same as the words and phrases (a–e).

a avoid   **b** expand   **c** bend
d explain step by step   **e** prevent from continuing

5 Which talk would you most like to see? Why? Watch the talk at TED.com.

AUTHENTIC LISTENING SKILLS
Linking: assimilation and reduction

6 🎧 1 22 You are going to hear a podcast in which a member of the *Keynote* team talks about Emily Balcetis's TED Talk, *Why some people find exercise harder than others*. Listen to this extract from the talk and mark how the sounds in the words in bold are assimilated or reduced.

… the **suggestion being** that we **ought to adopt what** the speaker calls an 'eye on the prize' strategy …

7 🎧 1 23 Listen to the sentence and underline the sounds that are assimilated and reduced.

I have to say, I'm also kind of curious about what other similar strategies could be developed …

LISTENING

8 🎧 1 24 Listen to the full podcast. Are these sentences true (T) or false (F)?

1 According to the podcaster, the purpose of Balcetis's research was to show how exercise could change your perception of the world. ☐

2 Nick is someone who has always liked to exercise and go to the gym. ☐

9 🎧 1 24 Listen again. Answer the questions.

1 According to the podcaster, what did the unmotivated participants in the experiment feel about the finish line?

2 Compared to the unmotivated participants, how did the motivated participants exercise?

3 How could the 'eye on the prize' strategy be transferable?

4 Why did Nick find the research in the talk compelling?

5 How did Nick use the 'eye on the prize' strategy in his own life?

VOCABULARY IN CONTEXT

10 Read the extracts from the podcast. Choose the correct meaning of the words in bold.

1 I watched Emily Balcetis's talk about how perception is ultimately **subjective**.
a unpredictable ☐   **b** imaginary ☐
c personal ☐

2 I am a person who **sets great store by** fitness and a healthy lifestyle.
a values highly ☐   **b** makes a lot of time for ☐
c invests a lot of money in ☐

3 … who lack the **requisite** willpower to see such a programme through.
a strong ☐   **b** personal ☐   **c** necessary ☐

4 I'm also curious about what other similar strategies could be developed and **deployed** …
a made use of ☐   **b** refined ☐
c promoted ☐

5 **Incremental** improvements to my levels of strength have been 'prizes' unto themselves, …
a poor ☐   **b** minor ☐   **c** small increasing ☐

4.2 How we communicate

GRAMMAR Past forms

1 Complete the extracts using the correct past form of the verbs in the boxes.

have	limit	make	measure	weigh

1 The first telephone call from a hand-held mobile phone _____ in 1973. Until then, mobile telephony _____ to phones installed in cars. The phone used for this call, produced by Motorola, _____ approximately 2 kg, _____ 23 × 13 cm and _____ a talk time of 30 minutes.

account	communicate	mark	propose
rise	will/become	work	

2 In the late 1980s, computer scientist Sir Tim Berners-Lee, who _____ for CERN (The European Organization for Nuclear Research) at the time, first _____ what _____ the World Wide Web. This _____ the beginning of the modern Internet as we know it today and it had immediate impact on global communication. In 1993, it _____ for 1% of all telecommunicated information, which _____ to 51% by 2000 and, by 2007, more than 97% of all information passing through telecommunications networks _____ by the Internet.

be	not/be	can/produce	can/also/produce
develop	discover	invent	require
seek	start	use	

3 People _____ a range of paper-like materials such as papyrus and parchment for a long time before paper _____ in ancient China around 2,200 years ago. However, these original materials _____ expensive, in limited supply or _____ extensive preparation, so an alternative _____ . People soon _____ that paper made from wood _____ easily, cheaply and in almost any location. And, after large scale manufacturing techniques _____ , it _____ in much larger quantities. Nevertheless, it _____ for another 1,000 years or so that papermaking and manufacturing _____ in Europe.

2 Choose the correct words or phrases to complete the text.

People [1] *had rhythmically beat / had been rhythmically beating* objects for a long time before then, but it [2] *wasn't / hadn't been* until around 7,000 years ago that an animal skin [3] *was first stretched / was first being stretched* over a hollow object. But the drum [4] *was / would be* for much more than simply creating music. Drums [5] *were / used to be* initially a means of communication, particularly over distance. In fact, the drum is possibly the world's first mass communication device. And historically, one of the main uses of the drum [6] *was / would be* military. Around 3,000 years ago, Chinese soldiers [7] *used / had used* drums to set a marching pace, and different rhythms or patterns [8] *would be giving / would give* orders or announcements. Different tempos [9] *were also to be used / would also be used* to influence the soldiers' mood and morale. In other parts of the world, Aztec armies [10] *were known to have used / had been known to use* drums to send orders and signals to warriors and ancient Sanskrit writings from India describe tribes charging into battle to the beat of the war drum. During the English Civil War, junior officers [11] *were carrying / would carry* drums and [12] *use / were using* them to relay commands over the noise of battle. Different regiments [13] *were having / would have* unique drum patterns that only they [14] *used to recognize / would recognize*. By the end of the 19th century the role of drums in the battlefield [15] *had all but ended / would all but end* and their use [16] *had become / would have become* limited to the parade ground and in marching bands.

3 🎧 **1 25** Complete the dialogues with the past forms of the words in brackets. Then listen and check your answers.

1 A: It was great to see you last night.
B: You too. It was great to catch up. And it's a shame we [1] _____ (have to) leave so soon. I wish we [2] _____ (could / stay) a little longer.

2 A: I really struggled with that last assignment.
B: I didn't realize. You [3] _____ (should / say) something. I [4] _____ (would / be) happy to help.
A: Thanks, anyway, but it's all done now. But if I [5] _____ (know) it would be difficult, I [6] _____ (might / well / choose) a different topic.

3 A: I was late for work again this morning. My phone alarm didn't work, again.
B: You [7] _____ (should / tell) me. I [8] _____ (could / give) you a lift.

4 A: Where is he?
B: Not here, that's for sure. He [9] _____ (might / not / get) the message.
A: But he was here earlier.
B: Well, he [10] _____ (might / not / pay) attention. You know what he's like.

4 Rewrite the sentences using the verbs in italics so the meaning is similar.

1 It's possible that the Internet wasn't working earlier. *might*

_____

2 It was a really bad move to phone him. I regret it now. *should*

_____

3 I couldn't get hold of them. I think I might have the wrong number. *able*

_____

4 My grandparents would often call me for a long chat at weekends. *used*

_____

5 I never used to want to go to bed as a child. *would*

_____

6 Sarah wasn't in the office yesterday so it's impossible that you spoke to her. *can't*

_____

7 Maybe you told me, but I can't remember to be honest. *could*

_____

8 He constantly used to be on his phone, whether it was WhatsApp or Facebook or whatever. *would*

_____

GRAMMAR Inversion with adverbial phrases

5 Complete the news extracts with the words in the box.

Hardly	Never before	No sooner	Not until
Only by	Only when	So	Such

1 _____ unexpected was the announcement that even the minister's own colleagues were taken by surprise.

2 _____ he arrived at the conference centre, did the minister realize the extent of ill-feeling he had generated.

3 _____ was the second edition of the book on sale than the third and fourth were being planned.

4 _____ was the hectic pace of the game, it came as no surprise when Miller quickly netted his second.

5 _____ both sides agree to and hold an unconditional ceasefire, will talks be possible.

6 _____ had the dust begun to settle on the expenses accusations when he was implicated in the cash-for-questions scandal.

7 _____ being united will they have any chance of defeating the government.

8 _____ , at all the meetings that I have attended, have I seen such enormous attendances as I have seen during this campaign.

6 Rewrite the sentences using inversion with adverbial phrases so the meaning is the same.

1 They opened the exam paper and immediately began to panic.
No sooner had they opened the exam paper when they immediately began to panic.

2 The central bank would consider the move only if the economy suddenly got much stronger.

_____

3 You cannot leave the exam room unescorted under any circumstances.

_____

4 He didn't feel nervous until he stood at the podium ready to speak.

_____

5 I was not only leaving a special place, but also my family and friends.

_____

6 He finally left the stage after he had fully soaked up the rapturous applause.

_____

DICTATION

7 🎧 **1 26** Listen to someone talking about the origins of Google. Complete the text.

Google started out in 1995 as a research project by two PhD students at Stanford University, Larry Page and Sergey Brin. Page [1] _____
as his research topic and, among his ideas, was
[2] _____ on the World Wide Web. His supervisor encouraged him to follow this idea, [3] _____ .
Page [4] _____ ,
but he decided to team up with Sergey Brin, whom Page
[5] _____ .

The pair soon developed a prototype search engine, which used the Stanford website and had the domain name google.stanford.edu.
[6] _____ , but the pair saw the commercial potential and the domain google.com was registered on September 15, 1997. By the end of 1998, Google [7] _____ .
The general feeling in the industry was that
[8] _____ , but it was also considered to be more user-friendly, simpler, faster and more technologically innovative.

Negotiate better

READING

1 Look at the definitions of the two words in the title. What do you think the article is going to be about?

Edwardian = relating to a period of British history from 1901 to 1914

Twitter = an online social networking service where users send and read short messages (140 characters maximum)

2 Read the article and match the headings (1–6) with the paragraphs (A–E).

1 Meteoric rise ☐
2 Nothing new ☐
3 Secret messages ☐
4 A passing fashion ☐
5 Snail mail ☐
6 A practical tool ☐

Edwardian **Twitter**

A

Instant messaging is seen very much as a phenomenon of 21st-century communications, but in fact the practice dates back over 100 years to what is known as the 'Golden Age' of the postcard between 1902 and 1914. According to Dr Julia Gillen of Lancaster University in the UK, postcards were 'something like the Twitter of the Edwardian Age'.

B

These days we associate postcards with holidays and view them as a rather slow, even redundant, way of communicating. In fact, it's not uncommon these days for a postcard to arrive after the sender has returned home. But in the early part of last century, the postal service was much more frequent and efficient. In some towns in Edwardian Britain, there were as many as six deliveries a day. This meant people could send a message on a postcard and be confident of receiving a reply the same day.

C

We also think of texting and tweeting as something of a communications revolution, but the postcard craze was similarly rapid and ground-breaking. The first known printed picture postcard was produced in France in 1870, but the postcard as we know it today – with a picture on

the front and a divided space on the back, one half for the message and the other for the address – did not appear in Britain until 1902. Over the next eight years, a staggering six billion cards were sent.

D

The reasons for the postcard's popularity were much the same as those for instant messaging today – it's a quick, cheap and effective way of transmitting a simple message. This can be seen in the type of messages that people sent each other in Edwardian times. 'Please meet me off the train tomorrow at 2pm' or 'George will come and fetch the peelings and bring you a bit of pork, so don't get any meat.' One obvious difference is that they were not private, since the postman, or anyone else who chanced to see the card before the receiver, could read it. But the Edwardians had a neat solution for this too.

E

By putting the stamp in a particular position on the card and at a particular angle, the sender could signify certain meanings. According to the Philatelic Database, a stamp placed in the top centre of the card meant 'Yes', a bottom centre meant 'no'; upside down in the top left-hand corner meant 'I love you'; at a right-angle in line with the surname meant 'I long to see you'; and upright on the right edge of the postcard meant 'Write back immediately'. Such codes were adopted in other countries too, but interestingly, the signification of stamp position was not universal.

F

Following the Great War of 1914–18, there was a shortage of labour and the number of postmen, who had comprised three-quarters of the Civil Service workforce before the war, declined dramatically. This, and the spread of the telephone, saw the end of the use of postcards for 'instant messaging'.

3 Read the article again. Are these sentences true (T), false (F) or unknown (U)?

1 The Edwardian era is known as the Golden Age of the postcard because it was the period when the Post Office made the most profit out of postcards. ☐

2 The writer suggests that the picture postcard is no longer a good way of communicating because modern day postal services are too inefficient. ☐

3 In the Edwardian era communication by postcard could be as quick as communication by text message is today. ☐

4 The author is clearly impressed with how quickly and widely the use of postcards grew in the period between 1902 and 1910. ☐

5 The format that is used in postcards today was established in 1870. ☐

6 The example content of Edwardian messages in the article and the use of a stamp code suggest postcards were the main way of transmitting romantic messages. ☐

7 The writer suggests that international communication using stamp codes may not have worked so well. ☐

8 The main reason for the interruption in the postcard craze was the invention of the telephone. ☐

4 🎧 1 27 Listen to a researcher talking about Edwardian postcards. Tick (✓) the reasons people at the time criticized them.

1 Offensive pictures on the cards ☐
2 Informal writing style ☐
3 Bad spelling and punctuation ☐
4 Lazy form of communication ☐
5 No legal control over what was written ☐
6 Communication was too open / not private ☐

5 🎧 1 27 Listen again. What two parallels does the speaker make with today's communication?

VOCABULARY Body language

6 Complete the extracts with the correct form of the verbs in the box.

clench	drum	fold	raise	roll
scowl	shake	shrug	tap	yawn

1 'Can I just ask a question?' he said, tentatively _____ his hand.

2 'I totally disagree,' she said firmly, _____ her head.

3 Stella stood there with her arms _____ and a disapproving look on her face.

4 He _____ his fists in a mixture of frustration and anger.

5 'OK, so what do we do now?' she asked, _____ her fingers on the desk.

6 'Don't _____ your eyes at me in that manner,' she told him.

7 'Well, I've no idea what to do,' he said, _____ his shoulders.

8 He _____ his feet nervously as he waited for his name to be called.

9 'Go away!' she _____ at him, 'and don't come back.'

10 'You've been _____ all morning. Try to get a good night's sleep before class tomorrow,' she said.

WORDBUILDING Negative prefixes with adjectives

7 Complete the words with a negative prefix (e.g. in-, dis-).

1 _____affected, _____escorted, _____ending, _____intentional

2 _____efficient, _____accessible, _____frequent, _____exact

3 _____legal, _____literate, _____legible (words beginning with l)

4 _____probable, _____balanced, _____mature (words beginning with p, b and m)

5 _____replaceable, _____rational, _____regular (words beginning with r)

6 _____honest, _____approving, _____allowed, _____advantageous

7 _____stop, _____alcoholic, _____verbal, _____violent

8 Rewrite the sentences using adjectives with the correct negative prefix.

1 These figures are not accurate.

2 What you're saying is not logical.

3 It's not advisable to do that.

4 Your explanation is not adequate.

5 He made a few comments that weren't tasteful.

6 They're often not obedient.

7 It's a nice idea, but not practical.

8 That is not proper behaviour.

9 The disease isn't usually curable.

4.4 Is that what you meant?

SAYING THE RIGHT THING

1 🎧 1 28 Listen to seven short dialogues. Match them with the topics (a–g).

- **a** Receiving a thank you gift ☐
- **b** Arranging a meeting ☐
- **c** Offering someone a lift ☐
- **d** Inviting someone for a drink ☐
- **e** Getting someone a coffee ☐
- **f** Offering to help someone ☐
- **g** Asking for time off work ☐

2 🎧 1 28 Complete the extracts from the dialogues in Exercise 1. Listen again and check your answers.

Conversation 1

1 B_____ n_____ . There's a problem with the RBC deal.
2 I'm n_____ a_____ Friday. Thursday s_____ me though.
3 I'd rather we meet i_____ p_____ .
4 Oh, b_____ t_____ w_____ , I said I'd tell Julia when we were meeting.
5 I can g_____ her a r_____ if you like.

Conversation 2

6 Can I g_____ you a h_____ with that?
7 Not a_____ a_____ . Don't m_____ it.

Conversation 3

8 Can I h_____ a q_____ w_____ ?
9 S_____ to h_____ that.

Conversation 4

10 I can g_____ you a l_____ to the station if you like.
11 I don't want to p_____ you o_____ .
12 I can d_____ you o_____ on my w_____ .

Conversation 5

13 Can I g_____ you a_____ ?

Conversation 6

14 Oh, really, you s_____ h_____ .

Conversation 7

15 OK, n_____ m_____ . A_____ t_____ .
16 And s_____ hi f_____ me.

3 Rewrite the responses by replacing the words and phrases in bold with words and phrases from Exercise 2.

1 A: Can I see Tamara Bartosz?
   B: I'm afraid she's **busy** at the moment.

2 A: I'll call you about it later in the week.
   B: I think we should discuss it **face to face**.

3 A: Shall we say 6.30?
   B: Yep, 6.30 **is good for** me.

4 A: Are you going to the shop?
   B: Yes. **Would you like** something?

5 A: You wanted to see me?
   B: Yes, can I **talk to you briefly**?

6 A: This is to say thanks for a lovely evening last night.
   B: Ah, **it really wasn't necessary for you to get me something**.

7 A: I've got so much to do.
   B: Let me **help you** with some of it.

8 A: Do you think I'll get to the station in ten minutes?
   B: I can **take you in my car if you like**.

   A: Are you sure? I really don't want to **cause you any extra effort**.

PRONUNCIATION Appropriate intonation

4 🎧 1 29 Listen to the dialogues. Does the intonation rise (↑), fall (↓) or stay the same (-)?

1 A: Bad news, I'm afraid. I didn't get the job.
   B: Oh, I'm sorry to hear that.

2 A: Hi, Richard.
   B: Ah, Lucas. Can I have a quick word?

3 A: This is for you. To say thank you.
   B: That's very kind of you, but you really shouldn't have.

4 A: Let me give you a lift.
   B: Are you sure? I really don't want to put you out.

5 A: See you tomorrow.
   B: Yeah, bye. Oh, by the way, I'll be a little late in tomorrow.

6 A: Can I give you a hand with anything?
   B: That's good of you to offer, but I'm fine, thanks.

7 A: Thanks again for all your help.
   B: Not at all. Don't mention it.

8 A: That seat's taken, actually.
   B: Oh sorry. I didn't realize.

WRITING SKILL Checking for errors

5 Read the sentences and correct the mistakes.

1 Thank you for taking a time to consider our proposal.

2 Thank you for agreeing meet with us on Friday, but I really don't want to put out you.

3 I think it's important that you and Susan meet in the person as soon as possible.

4 We feel that the proposed relocation is unpractical and could in fact be unadvantageous.

5 He has fully admitted that his conduct was unproper.

6 I am sorry hear that the arrangements was not to your satisfaction.

7 I had quick word with Julian and he has agreed go ahead with the proposal.

8 Only when we have the full facts we can begin to assess the situation.

6 Read the letter. Correct 20 mistakes in the email.

TO: FROM:

SUBJECT:

Dear Alison,

I am writing to request your approval for attend the London Business Conference, which being held from 15–17 January next year. Conference theme is Risk Management and is aimed to industry stakeholders as forum for discuss the current state of risk management in private equity. Of particularly interest to us, is a focus to co-investments versus fund investments. As well as main conference talks, there is a number of workshops.

You may to recall that Samantha Mitchell had attended the conference last year and she found extremely relevant and useful. I believe she was presenting some of the key issues to the senior management team, which I think you might attended. This is something that I am of course prepared to do.

I have included an approximate breakdown of the costs to attend below:

• Conference Registration: £300.00

• Travel, accommodation and meals: £350.00

If you would like to find more about conference, their website is Londonbusiness.org.

Thank you in advance for take a time to consider this and I look very much forward hearing from you.

Best wishes,

Tom

7 Put the sentences in the correct order to complete the email.

a Marta Masini had joined Waterwells Books January last year and since then she is reliable, effective and valuable member in sales team. ☐

b Below is my reference for Ms Marta Masini. ☐

c I believe that Marta is going to be valuable addition to some organization that she may to join. While we regret the decision of Marta for moving on, I would recommend her without to hesitate. ☐

d Yours faithful, Carmen Napoli ☐

e Please be in touch if should you require the further information. ☐

f Dear Sir or Madam, ☐ 1

g She was consistently showing that both she able work independently and as part of team. Her communication skill is excellent and she very well is liked with her colleagues and has always good rapport with customers and other clients. ☐

h Marta is professional and efficient in approach to her work and having sound knowledge and understanding both the book-selling business and wider retail industry. ☐

8 Reread the email in Exercise 7 and correct the mistakes. Then write the complete email.

TO: FROM:

SUBJECT:

Writing 2 | AN ESSAY

IDEAS

You will read an essay responding to the two sources below.

Source 1

> If your job requires you to do a lot of travelling, meeting people from all over the world, you need to make a good impression. To do this, it's important to consider the culture you're trying to do business in. One example would be to greet people in a culturally appropriate way, such as a *namaste* in India.
>
> However, sometimes there is a risk of offending people by inadvertently using greetings incorrectly, for example by not bowing low enough to a senior Japanese businessman.

Source 2

> A lot of cultural differences are not immediately obvious. For instance, research has shown that requirements for personal space vary from culture to culture. This means that for North Americans 1.2m is a necessary range of personal space, but for South Americans it can be much smaller.
>
> It is a shame that these kinds of cultural differences are often not taught to those involved in global business, despite the fact that being aware of other cultures can make business run more smoothly.

Write your essay in **240–280 words** in an appropriate style.

1 In the essay you need to address the four points covered in the sources. List them in the order they appear in the sources.

  a _____

  b _____

  c _____

  d _____

MODEL

2 Read the essay. Match the four sections with a description (a–d) from Exercise 1.

  1 ☐   **2** ☐   **3** ☐   **4** ☐

'Culture' is a term that can be challenging to define. For many, it is the 'high culture' of art or literature, but for those in business, it is the subtle differences in the ways people act that differ from one social group to another.

[1] One example is the handshake: a strong handshake from an English supplier may be considered overly dominant by a Filipino customer. However, unless these differences are explicitly pointed out, it can be incredibly difficult to know what to research when you begin doing business abroad.

[2] In order to reduce the potential difficulties caused by a lack of cultural awareness, it is vital that business people who work with those from other cultural backgrounds are taught about these variations in social interaction. [3] This will reduce the likelihood of committing a faux pas. For example, an executive attending a business dinner in China should know that the dishes in the centre of the table are for everyone to share throughout the meal, and they should not pile food onto their plate before they begin, as you might in many Western countries. Such a mistake made during a negotiation could change people's impressions, and therefore influence prices they are willing to pay, to give just one example.

[4] People will obviously understand you are a foreigner and cannot be expected to be familiar with all of the nuances of their culture. Nevertheless, attempting to increase awareness of the norms of the culture you are doing business in shows a level of respect which reflects well on your company.

I believe that learning more about other cultures can only be a benefit to international business, and will ease the job of negotiators around the world.

3 Correct the following statements.

  1 'Culture' is defined as the art or literature of a group of people.
  2 Filipino people prefer a strong handshake.
  3 In China, you should take all of the food that you want to eat at the start of the meal.
  4 If you make a cultural mistake during negotiations, it doesn't matter.
  5 Many people expect you to understand their culture completely if you're doing business with them.

USEFUL LANGUAGE

4 Find words in the model essay which match the definitions.

1 small and not easily noticed (adjective)
2 too; very (adverb)
3 clearly or directly, so it is easy to understand (adverb)
4 an action or mistake that is embarrassing because it is socially incorrect (phrase)
5 very small differences that are not usually very obvious (noun)
6 behaviours that are usual or expected within a culture (noun)

5 Add prepositions to complete the paragraph.

When historians look ¹_____ on the beginning of the 21ˢᵗ century, they are bound ²_____ mention the role of technology and how it has revolutionized our lives. ³_____ name just one example, virtual reality headsets now allow us to immerse ourselves ⁴_____ completely different surroundings. As this technology gets cheaper, it will become accessible ⁵_____ more and more people, and the desire ⁶_____ films and games that exploit these headsets will increase. Of course, there is also the question ⁷_____ how to deal ⁸_____ the downsides of such technology, like the motion sickness some people experience on wearing a VR headset, but it is only a matter ⁹_____ time before solutions are found to these problems.

6 These words (1–5) could be used in the essay in Exercise 8. Match them with their definitions (a–e).

1 beneficial ☐
2 instant ☐
3 frankly ☐
4 patently ☐
5 creativity ☐

a without doubt
b happening immediately
c being able to think of something new or imaginative
d with a helpful or useful effect which improves a situation
e said in an honest or direct way, but which people might not like

7 Use the words (1–5) from Exercise 6 and those below (a–e) to create collocations.

a unrealistic
b blossoms
c gratification
d true
e change

PLANNING

You will respond to the following two sources.

Source 1

> The advent of the smartphone has led to a world of people constantly looking down to check what's happening on social media or to play mindless games, instead of engaging with the world around them. This is particularly true of young people who have grown up with mobile phones. Whether it's at home with the family or in the middle of a business meeting, attention is constantly divided and nobody seems to focus on one thing at a time any more.

Source 2

> It's now possible for everyone to have the whole world in their pockets. No longer do you have to agonize for days over an elusive piece of information; you can simply pull out your phone and 'ask the Internet'. Communication and trade are easier than ever before, with products from around the world at the tips of your fingers and a huge range of options for communicating with the outside world.

Write your essay in **240–280 words** in an appropriate style.

8 Plan your essay. Identify the four key points from the sources. Write notes to decide how you will respond to them. Don't write full sentences yet.

WRITING

9 Write an essay to respond to the sources in Exercise 8. In your essay you should:
- refer to all four of the key points you have identified
- make your own opinion on the topic clear in the conclusion
- use a neutral or formal style

Write **240–280 words**.

ANALYSIS

10 Check your essay. Answer the questions.
- **Content:** Does the essay respond to all four points in the sources? Is it 240 to 280 words long?
- **Communicative achievement:** Is it written in a neutral or formal style? Is it clear to the reader what your opinion on the topic is?
- **Organization:** Is the essay logically organized? Does it use appropriate linking devices?
- **Language:** Does it use correct grammar and vocabulary? Is a good range of structures used?

5 Economic resources

5.1 The magic washing machine

TEDTALKS

HANS ROSLING was born in Uppsala, Sweden, in 1948. He studied statistics and medicine at Uppsala University, and then public health at St. John's Medical College, Bangalore, India. He became a licensed physician in 1976 and, from 1979 to 1981, he worked as a Medical Officer in Mozambique. In 1981, Rosling encountered an outbreak of a paralytic disease called konzo. He then spent two decades studying outbreaks of this disease in remote rural areas across Africa. His work in this area earned him an honorary PhD from Uppsala University. Among a number of other roles and achievements, Rosling has been health adviser to the WHO, UNICEF and a number of aid agencies and was one of the initiators of Médecins Sans Frontières in Sweden. He has co-authored a textbook on global health and has presented and appeared in a number of television programmes. Rosling is currently professor of global health at the Karolinska Institute in Stockholm.

Having always had a deep interest in the use of statistics, in 2005 Rosling co-founded the Gapminder Foundation together with his son and daughter-in-law. Gapminder developed the Trendalyzer software that converts statistics into moving, interactive graphics. Rosling's lectures using Gapminder graphics gained a global reputation for their creativity and originality and have won numerous awards. In 2007, Google acquired the Trendalyzer software.

Rosling has received a number of awards, including 'Speaker of the Year' from the Swedish Event Academy, one of *TIME Magazine's* '100 most influential people' and, in 2012, he was named 'International Swede of the Year'. He has also received honorary degrees from universities in Sweden, Norway and the UK and is a member of the Swedish Academy of Sciences.

Hans Rosling

CAREER PATHWAYS

1 Read the text. Are these statements true (T) or false (F)?

1 Rosling has qualifications from academic institutions in Sweden, India, Mozambique, Norway and the UK. ☐
2 Rosling discovered a new disease called konzo. ☐
3 Rosling was one of the founders of the global organization Médecins Sans Frontières. ☐
4 Today, Rosling's main field is the presentation and interpretation of statistics. ☐
5 Rosling is known for his presentation techniques. ☐

TED PLAYLIST

2 Other TED speakers are interested in topics similar to Hans Rosling's TED Talk. Read the descriptions of four TED Talks at the top of page 145. In your opinion, which is the best title for this playlist, a, b or c?

a Celebrating innovation
b Affordable, practical technology
c Technology without resources

3 Read the TED playlist again. Find a speaker who ...

1 talks about improvising with old technology to make new technological solutions.
2 advocates a democratic approach to technological innovation.
3 made a technological solution for a domestic problem.
4 questions our assumptions about the universal benefits of technology.

4 Read the TED playlist again. Find five compound adjectives.

▶ **Richard Turere: My invention that made peace with the lions**

In the Maasai community where Richard Turere lives with his family, cattle are all-important. But lion attacks were growing more frequent. In this short, inspiring talk, the young inventor shares the solar-powered solution he designed to safely scare the lions away.

▶ **Jon Gosier: The problem with 'trickle-down techonomics'**

Hooray for technology! It makes everything better for everyone! Right? Well, no. When a new technology, like ebooks or health trackers, is only available to some people, it has unintended consequences for all of us. Jon Gosier explains how 'the real innovation is in finding ways to include everyone'.

▶ **William Kamkwamba: How I built a windmill**

When he was just 14 years old, Malawian inventor William Kamkwamba built his family an electricity-generating windmill from spare parts, working from rough plans he found in a library book.

▶ **Vinay Venkatraman: Technology crafts for the digitally underserved**

Two thirds of the world may not have access to the latest smartphone, but local electronic shops are adept at fixing older tech using low-cost parts. Vinay Venkatraman explains his work in 'technology crafts', for example, how a mobile phone, a lunchbox and a flashlight can become a digital projector for a village school.

5 Which talk would you most like to see? Why? Watch the talk at TED.com.

AUTHENTIC LISTENING SKILLS
Prediction

6 🎧 **1 30** You are going to hear a podcast in which a member of the *Keynote* team talks about Richard Turere's TED Talk, *My invention that made peace with the lions*. Listen to the first part. What did the podcaster notice about the speaker before watching the talk?

LISTENING

7 🎧 **1 31** Listen to the full podcast. Choose the correct words or phrases to make true sentences.

1 According to the podcaster, Richard Turere describes how he arrived at an answer to his problem *purely by chance / by trying out different solutions*.

2 Ruth likes the message of the talk because it's about *not giving up / not being satisfied with less*.

8 🎧 **1 31** Listen again. Choose the correct option to complete the sentences. Sometimes both answers are possible.

1 At a young age Richard Turere was given the task of managing his father's *farm / animals*.

2 Ruth can relate to *being given big responsibilities as a child / being determined in the face of a challenge*.

3 Ruth wonders if Richard is so mature because he wants to *win his family's respect / take care of his family*.

4 She also wonders if he is so resourceful because *resources are limited / his family trained him to be resourceful*.

VOCABULARY IN CONTEXT

9 Read the extracts from the podcast. Choose the correct meaning of the words in bold.

1 He was then faced with a major issue and **set about** trying to work out a way to resolve it.
  a worked tirelessly ☐
  b decided on positively ☐
  c started determinedly ☐

2 What's nice about his talk is how he **takes us through** his process of trial and error.
  a demonstrates to us ☐
  b explains to us ☐
  c doesn't boast to us about ☐

3 .... rather than giving up and **becoming down** about a difficult situation.
  a becoming frustrated ☐
  b becoming depressed ☐
  c feeling overwhelmed ☐

4 Was he motivated by not wanting to **let** his father and the rest of his family **down**?
  a disappoint ☐
  b seem superior to ☐
  c do the same job as ☐

5 Is that a result of always having only limited resources to **fall back on**?
  a rely on ☐
  b spend money on ☐
  c improvise with ☐

5.2 Energy-hungry world

GRAMMAR Passive forms

1 Read the extracts and decide if the verb in bold would be better in the passive voice. If it would, rewrite the extract.

1 In 1954, the Obninsk Nuclear Power Plant in the USSR was the world's first nuclear power plant to produce electricity for a power grid. It **generated** around five megawatts of power.

_____

_____

2 Piezoelectricity is the electrical charge produced in certain materials (such as crystals and ceramics) when someone or something **applies** physical pressure.

_____

_____

3 The United States is the world's second largest energy consumer. It **obtains** the majority of this energy (around 68%) from fossil fuels.

_____

_____

4 The existence of the greenhouse effect was first proposed in 1824. However, we didn't **use** the term 'greenhouse' in this way until the beginning of the 1900s.

_____

_____

2 Rewrite the sentences using the passive. Include the agent if it is needed.

1 Nuclear power currently delivers around 12% of the world's electricity demand.
Around 12% of the world's electricity demand is currently delivered by nuclear power.

2 World energy consumption is the total energy that humans use. Authorities and agencies usually calculate and measure it per year.

_____

_____

3 More than 80 countries are currently using wind power. In 2013, wind generated almost 3% of the world's total electricity.

_____

_____

4 Humans have used solar energy since ancient times and today experts predict that, by the middle of the century, solar power could provide a third of all global energy. This would consequently reduce CO_2 emissions to 'very low levels'.

_____

_____

_____

5 They expect to complete construction of the new nuclear power plant by 2025. The government insists that the plant will generate enough energy to power six million homes.

_____

_____

_____

6 People generally agree that energy independence and security is one of today's key political issues and one which we need to address urgently.

_____

_____

3 Complete the news extracts using the passive infinitive or passive -ing form of the verb.

1 The forum gave a clear message that the current global guidelines on carbon emissions need _____ (reassess).

2 A number of MPs said they were angry _____ (not/inform) of the apparent U-turn before it was announced by the Prime Minister on Monday.

3 The majority of local residents are angry at _____ (not/consult) on the matter.

4 Thousands of doctors gathered outside parliament yesterday to protest against _____ (force) to work at weekends. A new law is _____ (introduce) which means all junior doctors are likely to have to work at least one weekend per month.

5 _____ (find) guilty, Ford will return to court _____ (sentence) on Friday.

6 _____ (beat) for the sixth game in a row was enough for chairman Tony Evans and Conway can expect _____ (sack) when the two meet tomorrow.

4 Complete the text using the passive form of the verbs in the box.

be	develop	embed	generate (×2)
~~introduce~~	place	test	

In 2010, in Toulouse, France, a pilot scheme [1] _was introduced_ to power street lights using energy [2]_____ by the feet of pedestrians passing by. A number of pressure-sensitive modules, [3]_____ with electricity-producing microsensors, [4]_____ under sections of pavement in the city centre. The idea of using human footsteps to generate electricity in this way had been around for a long time, but this was the first time that such a scheme was able [5]_____ on the street. Until then, the modules were unsuitable for street use as, according to the designers, Dutch company SDC, they needed [6]_____ 'virtually jumped on' for enough power to [7]_____ . However, a model [8]_____ on which you could walk normally and still produce enough energy to power nearby lights.

5 Rewrite the sentences in two ways using passive structures.

1 They offered compensation to everyone.
Everyone was offered compensation.
Compensation was offered to everyone.

2 They gave the award to Professor Helen Stephenson for her work on climate change.

_____

_____

3 The prosecution lawyer showed the court CCTV footage of the incident.

_____

_____

4 I guess someone sent me the email by mistake.

_____

_____

5 In total, people gave the charity over a million dollars.

_____

_____

GRAMMAR Nominalization in passive sentences

6 Match the words in the box with *make*, *reach* or *give*.

agreement	an allowance	an announcement
an answer	an assessment	~~an attempt~~
a complaint	a compromise (×2)	a conclusion
consideration (to)	a decision (×2)	information
an order	preference (to)	priority (to)
progress	thought (to)	

1 make   _an attempt_ / _____ / _____ / _____ / _____ / _____ / _____ / _____

2 reach   _____ / _____ / _____ / _____

3 give   _____ / _____ / _____ / _____ / _____ / _____ / _____

7 Rewrite the sentences using nominalization. Use phrases from Exercise 6 with the verb in the correct passive form.

1 It looks like they didn't think about the design very much. It doesn't look like _much thought was given to the design_.

2 They didn't allow for any delays in the development process.
No _____

3 We have duly considered everything in making this decision.
Due _____

4 A number of people complained about the service.
A number of _____

5 I'm pleased to say that we have agreed on most aspects of the deal.
I'm pleased to say that _____

6 It is clear that we need to prioritize renewable energy sources.
It is clear that _____

7 Initial reports suggest that the parties seem to have compromised regarding CO_2 emission quotas.
Initial reports suggest _____

8 We progressed significantly regarding trade in ozone-depleting substances.
Significant _____

DICTATION

8 🎧 **1 32** Listen to an extract from a student presentation about biofuels. Complete the text.

It is thought by many of today's leading scientists that biofuel is one solution to our future energy needs. Biofuel involves chemical energy [1]_____ such as wood, crops, animal and even human waste. The organic matter [2]_____ thermally, chemically or biochemically into energy-containing substances which are able to be stored in either solid, liquid or gas form, depending on [3]_____ . An example of biochemical conversion is the use of bacteria to break down organic matter, which [4]_____ , which in turn can be used as a fuel. Among a number of potential uses as a fuel, hydrogen [5]_____ as a means of powering or propelling vehicles and other modes of transport. A number of hydrogen-powered cars [6]_____ .

5.3 Land for all

READING

1 Look at the title of the article. What do you think is meant by a 'resilient city'?

2 Read the article and choose the statement (a–c) that best describes what a resilient city is.
  a A large city that is completely independent of national government control
  b A city that coordinates with other cities to find solutions to everyday urban issues
  c A city that plans its own responses to long-term and short-term urban problems

3 Read the article again and answer the questions.
  1 What is the size of Chennai in India?
  2 What is the population of Australia?
  3 How is the identity of individual cities changing?
  4 What type of extraordinary negative events do cities face?
  5 What kind of problems do national government initiatives seem less good at tackling?
  6 What is Bristol's traditional approach to life?
  7 What was the focus of Bristol's 'resilient cities' first meetings?
  8 What used to be the focus of such meetings about Bristol's problems?
  9 What specific issue did the meeting in Bristol highlight?
  10 What is the main advantage of the resilient city approach?

Resilient cities

Urbanization is the great trend of the late 20th and early 21st centuries. Half the world's population now live in cities and there are already 35 mega-cities in existence (cities with over 10 million inhabitants), the latest to join the list being Chennai in India. Some of these, like Greater Tokyo with 37 million and Shanghai with 25 million, have populations larger than the whole of Australia. While the economic importance of these urban hubs has been discussed for some time, the question of cities' independence and their power to determine other aspects of policy – education, transport, security and environmental protection – has moved up the agenda more slowly. But the more that globalization diminishes the significance of international borders for trade and migration, the stronger the identity of individual cities and the loyalty shown by inhabitants to them become. Ask a Londoner or New Yorker where they come from and they are far more likely to answer London or New York City than the UK or the USA.

Alongside this growth in the importance of cities has come a movement called '100 Resilient Cities', pioneered by the Rockefeller Foundation. 100RC is dedicated to helping cities become more capable of withstanding 'the physical, social and economic challenges that are a growing part of the 21st century.' This means not only preparing them for one-off 'shocks', such as flooding, earthquakes and epidemics, but also bolstering them against daily stresses such as unemployment, urban poverty, crime, road congestion, inefficient public transport and shortages of food or water. Evidence has shown that inter and intra-city networks set up to tackle the latter type of problem are much more effective at combatting them than national government initiatives.

Bristol in the UK, a city with a history of trying to do things differently, is one of the cities in the 100RC network committed to developing a resilience plan. Early meetings brought together local government representatives from different departments (transport, emergency services, public health, education, social care, etc.) and infrastructure-related businesses (e.g. water companies, road builders) to look more closely at the city's needs and to see how these could be addressed. The delegates were asked to think about worst-case scenarios for their particular area of concern. But, far from creating an atmosphere of doom and gloom, the meetings generated a lot of positivity, because there was a general feeling that they were taking matters into their own hands, rather than just complaining about inadequate national government policies and budgets as they had done previously.

One issue that came to light in Bristol was inequality of life expectancy. Bristol is a wealthy city, but delegates discovered that the poorest in the community were living eight to nine years less than the richest. Righting this injustice of wealth inequality has now become a target for the city's governors as part of their new 'social resilience' plan. This measure illustrates very well the real benefit of resilient city planning: it focusses minds on key issues and then looks at long-term, rather than short-term solutions for them.

4 Complete the definitions of the words from the article.

1 hub (paragraph 1)
the _____ of a region or activity

2 agenda (paragraph 1)
a list of points to be discussed at a _____

3 diminishes (paragraph 1)
makes _____

4 one-off (paragraph 2)
happening only _____

5 bolstering (paragraph 2)
making them _____

6 doom and gloom (paragraph 3)
a general feeling of _____

7 came to light (paragraph 4)
became _____

VOCABULARY Economics

5 Complete the headlines. Use the words in the box.

bankrupt	boom	debts	employees
interest	meet	operations	recession
recovery	unemployment		

1 Chancellor to cut _____ rates

2 Twenty firms a day going _____

3 Japan comes out of _____ , but growth still disappoints

4 One in five unable to make ends _____

5 Weak exports stifling economic _____

6 _____ rising at fastest rate for a generation

7 Most students don't ever pay off _____

8 Gaming industry enjoying _____ thanks to new 4D technology

9 American firm TRF to expand _____ into Europe

10 New government incentives for firms to take on more _____

WORD FOCUS *land*

6 Complete the sentences. Use the words and phrases in the box.

dry land	landlocked	landmark
landslide	live off the land	plot of land
strip of land	wasteland	

1 Bolivia and Paraguay are the only _____ countries in South America. All the others have a coastline.

2 The Eiffel Tower is probably the most famous _____ in Paris.

3 The first person to row the Pacific Ocean solo was Peter Bird of Britain. Bird set off from San Francisco, California, and reached _____ in Australia 294 days later.

4 They've bought a _____ and are going to build a house on it.

5 An isthmus is a narrow _____ that connects two larger landmasses, such as the Isthmus of Panama that joins Central and South America.

6 Many people are giving up their urban lives to return to nature and _____ .

7 The area round Chernobyl has been a _____ ever since the nuclear disaster in 1986.

8 The main natural causes of a _____ are excessive water caused by prolonged rainfall, vibrations caused by earthquakes, wave or river erosion and volcanic eruptions.

7 Match the words (1–3) with their definitions (a–c).

1 landscape
2 landmark
3 landslide

a an event that marks an important stage in something
b getting many more votes than an opponent in an election
c the features or current conditions of something

8 Complete the sentences with *landscape, landmark* or *landslide*.

1 The political _____ of Europe has changed enormously in the last 30 years.

2 After a _____ ruling by the European Court of Justice, hundreds of thousands of people could now demand to be paid for travelling to and from work.

3 The Middle East has a rich and varied cultural _____ .

4 Ronald Reagan's _____ victory, beating Walter Mondale by 525 to 13 in 1984, is the biggest margin ever in a US presidential election.

5 Elvis Presley's first hit single *That's All Right* is a _____ in the history of pop music.

5.4 I can well believe that

EXPRESSING BELIEF AND DISBELIEF

1 🎧 **1 33** Listen to eight extracts from discussions about the environment. For each, does the second person express belief/agree (✓) or express disbelief/disagree (✗)?

1 ☐ 2 ☐ 3 ☐ 4 ☐ 5 ☐ 6 ☐ 7 ☐ 8 ☐

2 🎧 **1 33** Complete the responses to the extracts in Exercise 1. Listen again and check your answers.

1 I can well b_____ that.
2 I'd take that with a p_____ of salt .... I'd be surprised if that was the c_____ .
3 That doesn't s_____ me at all.
4 I very much d_____ that.
5 That's just an o_____ wives' tale. I don't think there's any t_____ in that.
6 I suspect that's t_____ .
7 That's a common m_____ , actually ...
8 Well, that's what they'd have you b_____ , isn't it?
9 Yeah, I think they've got that _____ on.

3 Complete the responses using the words in brackets.

1 A: Apparently there's a 50/50 chance an asteroid's going to hit the Earth in 2020.
   B: _____ (pinch/salt)
2 A: They say that if all the cows in a field are lying down, then it's going to rain.
   B: _____ (wives')
3 A: They reckon that if you turn your TV off at the mains rather than leaving it on standby, then you can save about £20 a year in electricity.
   B: _____ (suspect/true)
4 A: Don't goldfish have a memory of just a few seconds?
   B: _____ (common/misconception)
5 A: They reckon there'll be no petrol or diesel in about five years.
   B: _____ (surprised/case)
6 A: Last year was the hottest year on record.
   B: _____ (well/believe)
   _____ (surprise/at all)
7 A: I heard the melting icecaps are going to cause huge tsunamis in the next few years.
   B: _____ (much/doubt)
   I think _____ (nonsense/honest)
8 A: I saw this ad that says that turning vegetarian before you're 30 can add on average five years onto your life.
   B: _____ (have/believe)
   _____ (some/reservations/that)

PRONUNCIATION Silent letters

4 🎧 **1 34** Underline the silent letter in the word in bold. Then listen and check your answers.

1 Many students take years to pay off their **debts**.
2 Can I have a **receipt**, please?
3 I **doubt** they'll reach an agreement today.
4 He was a **colonel** in the army.
5 Can I have an **aisle** seat, please?
6 We need a more **subtle** approach.
7 Can you pass me the **scissors**?
8 Would you like a **biscuit**?
9 My sister's an **architect**.
10 He was found **guilty** of all charges.

WRITING SKILL Using passive reporting verbs

5 Underline five examples of passive reporting structures in the text. Write them in the table.

It + passive reporting verb + that clause	Subject + passive reporting verb + to
1 _____	3 _____
2 _____	4 _____
	5 _____

Deforestation, the clearing of wooded or forested areas for human gain, is believed to have begun around half a million years ago. It is thought to have started with the simple cutting down of a few trees, but was soon followed by the use of fire to clear larger areas of land. Today, about 30% of the world's land remains covered with woodland or forests, with tropical rainforests accounting for about 7%, but at the current rate of destruction, it is predicted that the rainforests of the world could be completely destroyed in less than 100 years. Forests are cut down for many reasons, but the biggest driver of deforestation is agriculture, with forested areas being cleared to provide land for planting crops or grazing livestock. Logging operations are thought to be the second biggest cause of deforestation, with urban sprawl being another. The most dramatic impact of deforestation is habitat loss. 70% of Earth's land animals and plants live in forests and it is estimated that around 50% of all land-dwelling species live in tropical forests.

6 Rewrite the conversation extracts in two different ways using the two passive reporting structures. Use the verb in bold.

1 Experts **believe** that global carbon emissions are decreasing.
It is believed that global carbon emissions are decreasing.
Global carbon emissions are believed to be decreasing.

2 They **think** that ten thousand people took part in the anti-fracking demonstration.

_____

_____

3 Everyone **expects** the minister to resign within the next 24 hours.

_____

_____

4 The authorities **fear** that thousands have been left homeless after the hurricane.

_____

_____

5 They **say** that a picture is worth a thousand words.

_____

_____

6 Unnamed sources have **alleged** that bribes had been offered.

_____

_____

7 Complete the news extracts with passive reporting structures using the verbs in brackets.

1 Big freeze continues
As the freezing temperatures continue, _____ (recommend) homeowners keep their central heating on during the night. The current cold snap _____ (think/be) the longest period of sub-zero temperatures for over 40 years.

2 Thousands homeless
The damage caused by yesterday's explosion at the Bilsborough power plant _____ (believe/be) much worse than expected. _____ (now/fear) over 30 nearby buildings, including several homes, have been totally or partially destroyed.

3 Tennis in crisis
The tennis world is in crisis after _____ (report) that at least five major tournaments in the last year have been fixed. _____ (claim) a number of as yet unnamed players were paid tens of thousands of dollars to deliberately lose games. The ITF _____ (expect/release) a statement tomorrow.

4 Lion escapes
A lion has escaped from Belmount Zoo. The animal _____ (say/be) highly dangerous and people have been warned to be vigilant. The lion _____ (think/escape) while it was being moved to a temporary enclosure.

8 Expand the notes and write the paragraph from a news article. Use passive reporting structures for the verbs in bold.

estimated / global energy consumption / increase by around 50% by 2050.
thought / half / growth / come from China and India.
Moment / China and India consume about 21% / world energy / but / **expected** / 31% / middle of the century.
Also / **calculated** / China / use around 60% more energy than the US by 2050.
Fossil fuels will still be the dominant energy source and will account for around 70% of world energy use in 2050.
Over the same period / **predicted** / renewable energy / increase globally / about 3% per year.
Despite this / energy-related carbon-dioxide emissions / **expected** / continue / rise / and / 30–40% higher in 2050 than at present.

_____

_____

_____

_____

_____

_____

_____

_____

_____

_____

_____

_____

_____

_____

_____

_____

_____

_____

YOUR IDEA

1 Read about three changes in people's lives. Match them with the summaries (a–c)

1 Pablo: It might seem unbelievable nowadays, but we didn't have a dishwasher at home up until last year. My partner and I had an unwritten rule – we took turns cooking meals, and whoever didn't do the cooking would do the washing up. And it worked quite well and I thought that washing the dishes, pots and pans was actually quite therapeutic. But one morning, my other half came home and said five words: 'I've just bought a dishwasher.' It was only when we had the thing installed that I realized just how much time I spent doing the dishes. We've both got so much spare time now that we've been able to do those things we always wanted to: I learned how to knit, which I've wanted to do ever since I was younger, but just never had the time before. ☐

2 Valérie: I always used to take public transport to get around. I'm a teacher and travelling to work I often thought that getting stuck in traffic jams was such a waste of time – I couldn't understand why anyone would want to put themselves in that position. That's why I was apprehensive when I was given driving lessons as a birthday present. It was difficult to get over, but now I can't imagine not driving. I love my car – I also realized that it meant I could leave my school job and set myself up as a private language teacher. Being able to drive to clients meant that I could set up a teaching company and work for myself. ☐

3 Chao-Xing: Coming from China, it can be strange when you first travel abroad. Coming from a place where you can generally understand what people are talking about wherever you are, to somewhere like Europe, where there are so many different languages, has been a challenge. Not only that, but the traditions are completely distinct from my own. I don't regret it, however. Since I moved to Madrid, I've learned Spanish and have even taken up flamenco classes. It hasn't all been plain sailing – there was some confusion about my name, because it sounds a bit like a word they use in Spanish to say 'bye'! ☐

a The change in my life allowed me to gain new skills, even though there were problems to begin with.

b I have a lot more freedom because of this change in my life – I was even able to start my own business.

c Making this change saves me so much time that I'm able to pursue new hobbies.

2 Write notes about changes you have made in your life, or the things you would like to change. Think of several ideas so you can choose the best one.

3 Choose one thing from your list. Answer these questions about it.

1 What is your change and what area of your life does it relate to?

2 How does/would this change affect your life?

3 What could you or people in your family do as a result of making this change?

4 Practise your presentation out loud. Focus on the structure of your presentation and the journey you take your audience on. You could do this by …

- establishing your idea right at the beginning and then unpacking it step by step.
- creating the need for an answer to a question or problem and then leading the listener to the answer nearer the end of the presentation.
- presenting certain benefits of your idea and revealing further or greater benefits later in the presentation.

ORGANIZING YOUR PRESENTATION

5 Match the five steps of a presentation with examples of useful language (a–e).

1 Greet the audience and introduce yourself ☐

2 Outline your change and what area of your life it relates to ☐

3 Describe how this change has affected or would affect your life ☐

4 Add a final point about your change ☐

5 Thank the audience and finish the presentation ☐

a We bought a bigger car and this has made it much easier for us to travel around.

b A big thank you for listening to me today. Are there any questions?

c Not only has it helped us with this, but my husband is now also able to act as a driver for the fans of the local football team.

d Making this change has meant that we are able to take a lot more of our children's things when we go on holiday.

e Welcome everyone. My name is Alice. In this talk I will tell you about a change I made.

6 Read the useful language on the left and make notes for your presentation.

1 Greet the audience and introduce yourself Hello … Today I would like … In this talk …	
2 Outline your change and what area of your life it relates to The change … which … I/We … and this …	
3 Describe how this change has affected or would affect your life This has meant … Now I/we can … This would mean … Then I/we could … As a result …	
4 Add a final point about your change Not only … What is more …	
5 Thank the audience and finish the presentation Finally, I'd like to thank you all … Are there … ? Do you have … ?	

7 Film yourself giving your presentation or practise in front of a mirror. Give yourself marks out of ten for …

- structuring your talk and taking the audience on a journey. ☐ /10
- following the tips in Exercise 4. ☐ /10
- following the five steps in Exercise 6. ☐ /10
- using correct grammar. ☐ /10

6 Practical design

6.1 Magical houses, made of bamboo

TEDTALKS

ELORA HARDY was born in Bali, Indonesia, and spent her childhood there. Her father is the Canadian-born jewellery designer John Hardy, who had first visited Bali in the mid-1970s and set up his business there in 1975. Hardy thus grew up surrounded by art and creativity, and spent a lot of her time with local village craftsmen, where she learned skills such as carving, painting and batik. When she was 14, Hardy left Bali to finish her schooling and to go to university in the United States. She first attended a boarding school for the arts in California and then studied fine arts at Tufts University near Boston. After completing her degree she then 'talked herself into' a job creating fabric prints for fashion designer Donna Karan in New York and spent five years there from 2005 to 2010.

In 2010, Hardy left the fashion world to return to Bali. Inspired by the design and bamboo construction of the award-winning Green School, a Balinese academy, that her father and step-mother had recently opened, she founded her own company and design brand Ibuku. Ibuku is a team of architects, designers, craftsmen and builders, many of them local Balinesians, that use locally-sourced bamboo and other sustainable natural materials to create homes and other buildings. Ibuku also designs and produces the furniture inside the buildings, much of which is bespoke. Hardy says that a large part of her motivation and inspiration in setting up Ibuku was being able to reconnect with the culture and landscape that she grew up in. At the same time, she says that she wanted to support local Balinese artisans and craftsmen in continuing their traditions alongside more contemporary and international designers and architects.

Following critical acclaim for their initial building projects, which include houses, bridges, auditoriums and even a car park, the Ibuku team have established themselves among the world leaders in bamboo design and construction. In 2013, Hardy was featured as an Architectural Digest Innovator.

Elora Hardy

CAREER PATHWAYS

1 Read the text. Answer the questions.

  1 What aspects of her childhood would you say influenced Hardy's career?
  2 Which phrase in paragraph 1 means she persuaded someone to give her a job?
  3 Which word in the text means 'made to order' or 'made to a specific requested design'?
  4 In what way could it be said that Hardy is following in her father's footsteps?
  5 What key aspects of her work contributed to her being featured as an Architectural Innovator?

TED PLAYLIST

2 Other TED speakers are interested in topics similar to Elora Hardy's TED Talk. Read the descriptions of four TED Talks at the top of page 155. In your opinion, which is the best title for this playlist, a, b or c?
  a The common mistakes of architects
  b Architectural forms from nature
  c Beyond traditional building materials

3 Read the TED playlist again. Find a speaker who …

  1 uses building material sourced from trees and plants.
  2 is designing buildings for city living.
  3 is working in a difficult environment.

▶ **Michael Green: Why we should build wooden skyscrapers**

Building a skyscraper? Forget about steel and concrete, says architect Michael Green, and build it out of … wood. As he details in this intriguing talk, it's not only possible to build secure wooden structures up to 30 storeys tall, it's necessary.

▶ **Magnus Larsson: Turning dunes into architecture**

Architecture student Magnus Larsson details his bold plan to transform the harsh Sahara desert using bacteria and a surprising construction material: the sand itself.

▶ **Mitchell Joachim: Don't build your home, grow it!**

TED Fellow and urban designer Mitchell Joachim presents his vision for sustainable, organic architecture: eco-friendly abodes grown from plants and – wait for it – meat.

▶ **Shigeru Ban: Emergency shelters made from paper**

Architect Shigeru Ban began experimenting with sustainable building materials, such as cardboard tubes, long before sustainability was a buzzword. His remarkable structures are often used as temporary housing in disaster-struck regions, but often the buildings remain a beloved part of the landscape long after they have served their intended purpose.

4 Find the words in the TED playlist that mean the same as a–d.

a unpleasant **b** homes **c** safe **d** amazing

5 Which talk would you most like to see? Why? Watch the talk at TED.com.

AUTHENTIC LISTENING SKILLS
Word boundaries

6 ∩1 35 You are going to hear a podcast in which a member of the *Keynote* team talks about Michael Green's TED Talk, *Why we should build wooden skyscrapers*. Listen to the sentence and mark the words that are merged.

My first reaction to this talk was not at all sceptical. I just thought – what a fantastic idea!

7 ∩1 36 Listen and complete the next sentence with the merged words.

But _____ began _____
_____ deforestation and about how safe a wooden skyscraper _____ during an earthquake.

LISTENING

8 ∩1 37 Listen to the full podcast. Answer the questions.

1 What two concerns did Karen have after seeing the title of the talk?
2 What reasons does Karen give for liking wood as a building material?
3 What two concerns did Karen have at the end of the talk?

9 ∩1 37 Listen again. Are these statements true (T), false (F) or unknown (U)?

1 Karen implies that skyscrapers are not very pleasant buildings to live in. ☐
2 Karen travels a long way to her yoga class because she likes the wooden building. ☐
3 She exchanged her plastic office furniture for some wooden IKEA furniture. ☐
4 She claims not to understand the economics of growing trees for timber. ☐
5 She implies Michael Green has not thought through the noise implications of using wood on a large scale. ☐

VOCABULARY IN CONTEXT

10 Read the extracts from the podcast. Choose the correct meaning of the words in bold.

1 … So I was pleased when the speaker addressed and **alleviated** both these fears in his talk.
   a understood ☐ **b** controlled ☐ **c** eased ☐
2 … what he says about people **hugging** the wooden columns in his buildings.
   a touching ☐ **b** embracing ☐ **c** loving ☐
3 … how much this has improved my work space – mentally and in a **tactile** way.
   Relating to **a** productivity ☐ **b** emotion ☐
   c sense of touch ☐
4 the size needed to mass-produce the timber **panels** he talks about.
   a flat sections ☐ **b** long supports ☐
   c thick covering ☐
5 makes other loud and sudden **unsettling** noises as the wood expands and contracts.
   a disturbing ☐ **b** breaking ☐
   c confusing ☐

6.2 Get someone else to do it

GRAMMAR Causatives

1 Look at the pictures and complete the sentences using the causative and the words in the box.

deliver	fit	redecorate	sand	service

1 They _____ at the moment.

2 They _____ yesterday.

3 They _____ tomorrow.

4 They _____ recently.

5 They _____ last week.

2 Choose the correct words or phrases to complete the sentences.

1 The boxes are quite heavy. I'll get someone *help/to help* us with them.

2 You didn't see me? I think you need to get your eyes *testing/tested*.

3 She's not here at the moment, but I'll get her *call/to call* you back later this afternoon.

4 How on earth did you get them *agree/to agree* to that? I thought they were adamant about it.

5 Did you manage to get the iron *working/work*?

6 We had someone *give/giving* us an estimate for the work last week. £3,000, can you believe?

7 We need to get the extension *finished/to finish* before we go away in June.

8 We had the flat *valuing/valued* the other day. Guess how much?

3 Complete the text using the correct causative form of the words in brackets.

In the UK, one in six of us like to think we are pretty good at DIY and would rather try ¹_____ (get / the job / do) ourselves than ²_____ (get / a professional / do) it. However, by ³_____ (not have / an expert / do) the work, we very often end up doing more harm than good. In fact, around 13% of DIY projects go wrong in some way, sometimes disastrously. National Insurance Association (NIA) spokesperson Ian Smith says 'People think they can easily ⁴_____ (get / the heating / work) again or ⁵_____ (get / that stuck window / unstick), but very often it's not as simple or straightforward as it seems.'

And it can be very costly. It is estimated that DIY disasters cost us £200 million a year in insurance excesses and increased premiums. 'The long bank-holiday weekends are when most DIY-related insurance claims are made. People see it as the perfect opportunity to ⁶_____ (get / those long-overdue jobs / do),' says Smith. 'Another problem is that when something goes wrong or breaks down, people often want to ⁷_____ (have / it / sort) and back up and running as soon as possible and don't have the time to wait for a professional.' According to the NIA, the most common claim is for damage to walls and ceilings, followed by damage to flooring and furnishings. Burst pipes is also high on the list. 'The sensible advice is only have a go if you know what you are doing. If not, ⁸_____ (get / a professional / do) it'.

4 🎧 1 38 Complete the dialogues using the causative form of the words and phrases in the box. Then listen and check your answers.

get/him/see	get/it/catch	get/it/decorate
get/Jack/change	get/one/cut	get/someone/do
have/it/finish		

1 A: We need a spare key. Is there anywhere _____ round here?

B: Yeah, there's a shop on George Road. I think they do it.

2 A: So, you finally managed _____ his mind about the flat.

B: Well, it wasn't easy I can tell you – you know what he's like. But yeah, I finally _____ sense.

3 A: How's the nursery going? Finished it yet?

B: Almost. I should _____ by the end of the week.

4 A: What have you done to your hand?

B: Oh, I _____ in a car door. I was just getting out and someone closed it.

5 A: When are you moving into the new flat? Do you know yet?

B: Well, everything's gone through and it's now ours. But we're hoping _____ before we move in, but we're not sure if we've got the time. We might have _____ it. Do you know any decorators in the area?

LANGUAGE FOCUS Expressions with go and get

5 Find 20 words that make expressions with go or get.

go	get
missing	ill
_____	involved
_____	_____
_____	_____
_____	_____
_____	_____
_____	_____
_____	_____
_____	_____

Z	M	I	S	S	I	N	G	Z	U
X	B	A	N	K	R	U	P	T	P
O	B	B	R	V	A	Y	K	I	S
Q	L	A	W	R	O	N	G	L	E
V	U	D	L	E	I	L	G	L	T
B	L	I	N	D	J	E	V	R	Z
D	J	R	E	A	D	Y	D	E	Y
E	L	O	S	T	A	R	T	E	D
A	P	R	E	G	N	A	N	T	X
F	Z	X	C	R	A	Z	Y	G	F

6 Complete the definitions with expressions from Exercise 5.

1 make a mistake _____
2 lose your eyesight _____
3 become embarrassed _____
4 stop speaking/making a noise _____
5 become not sensible/insane _____
6 become sick _____
7 lose your hair _____
8 don't know where you are _____
9 have no money (for a business) _____
10 prepare yourself _____

7 Complete the sentences with an expression using the correct form of go or get and the words in the box.

anywhere	anywhere	dark	involved
missing	a bit old	rusty	started
a new TV			

1 The office lights are programmed to come on when it starts _____. That's around three or four in the afternoon at this time of year.
2 I'll _____ with the tidying up. Can you have a go at cleaning the mess in the bathroom?
3 Some of my old records _____. You haven't lent them to anybody, have you?
4 We don't seem _____ with this. Let's have a rethink and start again. Maybe try a different approach.
5 Look at this traffic! I don't think we _____ in a hurry.
6 We need to think about _____. This one _____ now. The sound keeps cutting out.
7 Your bike chain's _____. You need to give it a bit of an oiling.
8 I wouldn't _____ if I were you. I'd leave them to sort it out themselves.

DICTATION

8 🎧 **1 39** Listen to someone talking about the term 'DIY'. Complete the sentences.

The term 'do-it-yourself', or DIY, has been in popular use since the mid-1900s. ¹_____ of a home-owner undertaking some form of home improvement, maintenance or repair themselves rather than ²_____. The term DIY has more recently, however, taken on a broader meaning and is today used in a number of ways ³_____, or doing something in their own way, rather than following the more traditional and established route ⁴_____.
Examples of this include the music industry, where bands can now produce their own music and promote it themselves, or pay ⁵_____, the recent increase in writers self-publishing, and, more generally, the myriad of websites enabling us to sell things, rent out properties and generally promote ourselves and our services on our own terms. From this has developed a more mainstream DIY ethic and culture, which refers across a whole range of areas to the idea of being self-sufficient and ⁶_____ without ⁷_____ it.

6.3 Better by design

READING

1 Look at the title of the article. Answer the questions.

   1 What is a manifesto?

   2 Who normally publishes a manifesto?

2 Read the first paragraph describing the life of Dieter Rams. Then answer the questions.

   1 How did his background and training differ from the work he ended up doing? How was it linked?

   2 What, in the descriptions, tells you that Dieter Rams' designs were fairly 'minimalist'?

3 Read the rest of the article. Match the statements (a–h) with eight of the principles (1–10).

   a 'A well-designed object should just blend into the background.' ☐

   b 'But that's not to say it can't be attractive too – in its own way.' ☐

   c 'Good design takes time, because you have to think so carefully about how all aspects of the object function to best effect.' ☐

   d 'Really good designs surprise you because although they're fresh and new, they seem somehow obvious.' ☐

   e 'The best designs just strip things back to their bare basics.' ☐

   f 'Good designs don't just try to make something look more exclusive and up-market.' ☐

   g 'I think Apple designs are great. Even young toddlers, when they pick up an iPad, seem to know immediately how to manipulate it.' ☐

   h 'You know something's a design classic when years later people are still using (or copying) the same design.' ☐

A design manifesto

Dieter Rams is one of the most influential figures in modern industrial design. Born in Wiesbaden, Germany, in 1932, he studied and worked originally as an architect and interior designer. In 1955, he was recruited by the industrial giant and maker of electrical goods, Braun, and remained there for 40 years, becoming their Chief Design Officer. His designs ranged from record players and film projectors for Braun to shelving units and chairs for the furniture maker, Vitsoe. His own design philosophy is summed up in the phrase 'Less, but better' and, accordingly, he is often placed within the functionalist school of architecture and design, whose guiding principle is that 'form should follow function'. In other words, if you pay attention to the function of an object, good design will naturally follow.

Troubled in the 1970s and 80s by the seeming lack of co-ordination or harmony in the world of industrial and architectural design, a situation Rams called 'an impenetrable confusion of forms, colours and noises', he developed his now famous ten principles of good design. These were as follows:

1 Good design is innovative. Innovative design should never be an end in itself, but the best designs are always innovative since they achieve a harmony between form and function that has not been achieved before.

2 Good design makes a product useful. The use of the object should be immediately apparent to the user and no feature should detract from what is useful about it.

3 Good design is aesthetic. Form and function are not exclusive qualities. Beauty arises from an object's simplicity and purity.

4 Good design makes a product understandable. If the user has to struggle to understand the purpose of a particular feature or part of the design, then the designer has failed. Everything should be intuitive.

5 Good design is unobtrusive. Design for practical objects should never be showy since their purpose is not to decorate but to perform a function.

6 Good design is honest. The aim of design is not to distinguish an object as a high-quality, high-tech or high-value item, but simply to reflect an object's function.

7 Good design is long-lasting. It must stand the test of time, not only in the sense of being durable, but also in the sense of being outside the world of transient fashions.

8 Good design is thorough down to the last detail. Each detail has to be refined and each detail must work with the user in mind.

9 Good design is environmentally-friendly. Good design is respectful of the need to conserve resources, both in the object's manufacture and in its eventual disposal or recycling.

10 Good design is as little design as possible. It is the job of the designer to focus on the essential elements and produce something that is both pure and simple.

4 Find adjectives in the text that mean the same as these words (1–8).

1 comprehensible _____
2 incomprehensible _____
3 comprehensive _____
4 passing _____
5 artistic _____
6 instinctive _____
7 inconspicuous _____
8 hard-wearing _____

5 ∩ 1 40 Listen to two people discussing the 'Henry Hoover' vacuum cleaner. Do they think it fits Dieter Rams' criteria? Yes (✓), no (✗) or not clear (?).

1 ☐ 2 ☐ 3 ☐ 4 ☐ 5 ☐
6 ☐ 7 ☐ 8 ☐ 9 ☐ 10 ☐

VOCABULARY Describing objects: collocations

6 Complete the sentences with adverbs using the adjectives in the box.

beautiful	bright	great	high	perfect
prohibitive	reasonable	scientific	shoddy	wide

1 You can tell that they're fakes as they're so _____ built. They look like they're going to fall apart at any minute.
2 The marketing tag of '_____ proven' has become pretty common these days. But what exactly does it mean?
3 Her work is _____ admired, particularly in the US, where her _____ original pieces can fetch upwards of $100,000.
4 Today, concrete is the most _____ used building material in the world.
5 It's usually the male bird which is _____ coloured, while the female of the species is often a more drab brown colour.
6 3-D televisions were _____ expensive when they first came out, but now, like a lot of similar technology, they're pretty _____ priced.
7 The song is _____ crafted and _____ put together, with lyrics and melody combining effortlessly.

WORDBUILDING The suffix -able/-ible

7 Rewrite the sentences using an adjective ending -able/ -ible to replace the words in bold. You may also need to use a negative prefix in some cases.

1 Designer Dieter Rams described the situation as a 'confusion of forms, colours and noises' that couldn't be **penetrated**.
Designer Dieter Rams described the situation as 'an impenetrable confusion of forms, colours and noises'

2 Rams said that good design makes a product easy to **understand**.

_____

3 Ibuku uses natural materials that can be **sustained** to create homes and other buildings.

_____

4 Even though it can be **broken**, carbon fibre is one of the strongest known materials currently used in manufacturing.

_____

5 His art is very hands-on and interactive with a number of exhibits with parts that can be **moved**.

_____

6 You cannot **imagine** the detail and the intricacy of the painting until you get up close and see it with your own eyes.

_____

7 The book is beyond **value** and is impossible to **replace**.

_____

8 You can instantly **recognize** the band as soon as you hear the first few bars of their songs.

_____

8 Match the adjectives (1–8) with their meanings (a–h).

1 malleable   a can be eaten
2 durable   b can burn easily
3 edible   c cannot be read
4 inflammable   d cannot be repaired
5 irreparable   e cannot be explained
6 inexplicable   f likely to last a long time
7 illegible   g can be shaped easily
8 pliable   h can be bent easily

9 Complete the sentences with the adjectives (1–8) from Exercise 8.

1 Gold is a very soft and _____ metal, which is why it has been used in jewellery making for thousands of years.
2 Modern furniture must adhere to strict safety standards and not be made of _____ material.
3 The appeal of some modern art is to me totally _____. I just don't get it at all.
4 My writing can be pretty _____ at the best of times. Even I sometimes can't read what I've written myself.
5 Fibreglass is one of the strongest and most _____ materials in the world.
6 The fire caused _____ damage to a number of the museum exhibits.
7 TVs of the future will be made from a _____ material so that you can roll them up and watch them anywhere.
8 His dishes are like _____ works of art. They're so beautiful, you don't want to eat them.

6.4 Common sense

INTERVIEW QUESTIONS

1 ⌒ 1 41 Listen to four extracts from job interviews. Are these statements true (T), false (F) or unknown (U)?

Extract 1: The candidate generally works well at home. ☐
Extract 2: The candidate likes working in open-plan offices. ☐
Extract 3: The candidate would never criticize a colleague. ☐
Extract 4: The candidate's answer surprised the interviewer. ☐

2 ⌒ 1 41 Complete the extracts from the interviews. Then listen again and check your answers.

1 A: D_____ you f_____
that working at home makes it easier or harder to be self-disciplined?
B: Well, t_____ d_____ ,
I guess.

2 A: In what environment do you work best,
w_____ you s_____ ?
B: Mmm, I s_____ I'd
s_____ , like, a small office or
workspace environment...
A: And w_____ d_____
you s_____ t_____ ?

3 A: In a s_____ w_____
you, for some reason, think ..., what
w_____ you d_____ ?
B: My f_____ i_____
i_____ to say that I'd keep quiet and ...
A: And how w_____ you
g_____ a_____ doing
this?

4 A: And one final question. I_____
t_____ you're on a deserted island and
can take with you just one book, w_____
w_____ it b_____ ?
B : Mm, t_____ 's a t_____
q_____ . L_____
m_____ h_____ a
t_____ .

3 Correct the mistakes in these interview extracts. Each exchange contains two or three errors.

1 A: In situation where you felt you were being undervalued, what do you do?
B: I suppose I talk to someone about it.

2 A: Would you find that you work differently at different times of day?
B: Well, that's depend on what I'm working on.

3 A: Imagining a colleague is not pulling their weight, what do you do?
B: That's trick question. But I guess it depends on how it is affecting things.

4 A: How would you go about appeal to and recruiting recent graduates?
B: Let me have think. I suppose the first thing would be to raise our profile and presence in the universities.

5 A: Would you say are a good motivating influence?
B: First instinct is say yes. But I suppose that's for others to say.
A: And why did you say that?
B: Well, I might think I'm helping with motivation, but that might not be the case.

PRONUNCIATION Word stress

4 ⌒ 1 42 Read the sentences. Underline the syllables in the words in bold that you think will be stressed. Then listen and check your answers.

1 She's got a strong **imagination** and has a lot of very good **ideas**.
2 He's got a lot of **international** experience.
3 She's got **excellent communication** skills.
4 He's **apparently** got a **photographic** memory.
5 He's got a **background** in **economics** and **politics**.
6 What experience and **qualifications specific** to **translation** do you have?
7 We need an **effective** and **creative public** speaker.
8 A lot of what we do **requires** a strong **instinct** and **intuition**.
9 The **salary** will **depend** on **various** factors.
10 I think I'm quite **assertive** and **enthusiastic**.

WRITING SKILL Reported speech

5 Read the online post. Rewrite what you think the speaker actually said for the extracts in bold.

1 _____
_____
_____
_____

2 _____
_____
_____
_____

3 _____
_____
_____

4 _____
_____
_____
_____

5 _____
_____
_____
_____

I'd like to share my recent interview experience. I was applying for a temporary job at a telemarketing company, or so I thought. There were two interviewers and they asked me the usual questions about why I wanted the job, what experience I had and what I could offer them. I think I answered quite well, and ¹**told them I had done it before the previous summer and that I'd managed to get some good sales figures**. Then they ²**asked me how I thought the recent changes to EU data protection law would affect the way the company operates**. I have to say I was a bit unprepared for this and couldn't really understand why they were asking me. Anyway, I said that while I was aware of the changes, I didn't know the details of the new law, and I ³**told them that I would be happy to look into it if they wanted me to**. They ⁴**said that if I was invited for a second interview, then we would probably need to talk about it**. I have to say, it threw me a fair bit and I was a bit confused why there would be a second interview. The job is basically ringing people up and reading from a script. Anyway, towards the end of the interview they ⁵**told me that because I'd just graduated in business and because I'd got experience and had done the job the year before, they thought I might be suitable as their new marketing manager**. It was nice to be considered, but I told them I wasn't interested. I did get the temporary job that I'd originally gone for though.

6 Rewrite the sentences using reported speech.

1 'What do you know about the company?'
She asked _____

2 'What do you think the main challenges will be if you get the job?'
They asked _____

3 'What do you think your colleagues would consider as your best qualities?'
They wanted _____

4 'We'll be in touch if we need any further information.'
He said _____

5 'You should look at other options before you make a decision.'
They advised _____

6 'Why aren't you applying for a more senior position?'
He questioned _____

7 'I think it'll be a week or so before we know anything.'
They told _____

8 'Do you know how many other candidates have been shortlisted?'
I asked _____

7 Rewrite the interview questions and answers using reported speech. Use reporting verbs (e.g. *said*, *told*, *asked*, *wanted to know*).

1 Interviewer: Why do you want to work here?
You: I see it as a positive move in my career to work for a leading company like yours.
They _asked me why I wanted to work there._ I said _that I saw it as a positive move in my career to work for a leading company like theirs._

2 Interviewer: What can you offer us that other candidates can't?
You: I'm very experienced, I've got a lot of insight into the sector and I know the market.
They _____.
I _____

3 Interviewer: Where do you see yourself in five years' time?
You: I hope to be heading up my own marketing team.
_____
_____
_____

4 Interviewer: What do you think is the number one key to successful marketing, of any product?
You: I think the number one thing is to have a clear strategy, which is implemented consistently.
_____
_____
_____

5 Interviewer: What do you see as your strengths?
You: I'm a good organizer and I plan everything in detail. I'm creative, and, as I mentioned, I know the market.
_____
_____

6 Interviewer: Can you think of any improvements to our products?
You: I think your products are second to none. But I do think the marketing and advertising can be freshened up a little.
_____
_____
_____
_____

IDEAS

You will read a review written to answer the question below.

An English-language magazine in your local area has a regular section where people submit reviews of their favourite apps. You decide to send in a review recommending an app you enjoy using. You should briefly describe its main features and why they are useful, as well as anything users should be aware of before they download the app.

Write your review in **280–320 words** in an appropriate style.

1 In the question, underline the three topics which need to be covered in the review. What points could be included in each topic?

MODEL

2 Read the article on the right. Match the functions (a–d) with the paragraphs (1–4). Are any of your ideas included?

- **a** Features of the app which the user likes and why they are useful ☐
- **b** Recommendations from the user ☐
- **c** Why the user wanted to download the app ☐
- **d** A potential problem with the app ☐

3 Correct the following statements.

1. The user is happy with the range of recipes they already know.
2. The user finds it easy to navigate the information available on recipe websites.
3. You have to copy the ingredients you need to your shopping list yourself.
4. It's easy to forget which ingredients you've used when using Recipe Record.
5. It's a simple process to download recipes from any website.
6. The user thinks Recipe Record is more expensive than it should be.

USEFUL LANGUAGE

4 Find phrases in the model text in Exercise 2 which mean the same as 1–6.

1. increase the range of things I cook
2. as far as shopping is concerned
3. look for something without finding it
4. a possible drawback to be aware of
5. My £6 was well-spent.
6. anyone who wants to

---

[1] I'm an avid cook and I'm constantly looking for new recipes to build my repertoire of dishes. As I'm sure is true of most people nowadays, the main way to do this is through the Internet. The problem is that recipes from different sites are all laid out in different ways, and it can be hard to find the information you need quickly.

[2] When my friend heard this complaint, she recommended Recipe Record, an app which allows you to clip recipes from websites and save them in one easy-to-search location. To use it, you simply search for a recipe within the app's browser, then tap to save it for later. When it comes to shopping, it couldn't be easier. You can automatically add ingredients from your chosen recipe to your shopping list with one tap. And no longer will you have to search in vain for your place in the recipe when you're in the kitchen: as you're cooking, cross ingredients off your list to show you've used them and use voice recognition software to listen to the step of the recipe you're on.

[3] A note of caution though: not every site allows Recipe Record to clip from it so easily. In that case, you have to manually tell the app where to find each piece of information in order to save it in the specified format. This can be time-consuming and takes a bit of practice, but it means you should be able to add recipes from any source you like.

[4] All of these functions don't come cheaply, however. Recipe Record is a mid-priced app, meaning you should be sure you're going to use it before taking the plunge. For me, it's completely changed the way I curate my recipe collection and was well worth the £6 I paid for it. I'd recommended it without hesitation to anyone looking to manage their recipes more efficiently – it really does make life easier.

5 Rewrite this review using the answers from Exercise 4.

Anyone who wants to get fit could do worse than download VidFitPlus. You can use it to increase the range of exercises you do quickly and easily. No longer will you have to look for videos showing you the safest way to stretch your quads or a new yoga breathing technique without finding them: they're all in one place within the app. Every minute you spend using VidFitPlus is time well-spent. As far as the price is concerned, it's a bargain at just 99p. It has one possible drawback though: it's addictive. Once you start using it, you won't be able to stop! I'd recommend it to all you fitness fans out there.

6 Complete the phrases so they mean the same as the sentences. Use the prompt words to help you.

1 Why is it so successful?

What _____ _____

secret _____ its _____?

2 You might think something different.

Contrary _____ _____

_____ might think…

3 It's very difficult to do this.

_____ far _____

_____ to do this.

4 The developer mostly manages to…

_____ _____ large, the

developer manages to…

5 The app I'm writing about…

The app _____ question…

6 The app deals with it in an unusual way.

The app _____ _____

_____ approach.

7 Find two replacements for the words 1–7. Use the words in the box.

> baffling   dull   entertaining   exceptional   extremely
> gripping   highly   hilarious   outstanding
> over-complicated   riveting   tedious   undeniably
> unquestionably

1 brilliant _____ _____
2 interesting _____ _____
3 boring _____ _____
4 funny _____ _____
5 confusing _____ _____
6 very _____ _____
7 definitely _____ _____

PLANNING

You will answer the following question.

> Your English teacher has asked you to write a review for a blog for English learners of a TED Talk you have seen. In your review you should briefly describe the topic of the talk and say why you chose it. You should also explain the reasons why watching TED Talks can be useful for English learners.

Write your review in **280–320 words** in an appropriate style.

8 Plan your review. Write notes to answer these questions. Don't write full sentences yet.

1 Which TED Talk will you write about?
2 What is the topic of the talk?
3 Why did you choose it?
4 Why is it useful for English learners to watch TED Talks?

WRITING

9 Write a review to reply to the message in Exercise 8. In your review you should:

- Clearly identify the talk you are writing about.
- Describe the topic of the talk.
- Make it clear why you selected this talk to review.
- Explain why TED Talks are useful for English learners.

Write **280–320** words.

ANALYSIS

10 Check your review. Answer the questions.

Content: Is the talk clearly identified? Is the topic of the talk described? Is it clear why you chose this talk? Does the review include an explanation of why TED talks are useful for English learners? Is the review 280 to 320 words long?

Communicative achievement: Is it written in a neutral style? Is your opinion about the talk clear to the reader?

Organization: Is the review logically organized? Does it use clear paragraphs?

Language: Does it use correct grammar and vocabulary? Is a good range of structures used?

Workbook
answer key

Answer key

UNIT 1

1.1 Do schools kill creativity?

1

1 Theatre / drama and education
2 In the development of creativity, innovation and human resources in education and in business
3 His TED Talk videos have been seen by a record estimated 250 million people in over 150 countries and his 2006 talk became the most viewed in TED's history.
4 Creativity and innovation, business, arts, education, UK/US cultural relations
5 He was knighted for 'services to the arts'

2

c Leaving the textbook at the classroom door

3

1 Musallam **2** Mulgan **3** Pierson, Musallam
4 Robinson, Mulgan

4

a rousing **b** poignant **c** fabled **d** fun
e succinct

6

I've <u>seen</u> this <u>talk</u> quite a <u>few</u> <u>times</u> and I <u>still</u> get really e<u>mot</u>ional <u>wat</u>ching it.

7

I <u>think</u> it has <u>something</u> to do with the <u>kind</u> of <u>overwhelming kindness</u> – <u>love</u> even – that <u>Rita F. Pierson shows</u> her <u>students</u>.

8

1 teacher trainer **2** connections

9

1 vulnerability / background; orator / speaker
2 engage / interest **3** poverty; surroundings / environment **4** every teacher

10

1 a **2** b **3** b **4** b **5** a

1.2 What've you been up to?

1

a 2, 6, 7, 8, 10
b 5, 9
c 1, 3, 4

2

1 made
2 leaped
3 have become
4 have ever created
5 has ever yet come
6 didn't see
7 turned out ('has turned out' is maybe also possible, suggesting that the reflection is grounded in the time of speaking, But the original has 'turned out' suggesting this was realized in the past, possibly shortly after the event)

8 was replaced
9 freed ('has freed' also possible, depending on Jobs' perspective)

3

1 has been **2** 've known **3** involved
4 found **5** 've been talking **6** have been
7 has been **8** 've been told **9** produced
10 had **11** painted **12** worked

4

1 a 's worked **b** 's been working **c** was working **d** worked
2 a 've been finalizing **b** finalized **c** Have they finalized **d** were finalizing
3 a were waiting **b** waited and waited **c** 've only been waiting **d** 've waited (or 've been waiting)
4 a was going **b** went **c** 've been going **d** 've been

5

1 small/tiny **2** vast **3** almost **4** significant
5 tiny/small **6** sizeable **7** Relatively
8 good

6

1 Globally, about one **in** eight males have some form of colour blindness, whereas only about one **in** 200 women is colour blind.
2 About one in **every** 16 Americans plays a musical instrument.
3 In **most** countries, over 99 **per cent** of all students graduating in medicine find jobs or enter further study within six months of graduating.
4 Geography is the worst degree for gaining employment in a number **of** countries, with only around three out **of** every ten graduates in subject-related employment six months after graduating.
5 Research suggests that only one **in** four employees believe they are allowed to fulfil their creative potential at work.
6 According to a study, about four **out** of every ten people consider themselves to be in some way artistic.

7

1 has won a number of awards
2 named him as one of the 100 most influential people
3 he became a Senator for Life
4 has collaborated with a number of other notable architects
5 designed the iconic
6 has been described as having
7 has been chairman of the
8 has also been working
9 was set up as a non-profit organization
10 most notable projects have been completed

1.3 How talent thrives

1

c

2

b

3

1 a 4 **b** 1 **c** 2 **d** 3
2 c (Based on each individual's letters, diaries and interviews and drawing on some secondary sources)
3 a Anthony Trollope **b** Gertrude Stein **c** Igor Stravinsky
4 a
5 b

4

a breaking down **b** drawing on **c** exacting
d procrastination **e** mundane **f** increment

5

2 had, inspiration
3 came, idea
4 came, angle
5 take, hobby
6 devoted, work
7 broke, convention
8 build, experience, follow, path

6

1 creation **2** creative **3** creator **4** Creativity
5 creatively **6** creation **7** recreating
8 Creationism, creationists

7

1 demonstrate **2** thinking **3** streak
4 force **5** impression **6** highly
7 stifling **8** foster

1.4 It's not really my thing

1

1 ✗ **2** ✓ **3** ✗ **4** ✓ **5** ✗ **6** ✓ **7** ✓
8 ✗ **9** ✓

2

1 into, not, thing
2 do, not, keen
3 into
4 a, fan, not, into, take, leave
5 a, fan
6 can't, excited, appeal

3

1 playing the piano ✓   singing ✗
2 teaching ✓   administrative tasks ✗
3 making tea ✗   cooking ✓
4 shopping ✓   saving money ✗

4

1 that's one thing I'm quite good at
2 I'm not great at singing
3 I think I'm quite a natural at teaching
4 I'm most definitely not a natural when it comes to
5 I can't make a cup of tea to save my life
6 I do have a talent for cooking
7 I'm pretty hopeless at saving it
8 I'm a born spendaholic

5

1 I'm not a fan of rock music.
2 Football's OK, but I can take it or leave it.
3 I can't get excited about modern art. It just doesn't appeal to me.

4 Anna's a natural when it comes to learning languages.
5 I can't cook to save my life.
6 He's a born leader.

6

1 I *do like* watching a good *film*.
2 I *really want* to learn the *piano* one day.
3 The lecture was *quite* good, but I thought it was a bit *slow* in places.
4 Modern art's *really* not my thing, I'm afraid.
5 I quite *like* modern art, actually. Especially *earlier* modern art.
6 Sam *does* tell a good story.
7 I *did* enjoy that *film* last night.
8 I know it's quite *expensive*, but I *really do* think it's worth it.

7

1 intention is
2 decision has been made
3 Clear and open communication
4 has been a significant increase in, the implementation of
5 was/has been a poor response, there were/ have been a number of complaints
6 further consultation, the distribution of

8

2 Insufficient sleep
3 There has been a number of changes to/in
4 Advances in technology are alarming.
5 the marketing department's proposal, an unnecessary complication.
6 your suggestion, on my return

9

the development of the two sites was not based on any kind of comprehensive e-commerce strategy. There was not enough thought put into the design and (the) functionality. In addition, there was no proper implementation of credit card transaction processing and order fulfilment was inefficient. Looking forward, we have been in consultation with a specialist e-commerce firm and we are currently in discussion with the board about the availability of additional financial and human resources.

PRESENTATION 1

1

a Tammy **b** Claudia **c** Joel **d** Joel, Claudia **e** Tammy **f** Claudia

5

1 b **2** d **3** c **4** a **5** e

6 (example answers)

1 Hello everyone. Welcome to my presentation. The purpose of this presentation is to talk about a talent I'd like to have.
2 I've always admired people who have an eye for a good photo. I'd really love to get better at using cameras and taking photos. I've been able to practise a little bit, though

I think the best thing would be attending classes.
3 I would need my family to help me with this. I'd need them to understand my goal to develop my photography. They could help me by helping me around the house so I have free time to go to evening classes.
4 I'd be able to take photos for my friends and family. Maybe one day I'd be able to sell my snaps or have them displayed in a picture gallery.
5 That brings us to the end of my talk. Thank you very much for listening to me. If you have any questions, please feel free to ask them.

UNIT 2

2.1 Why I live in mortal dread of public speaking

1

1 F – (Early in her career, she played jazz piano with a number of acts and before going solo, founded a band called Washington.)
2 F – (the lyrics to her songs have been described as having a beautiful and confessional tone.)
3 F – (Washington has won a number of awards, including Australia's 'Best Female Artist' and 'Breakthrough Artist' following the release of her debut platinum-selling album in 2010. ... Since her breakthrough solo album, which reached number three in the Australian charts, she has attracted the attention of a wider audience by appearing on a number of Australian TV music shows.)
4 T
5 T

2

c

3

1 Sting and Tillemann-Dick **2** The Lady Lifers and Sting **3** Tillemann-Dick **4** Gupta

4

a conventional **b** moving **c** nasty
d unwavering

6

eyes, stones, load, shoes, do

7

1 the homeless, the marginalized, people in difficult circumstances **2** the combination of the talk and music adds something more to the experience of listening to Gupta

8

1 medicine; violin **2** hope **3** teaching
4 musician; power

9

1 a **2** c **3** b **4** b **5** b

2.2 Optimist or pessimist?

1

1 P **2** G **3** F **4** F **5** P **6** P **7** F **8** G/P

2

1 will continue **2** will have reached
3 is likely to be **4** will still be growing
5 is going to peak **6** are holding
7 is slowed **8** is going to cause
9 don't take **10** will very likely be facing

3

1 is likely to have, will not/won't be able, may have doubled/may double.
2 continues, will live
3 is/are meeting, will focus/will be focussing
4 will soon be able, will only be, proves, may eventually follow
5 will have started / will start, will be travelling

4

1 to do
2 'll call back
3 's having
4 's
5 starts
6 're going to make
7 'll be having, 'll have finished
8 Are, going to say, 'm going to tell

5

1 In all likelihood, the population will reach eleven million by the year 2100.
2 We're bound to find a cure for cancer sooner or later.
3 A third world war may very well happen one day.
4 It's a foregone conclusion that we'll one day colonize Mars/colonize Mars one day.
5 The US is likely to remain the world's biggest economy for a long time.
6 It's by no means certain that there is life on another planet.

6

1 She's bound to know what to do.
2 It's by no means certain (that) they'll agree.
3 It may well have been/be my fault.
4 It's highly unlikely to be here/(that) it'll be here.
5 In all likelihood/There's a strong likelihood we'll never hear from them again.

7

1 highly/quite/pretty/very
2 It's, guess
3 may/might/could, out
4 foregone
5 by, certain

8

1 the current birth rate persists
2 will decline significantly
3 may have shrunk by as much as
4 does start to look likely
5 will have one of the worst
6 will have reached retirement
7 will no longer be working and contributing
8 will be increasing

2.3 Expanding your horizons

1

a 2, 3, 4   **b** 5   **c** 1

2

2 serious back pain
3 dyslexia, having to leave school early to work, motor neurone disease
4 financial problems
5 chronic poverty, social discrimination

3

1 natural   2 isn't   3 generally have
4 makes us better able   5 generally learn from   6 relieve the tension   7 minority
8 are overwhelmed

4

1 difficult   2 bigger   3 resist   4 high
5 weight   6 expressed   7 long   8 duty

5

2 and 3

6

1 trying to make ends meet from being a songwriter
2 depression after her mother's death (and being a single mother)
3 in local cafés
4 stick at what you love doing and believe in

7

1 pin   2 dashed   3 giving   4 cold
5 plucked   6 nerves   7 leap   8 limit

8

1 takes   2 favours   3 brave   4 up
5 convictions   6 brave   7 hands   8 have

9

1 braved the elements
2 has / will have the courage of his convictions
3 put up a brave fight
4 It takes guts
5 putting a brave face on it
6 have the guts

2.4 Worst-case scenario

1

1 T   2 F   3 T   4 F   5 T

2

1 aware   2 advise against   3 event of
4 best thing   5 way, 'll   6 advisable to
7 Avoid, chances   8 ensure

3

1 take (my) time to think, Talking to someone is also a good idea.
2 to consider looking for
3 opt for location over facilities
4 For your own peace of mind
5 the best thing is to say, That way you won't

6 'd advise against doing, avoid being, The chances are (that)

4

1 sixth   2 through   3 spring   4 asked
5 clothes   6 length   7 months   8 depth
9 twelfth   10 breathes   11 hundredth
12 filmed   13 health   14 crisps   15 helpful
16 splendid   17 explained   18 instincts
19 facts   20 rejects

5

1 were just going to stay
2 wasn't going to say
3 were originally going to get
4 was going to tell
5 were originally going to hold

6

1 She looked as though she was going to say something
2 The two leaders were going to meet tomorrow
3 Jones was originally going to be discharged yesterday
4 It wasn't supposed to rain
5 Play was due to resume at three
6 It was meant to be a working lunch
7 I was sure he would be waiting for us
8 We were supposed to meet at nine o'clock

7

1 We were going to leave at about six, but we were still there at seven.
2 They were supposed to arrive on Tuesday.
3 I expected (that) they would leave early, but they stayed until the early hours.
4 We weren't going to take a taxi, but it was raining.
5 The flight was due to take off at 5.30, but it was delayed again until seven o'clock.
6 We didn't anticipate/hadn't anticipated (that) it would take so long.

8

1 was supposed to meet
2 were going to have to make
3 would take
4 was going to improve
5 wouldn't recognize
6 were originally going to stay
7 were due to move

WRITING 1

1

a description of their work-life balance, the importance of maintaining an appropriate work-life balance, what companies can do to help their employees achieve this
Points to include: student's own ideas

2

Paragraph 1/4 – description of work-life balance; Paragraph 2 – importance of maintaining an appropriate work-life balance; Paragraph 3 – what companies can do to help their employees

3

a 3   **b** 1   **c** 4   **d** 2

4

1 a, b, f   2 c, g, i   3 d, e, h

5

1

Example – **(a)** I came to realize that if I didn't . . .
(b) It suddenly occurred to me that if I didn't . . .
(f) It dawned on me that if I didn't . . .

2

(c) The essence of changing employees' mindsets lies in the way companies encourage them to use their time at work.
(g) A key ingredient of changing employees' mindsets is the way companies encourage them to use their time at work.
(i) The way companies encourage employees to use their time at work is vital to change their mindsets.

3

(d) A possible route to achieve this would be to follow the example of…
(e) One way to approach this is to follow the example of…
(h) A possible course of action for this is to follow the example of…

6

Exhausted, depressed and coming down with a cold

Their stress levels are lower, they take fewer sick days and they are able to complete tasks more efficiently.

I'm happier, healthier and have more of a social life than ever before.

7

by organizing a night out, a weekend away or simply lunch at a local restaurant

by allowing flexi-time, encouraging job shares or letting staff leave early on Fridays

having been awake since six, at my desk since eight, and not likely to get home until seven

they are more productive, more creative and their imaginations are given free rein

living, sleeping and breathing their jobs

10 Sample answer

Seeing the world through new eyes

My fascination with photography began when I opened a beautifully wrapped eighteenth birthday present. At a time when most people, including me, still relied on film cameras, the sight of a brand new digital camera was a real treat. I couldn't wait to try it out.

As time passed, I sought out advice from more experienced photographers through reading magazines and blogs. One of the most useful tips I found was to slow down. By spending a little more time framing each shot, considering the light conditions and positioning the camera exactly, my photos became much more striking. I dedicated time to looking for places to take the perfect photo and I developed a greater appreciation for the small details of life, like dew shining on a spider's web or tiny architectural flourishes on huge buildings.

Encouraging you to take time and notice detail are just two of the manifold benefits that digital cameras have. Unlike with film cameras, there are no limits to the number of photos you can take. That, plus the fact that you don't have to pay for photos to be developed before you can see the results of your efforts, means that it is possible for everyone to experiment with photography in a way that was never possible before the advent of this technology.

Of course, nowadays everyone has a camera on their phone and there is a constant stream of photos being uploaded to social media. Some people say that this obsession with photography, and the 'selfie' culture that has developed, have removed people's appreciation of a carefully crafted image. While it remains to be seen whether the ease of taking photos nowadays really has made our society more narcissistic, I can't deny that box I opened, all those years ago, changed the way I looked at the world in a profoundly positive way.

UNIT 3

3.1 The 4 ways sound affects us

1

1 Economics, advertising and publishing
2 TPD Publishing, which Treasure started, was very successful (went on to become one of the UK's leading contract magazine publishing companies). He held a number of senior posts in the publishing industry (in various publishing associations and agencies) and in 2002 he received a (Professional Publishers Association) Award for services to the UK magazine publishing industry.
3 His passion for sound and his interest in music led to his interest in 'the noise of modern life'. (As a drummer and musician ... he had for a long time been interested in the noise of modern life, and in particular that produced by the business world and other organizations.)
4 He realized that businesses could improve their performance by becoming more sound-conscious. (As he researched this, he realized that most business sound was having a negative effect on people and he realized there was an opportunity for businesses to improve their results by becoming more sound-conscious.)
5 It has advised on (i) the use of ambient sound to reduce crime in urban areas and (ii) in-store soundscapes that increase both sales and customer satisfaction.

2

c

3

1 Treasure   2 Lee   3 Calix (and Treasure and Lee)

4

a gnawing away at   b assault   c spectrum
d heed   e handy

6

4, 2 (4 again)

7

1 – she says that Calix is a composer
2 fascinating   3 & 4 how she uses music to add to people's perceptions

8

fixed She is open about the fact we don't really understand the relationship between music and emotions; she doesn't try to be too scientific or to analyze it too deeply.

9

1 tunnel   2 commuters and leisure
3 installations   4 emotion   5 Lisbon
6 singer   7 (scientific) explanation / words

10

1 c   2 b   3 a   4 a   5 a

3.2 Judging by appearances

1

1 S   2 S   3 S   4 D   5 S   6 D   7 S   8 S
9 D   10 S   11 S   12 S (used in the continuous to give a more dynamic sense)
13 S (used in the continuous to give a more dynamic sense)   14 S   15 S   16 S   17 D
18 S   19 D   20 S (used in the continuous to give a more dynamic sense)   21 S   22 D

2

1 depends, mean, think, seems, counts
2 're thinking, looks, realize, think, seem, prefer, guess/'m guessing, depend, see
3 is, must've cost, own, rent/'re renting, get

3

1 Do you know, don't look, don't know, know, haven't been working, don't recognize, don't think, work, haven't seen
2 've been meaning, trust, are settling, seems, be going, 'm really enjoying, are you getting on, Have you worked, seems, sounds (also possible is sounding), is going, 'll leave, don't forget, 's, need
3 Do you know, belongs, looks, think, imagine, 'll come back (also possible: be coming back), don't suppose, 'll get

4

1 is, don't get, has
2 matter, say, size
3 don't know, come from, mean, don't always appreciate

5

2 What I don't understand is how on earth this was allowed to happen. / How on earth this was allowed to happen is what I don't understand.

3 I did enjoy that meal.
4 It's not knowing the dangers that worries me.
5 The thing I want to know is where he got all his information from.
6 What surprised me wasn't what he said, but the timing of it.

6

1 struck me is his energy and drive.
2 's the commuting (that) I'm not so keen on.
3 I can't understand is why they are so popular.
4 I really like is that you can get everywhere on foot.
5 enthusiasm for the project is what really impressed me.

7

1 The most important thing in an interview is
2 it's important that
3 The thing that your interviewers will notice next is
4 It's then the next few minutes, the beginning of the actual interview, that
5 And what is particularly vital is
6 This initial impact is what
7 it's often a candidate's performance in the first two minutes of an interview that

3.3 Lights, music, action

2

a passion and excitement; also warnings and 'Stop'
b elegance and power
c health and nature; also friendly and 'Go'; also simplicity and modernity
d calm and stability; also simplicity and modernity
e friendliness and fun

3

1 a   2 c   3 a   4 a   5 a   6 c

4

1 mourning   2 stimuli   3 a (whole) host
4 reverted   5 shades   6 eye-catching

5

1 c   2 f   3 g   4 h   5 i   6 a   7 b   8 d   9 e

6

1 sensible   2 sensitive   3 sensitivity
4 sensory   5 sensor   6 sensuous   7 senseless
8 sensibility   9 sensitize   10 sensation

7

1 sensor   2 sensible   3 sensitive
4 sensory   5 sensitivity   6 sensation
7 sensibility   8 senseless   9 desensitized
10 sensuous

3.4 Contrary to popular belief

1

1 F   2 F   3 T   4 F

2

1 conventional, actual

2 Supposedly, reality, seems
3 case, face, apparently, allegedly
4 belief, truth, fact

3

1 You would think that, in actual fact
2 On the face of it.
3 But the truth of the matter, behind the surface lies
4 The popular belief is, The truth, however, is, It seems that
5 the conventional wisdom is, But that's not always the case
6 He gives the outward appearance of, If truth be told

4

1 In terms of light, mixing red and green makes yellow. But with <u>paint</u> it makes a sort of <u>brown</u> colour.
2 They say you can see the Great Wall of China from the moon. But, in <u>fact</u>, you <u>can't</u>.
3 Contrary to popular belief, Thomas Edison didn't invent the light bulb. He <u>did</u>, however, <u>patent</u> and <u>improve</u> an <u>existing</u> <u>design</u>.
4 Bats are not blind. All bat species have <u>eyes</u> and <u>can</u> <u>see</u> and, in fact, some have <u>excellent</u> <u>vision</u>.
5 Humans have more than the five commonly cited senses of sight, smell, taste, touch and hearing. Among <u>other</u> <u>things</u>, humans can sense <u>balance</u>, <u>acceleration</u>, <u>pain</u> and <u>relative</u> <u>temperature</u>.
6 Chameleons do not change colour to match their background. But they <u>do</u> change colour to <u>communicate</u> and as a response to <u>mood</u>, <u>temperature</u> and <u>light</u> <u>conditions</u>.

5

1 In term**s** of communication and collaboration, an open-plan workspace may have positive results. However, research suggests that it may have an adverse effect when **it** comes to concentration and productivity.
2 From **the** point of view **of** office equipment, heating and electricity costs, an open-plan workspace can benefit **a business** economically.
3 The chairless office has a number of benefits for the employee, notably when **it comes** to reported physical well-being.
4 **Financially** speaking, family-run businesses tend to have long-term rather than short-term goals.
5 From **a** purely business perspective, the aim is simply to maximize the value of the organization.
6 **Statistically**, there are more billionaires in London than in any other city in the world, with over 80 claiming the city to be their home.

6

From a(n) historical perspective
In terms of flexibility
Technically (speaking)
Environmentally speaking

5 factually (speaking)
6 From a safety perspective

7

1 Historically   **2** socially   **3** Commercially
4 From a business point of view   **5** From a social science perspective   **6** in terms of engineering

PRESENTATION 2

1

1 b   **2** c   **3** a

3 (example answers)

1 This piece of advice will help you become a better cook. It's a tip to help you manage in the kitchen.
2 This advice will be most helpful for people cooking for a medium-sized family.
3 This will help save you time in the kitchen, so you can focus on cooking the best food you can.

5

1 d   **2** e   **3** b   **4** a   **5** c

6 (example answers)

1 Hello. My name's (name) and today I'm going to give you a useful piece of advice for when you are studying.
2 Have you ever been overwhelmed by the amount you have to read for an academic assignment? Well don't give up – the solution is actually very simple. You have to be selective in what you read.
3 You do have to really read your assignment carefully. You'll need to work out exactly what the focus is, so that you can decide what you really need to read from the book list. It should help you to read in more detail and save you time because you're not reading material that is not relevant.
4 Going over the main points again, be very selective in what you read and base this on what the assignment is asking you to do. Use this knowledge to plan your reading better.
5 Thank you for listening. If you have any questions, I'll do my best to answer them.

UNIT 4

4.1 Your body language shapes who you are

1

1 From her experiences after her accident, in particular her knowledge of how the brain functions.
2 two (graduated from the University of Colorado in 1998 ... completed an MA in social psychology and earned her PhD in the same subject from Princeton in 2005)
3 'studied circles around everyone'
4 Her professional interests in negotiation, power, influence, empowerment,

stereotyping and discrimination are possibly influenced by her experiences after her road accident, when she possibly faced such challenges herself.
5 The nonverbal communication and body posture aspects of ballet have influenced her interest and specialization in nonverbal communication and how body posture can be empowering ('power posing').

2

c

3

1 Ramsey and Balcetis   **2** Dweck and Ramsey   **3** Gutman

4

a keep off   **b** grow   **c** flex   **d** walk someone through   **e** disrupt

6

the suggestio**mb**eing that we **oughtowadop whathe** speaker calls an 'eye on the prize' strategy

7

I **hafda** say, I'm also **kinda** curious about what other similar strategies **coube** developed.

8

1 False – it was to show how motivation can change your perception of your goals when exercising   **2** True

9

1 it was further away   **2** more quickly
3 to other daily habits, a similar strategy could potentially help people cultivate other healthy habits in their lives   **4** because he values exercise and having a healthy lifestyle
5 the appreciation of his progress in weightlifting, the prize of his personal records and incremental improvements

10

1 c   **2** a   **3** c   **4** a   **5** c

4.2 How we communicate

1

1 was made, had been limited, weighed, measured, had
2 was working, proposed, would become, marked, accounted, had risen, was communicated/was being communicated
3 had been using, was invented, were, required, was sought, discovered, could be produced, had been developed, could also be produced, wasn't, started

2

1 had been rhythmically beating   **2** wasn't
3 was first stretched   **4** was   **5** were   **6** was
7 used   **8** would give   **9** would also be used

10 were known to have used   **11** would carry
12 use   **13** would have   **14** would recognize
15 had all but ended   **16** had become

3

1 had to   **2** could've stayed   **3** should've
said   **4** would've been   **5** 'd known
6 might well have chosen   **7** should've told
8 could've given   **9** might not've got
10 might not've been paying

4

1 The Internet might not have been working
earlier. / It might be that the Internet wasn't
working earlier.
2 I shouldn't have phoned him. I regret it
now.
3 I wasn't able to get hold of them. I think I
might have the wrong number.
4 My grandparents often used to call me for
a long chat at weekends.
5 I would never want to go to bed as a
child.
6 Sarah wasn't in the office yesterday so you
can't have spoken to her.
7 You could've told me, but I can't remember
to be honest.
8 He would constantly be on his phone
whether it was WhatsApp or Facebook or
whatever.

5

1 So   **2** Not until / Only when   **3** No sooner
4 Such   **5** Only when / Not until   **6** Hardly
7 Only by   **8** Never before

6

2 Only if the economy suddenly got much
stronger would the central bank consider
the move.
3 Under no circumstances can you leave the
exam room unescorted.
4 Not until he stood at the podium ready to
speak did he feel nervous.
5 Not only was I leaving a special place, but
also my family and friends.
6 Only after he had fully soaked up the
rapturous applause did he finally leave the
stage.

7

1 had been trying to decide what to focus on
2 exploring how certain pages linked with
other pages
3 which Page later described as the best
advice he ever received
4 could have focussed on his research alone
5 had first met when Brin was showing a
group of new students around the campus
6 That might well have been the end of it
7 had an index of about 60 million pages and
this was growing rapidly
8 not only were Google's search results
better than its competitors at the time

4.3 Negotiate better

2

1 C   **2** A   **3** E   **4** F   **5** B   **6** D

3

1 U – we only know it was the period when
postcards had their greatest success
among users
2 True
3 False – messages could be sent and replied
to within a day (text messages within
minutes)
4 True
5 False – it was established in 1902 with the
divided back postcard
6 U – they were used for romantic purposes
(secret messages), but it doesn't say if this
was the preferred way of sending such
messages
7 True
8 False – it was the war that interrupted
the practice and it was never resumed
because of a shortage of postmen and the
spread of the telephone

4

2, 3, 4, 5, 6

5

Informal writing style in text messaging
and its effects on literacy; governments'
struggles to control content on the World
Wide Web

6

1 raising   **2** shaking   **3** folded   **4** clenched
5 drumming   **6** roll   **7** shrugging   **8** tapped
9 scowled   **10** yawning

7

1 un   **2** in   **3** il   **4** im   **5** ir   **6** dis   **7** non-

8

1 These figures are inaccurate.
2 What you're saying is illogical.
3 It's inadvisable to do that.
4 Your explanation is inadequate.
5 He made a few comments that were
distasteful./He made a few distasteful
comments.
6 They're often disobedient.
7 It's a nice idea, but impractical.
8 That is improper behaviour.
9 The disease is usually incurable.

4.4 Is that what you meant?

1

a 6   **b** 1   **c** 4   **d** 7   **e** 5   **f** 2   **g** 3

2

1 Bad news   **2** not available, suits
3 in person   **4** by the way   **5** give, ring
6 give, hand   **7** at all, mention   **8** have,
quick word   **9** Sorry, hear   **10** give, lift
11 put, out   **12** drop, off, way   **13** get,
anything   **14** shouldn't have   **15** never
mind, Another time   **16** say, from

3

1 I'm afraid she's **not available** at the
moment.
2 I think we should discuss it **in person**.
3 Yep, 6.30 **suits** me.
4 Yes. **Can I get you** something?
5 Yes, can **I have a quick word**?
6 Ah, **you shouldn't have**.
7 Let me **give you a hand** with some of it.
8 I can **give you a lift**. I really don't want to
put you out.

4

1 **A:** Bad news, I'm afraid. (↓) I didn't get the
job. (-)
   B: Oh, I'm sorry to hear that. (↓)
2 **A:** Hi Richard.
   B: Ah, Lucas. Can I have a quick word? (↑)
3 **A:** This is for you. To say thank you.
   B: That's very kind of you, but you really
shouldn't have. (-)
4 **A:** Let me give you a lift. (-)
   B: Are you sure? (↑) I really don't want to
put you out. (-)
5 **A:** See you tomorrow. (↑)
   B: Yeah, bye. Oh, by the way, I'll be a little
late in tomorrow. (↓)
6 **A:** Can I give you a hand with anything? (↑)
   B: That's good of you to offer, but I'm fine
thanks. (↓)
7 **A:** Thanks again for all your help. (-)
   B: Not at all. Don't mention it. (↓)
8 **A:** That seat's taken, actually. (↓)
   B: Oh sorry. I didn't realize. (-)

5

1 Thank you for <u>taking the time</u> to consider
our proposal.
2 Thank you for <u>agreeing to meet</u> with us on
Friday, but I really don't want to <u>put you out</u>
3 I think it's important that you and Susan
meet <u>in person</u> as soon as possible.
4 We feel that the proposed relocation
is <u>impractical</u> and could in fact be
<u>disadvantageous</u>.
5 He has fully admitted that his conduct
was <u>improper</u>.
6 I am <u>sorry to hear</u> that the arrangements
<u>were</u> not to your satisfaction.
7 I <u>had a quick word</u> with Julian and he has
<u>agreed to go</u> ahead with the proposal.
8 Only when we have the full facts <u>can we</u>
begin to assess the situation.

6

Dear Alison,

I am writing to request your approval <u>to atten</u>
the London Business Conference, which <u>is</u>
being held from 15–17 January next year. <u>The</u>
conference theme is Risk Management and <u>is</u>
aimed <u>at</u> industry stakeholders as <u>a</u> forum <u>to</u>
discuss the current state of risk management
in private equity. Of <u>particular</u> interest to us,
is a focus <u>on</u> co-investments versus fund
investments. As well as <u>the</u> main conference
talks, there <u>are</u> a number of workshops.

You <u>may recall</u> that Samantha Mitchell
<u>attended the</u> conference last year and she
found <u>it</u> extremely relevant and useful. I
believe she <u>presented</u> some of the key issues
to the senior management team, which I thin
you <u>might have attended</u>. This is something
that I am of course prepared to do.

I have included an approximate breakdown of the costs to attend below:

- Conference Registration: £300.00
- Travel, accommodation and meals: £350.00

If you would like to find out more about the conference, their website is Londonbusiness.org.

Thank you in advance for taking the time to consider this and I very much look forward to hearing from you.

Best wishes,

Tom

7

a 3   b 2   c 6   d 8   e 7   f 1   g 5   h 4

8

Dear Sir or Madam,

Below is my reference for Ms Marta Masini

Marta Masini joined Waterwells Books in January last year and since then she has been a reliable, effective and valuable member of the sales team.

Marta is professional and efficient in her approach to her work and has a sound knowledge and understanding of both the book-selling business and the wider retail industry.

She has consistently shown that she is able to work both independently and as part of a team. Her communication skills are excellent and she is very well-liked by her colleagues and always has a good rapport with customers and (with) other clients.

I believe that Marta will be a valuable addition to any organization that she may join. While we regret Marta's decision to move on, I would recommend her without hesitation.

Please get in touch if you should require (any) further information.

Yours faithfully,

Carmen Napoli

WRITING 2

1

a Being culturally appropriate makes a good impression.

b If you make a mistake with cultural norms, it can offend.

c Cultural differences can be difficult to spot.

d They need to be taught to business people to make business run more smoothly.

2

1 c   2 d   3 b   4 a

3

1 'Culture' is the differences in how people act in different social groups.

2 A strong handshake can be too dominant for Filipino customers.

3 You should take small amounts of food throughout the meal, not all of your food at the start.

4 It can influence the negotiations, for example the prices people are willing to pay.

5 They don't expect you to understand everything, but it can increase their respect for you.

4

1 subtle   2 overly   3 explicitly   4 a faux pas
5 nuances   6 norms

5

1 back   2 to   3 To   4 in   5 to   6 for
7 of   8 with   9 of

6

1 d   2 b   3 e   4 a   5 c

7

a 3: frankly unrealistic
b 5: creativity blossoms
c 2: instant gratification
d 4: patently true
e 1: beneficial change

8

People don't engage with the world around them.

Attention is divided and there is a lack of focus.

The Internet gives you access to a lot of information.

It is easy to communicate and work with people in other places.

10   Sample answer

When historians look back on the invention of the smartphone, they may well say that it was revolutionary. The key question, however, is whether this is a beneficial change or not.

Firstly, the fact that people can access the Internet from wherever they are has led to a desire for instant gratification. There is an impatience in society that demands an instant answer to any question and an instant solution to any problem, creating a frankly unrealistic impression of what knowledge is available to us and what we are currently able to use it for. Some people undoubtedly believe that you can find anything on the Internet, even though that is patently not true.

That is not to say that having a powerful computer in our pockets at all times is entirely a bad thing. On the contrary, it is a valuable tool in many situations, from finding directions in an unfamiliar city to telling people you are alive and safe after a natural disaster.

The biggest change that smartphones have brought with them is a new inability for their owners to deal with boredom. No longer are people's minds allowed to wander and their creativity to blossom. As soon as they start to feel the smallest hint that the situation they are in might not interest them, they immerse themselves in the world of their phones, rather than focussing on what is in front of them. To the detriment of relationships, they split their attention between this small device and the people they are with.

In conclusion, I believe that, while the smartphone brings many advantages, we must ensure that we do not allow it to take over our lives completely.

UNIT 5

5.1   The magic washing machine

1

1 F – (There is no information about qualifications gained in Mozambique – He studied statistics and medicine at Uppsala University, and then public health at St. John's Medical College, Bangalore, India ... He has also received honorary degrees from universities in Sweden, Norway and the UK and is a member of the Swedish Academy of Sciences.)

2 F – (In 1981, Rosling encountered an outbreak of a paralytic disease called konzo.)

3 F – (... was one of the initiators of Médecins Sans Frontières in Sweden – not the global organization)

4 F – (his main field is global health)

5 T – (Rosling's lectures using Gapminder graphics have gained a global reputation for their creativity and originality and have won numerous awards ... Rosling has received a number of awards and accolades, including 'Speaker of the Year')

2

a

3

1 Kamkwamba and Venkatraman
2 Gosier and Venkatraman   3 Turere and Kamkwamba   4 Gosier

4

1 all-important, solar-powered, trickle-down, electricity-generating, low-cost

6

She talks about how young he is and how his age made her curious to hear him. She describes how he had to deal with solving a major problem.

7

1 by trying out different solutions   2 not giving up

8

1 animals   2 being determined in the face of a challenge   3 win his family's respect
4 both

9

1 c   2 b   3 b   4 a   5 a

5.2 Energy-hungry world

1

2 More appropriate in the passive: Piezoelectricity is the electrical charge produced in certain materials (such as crystals and ceramics) **when physical pressure is applied**.

3 Both active and passive would be appropriate: The United States is the world's second largest energy consumer. It **obtains** the majority of this energy (around 68%) from fossil fuels. / The United States is the world's second largest energy consumer. **The majority of this energy (around 68%) is obtained from fossil fuels.**

4 More appropriate in the passive: The existence of the greenhouse effect was first proposed in 1824. **However, the term 'greenhouse' was not used in this way until the beginning of the 1900s.**

2

2 World energy consumption is the total energy (that is) used by humans. It is usually calculated and measured per year.

3 Wind power is currently being used by more than 80 countries. In 2013, almost 3% of the world's total electricity was generated by wind.

4 Solar energy has been used (by humans) since ancient times and today it is predicted that, by the middle of the century, a third of all global energy could be provided by solar power. CO_2 emissions would consequently be reduced to 'very low levels'.

5 Construction of the new nuclear power plant is expected to be completed by 2025. The government insists that enough energy will be generated to power six million homes.

6 It is generally agreed that energy independence and security is one of today's key political issues and one which needs to be addressed urgently.

3

1 to be reassessed/reassessing
2 not to have been informed
3 not having been consulted
4 being forced, to be introduced/being introduced
5 Having been found, to be sentenced
6 Being beaten, to be sacked

4

2 generated 3 embedded 4 were placed
5 to be tested 6 to be 7 be generated
8 was developed / has been developed

5

2 Professor Helen Stephenson was given the award for her work on climate change. / The award was given to Professor Helen Stephenson for her work on climate change.

3 The court was shown CCTV footage of the incident (by the prosecution lawyer). / CCTV footage of the incident was shown to the court (by the prosecution lawyer).

4 I guess I was sent the email by mistake. / I guess the email was sent to me by mistake.

5 In total, the charity was given over a million dollars. /In total, over a million dollars was given to the charity.

6

1 make an attempt/a decision/an announcement/an assessment/a complaint/an allowance/progress/a compromise
2 reach agreement/a compromise/a decision/a conclusion
3 give consideration (to)/priority (to)/preference (to)/thought (to)/information/an order/an answer

7

2 allowance was made for any delays in the development process.
3 consideration has been given to everything in making this decision.
4 complaints were made about the service.
5 agreement has been reached on most aspects of the deal.
6 priority needs to be given to renewable energy sources.
7 that a compromise seems to have been reached regarding CO_2 emission quotas.
8 progress was/has been made regarding trade in ozone-depleting substances.

8

1 being released from organic matter
2 can be converted
3 which conversion process has been used
4 results in hydrogen being produced
5 is currently being developed
6 have already been developed

5.3 Land for all

2

c

3

1 Over 10 million
2 Under 25 million
3 it's becoming stronger
4 Floods, earthquakes, epidemics
5 unemployment, urban poverty, crime, road congestion, inefficient public transport and shortages of food or water
6 do things differently
7 worst case scenarios
8 complaining about government policy / government policies and budgets
9 (injustice of) wealth inequality
10 encourages long-term solutions

4

1 centre 2 meeting 3 smaller 4 once
5 stronger 6 pessimism 7 apparent/clear

5

1 interest 2 bankrupt 3 recession 4 meet
5 recovery 6 Unemployment 7 debts
8 boom 9 operations 10 employees

6

1 landlocked 2 landmark 3 dry land
4 plot of land 5 strip of land 6 live off the land 7 wasteland 8 landslide

7

1 c 2 a 3 b

8

1 landscape 2 landmark 3 landscape
4 landslide 5 landmark

5.4 I can well believe that

1

1 ✓ 2 ✗ 3 ✓ 4 ✗ 5 ✗ 6 ✓ 7 ✗
8 ✓

2

1 believe 2 pinch, case 3 surprise
4 doubt 5 old, truth 6 true
7 misconception 8 believe 9 spot

3

1 I'd take that with a pinch of salt.
2 That's (just) an old wives' tale.
3 I suspect that's true.
4 That's a common misconception.
5 I'd be surprised if that was the case.
6 I can well believe that. It doesn't/wouldn't surprise me at all.
7 I very much doubt that. I think it's nonsense, to be honest.
8 That's what they'd have you believe. I'd have some reservations about that.

4

1 Many students take years to pay off their de<u>b</u>ts.
2 Can I have a recei<u>p</u>t please?
3 I dou<u>b</u>t they'll reach an agreement today.
4 He was a co<u>l</u>onel in the army.
5 Can I have an ai<u>s</u>le seat please?
6 We need a more su<u>b</u>tle approach.
7 Can you pass me the s<u>c</u>issors?
8 Would you like a bisc<u>u</u>it?
9 My sister's an arc<u>h</u>itect.
10 He was found g<u>u</u>ilty of all charges.

5

1 it is predicted that 2 it is estimated that
3 is believed to 4 It is thought to
5 are thought to

6

2 It is thought that ten thousand people took part in the anti-fracking demonstration. Ten thousand people are thought to have taken part in the anti-fracking demonstration.
3 It is expected that the minister will/is to resign within the next 24 hours. The minister is expected to resign within the next 24 hours.
4 It is feared that thousands have been left homeless after the hurricane. Thousands are feared to have been left homeless after the hurricane.

5 It is said that a picture is worth a thousand words.
A picture is said to be worth a thousand words.
6 It is/has been alleged that bribes had been offered.
Bribes are alleged to have been offered.

7

1 it is recommended that, is thought to be
2 is believed to be, It is now feared that
3 it was reported, It is/has been claimed that, is expected to release
4 is said to be, is thought to have escaped

8

It is estimated that global energy consumption will have increased by around 50% by 2050. It is thought that half of that growth will come from China and India. At the moment China and India consume about 21% of world energy, but this is expected to increase to 31% by the middle of the century. It is also calculated that China will use around 60% more energy than the US by 2050. Fossil fuels will still be the dominant energy source and will account for around 70% of world energy use in 2050. Over the same period it is predicted that renewable energy will increase globally by about 3% per year. Despite this, energy-related carbon-dioxide emissions are expected to continue to rise and be 30–40% higher in 2050 than at present.

PRESENTATION 3

1

1 c   **2** b   **3** a

3 (example answers)

1 I decided to take up yoga classes five years ago because I was feeling unfit. I needed to find a way of being healthier.
2 As a result of going to yoga, I feel a lot calmer. I've also noticed that I've become much more flexible and stronger.
3 What is more, another thing I've been able to do is to teach my children a little bit about practising yoga.

5

1 e   **2** a   **3** d   **4** c   **5** b

6 (example answers)

1 Hello, I'm (name). Today I would like to talk about a change in my life I'm planning to make.
2 The change would be learning a new language. I'd really like to learn Arabic as I think this would open up a lot of new cultures and experiences for me. I would love to travel around northern Africa and knowing a bit of Arabic would help me a lot.
3 Learning this language would give me a new outlook on life. I think it's totally different to the other languages I speak – English and Spanish. I know that it isn't exactly the same Arabic that is spoken in

different countries, but it would mean that I could communicate at least a little bit.
4 Not only would it help me when travelling, but I think it could also be of benefit in my job – I'm a language teacher and a lot of my students come from countries where they speak Arabic. Understanding the language might mean I am able to help them learn English better.
5 Finally, I'd like to thank you all for listening. Do you have any questions?

UNIT 6

6.1 Magical houses, made of bamboo

1

1 Her father was a jewellery designer and she grew up surrounded by art and creativity and spent a lot of her time with local village craftsmen, where she learned skills such as carving, painting and batik. She says in setting up Ibuku that she wanted to reconnect with the culture and landscape that she grew up in.
2 *talked herself into* It means she managed to persuade the company to give her a job, even though they perhaps initially didn't want to or didn't have a job available.
3 *bespoke*.
4 He was a designer, albeit of jewellery, and he also designed and built buildings out of bamboo. In fact she was directly inspired by the design and bamboo construction of a building her father and step-mother had recently opened.
5 The innovative aspect of her constructions is that she uses locally-sourced bamboo and other sustainable natural materials, often with bespoke furniture.

2

c

3

1 Green, Joachim and Ban   **2** Joachim (and Green)   **3** Larsson (and Ban)

4

a harsh   **b** abodes   **c** secure   **d** remarkable

6

My firsreaction to this talk was notatall sceptical. I justhought – whata fantastic idea!

7

But **then I** began **to wonder about its impact on** deforestation and about how safe a wooden skyscraper **would be** during an earthquake.

8

1 impact on deforestation; safety in an earthquake
2 it's warm, welcoming and natural; it's environmentally friendly
3 its financial viability; the noises it makes

9

1 T   **2** T   **3** F   **4** U   **5** T

10

1 c   **2** b   **3** c   **4** a   **5** a

6.2 Get someone else to do it

1

1 They're having the floor sanded
2 They had the boiler serviced
3 They're having/going to have a sofa delivered
4 They've had/had an alarm fitted
5 They had the office redecorated

2

1 to help   **2** tested   **3** to call   **4** to agree
5 working   **6** give   **7** finished   **8** valued

3

1 to get the job done
2 get a professional to do
3 not having an expert do
4 get the heating working
5 get that stuck window unstuck
6 get those long-overdue jobs done
7 have it sorted
8 get a professional to do

4

1 to get one cut
2 to get Jack to change, got him to see
3 have it finished
4 got it caught
5 to get it decorated, to get someone to do

5

go: missing, wrong, blind, red, quiet, crazy, bald, bankrupt, deaf, bad
get: ill, involved, lost, ready, started, pregnant, upset, married, angry, old

6

1 go wrong   **2** go blind   **3** go red   **4** go quiet
5 go crazy   **6** get ill   **7** go bald   **8** get lost
9 go bankrupt   **10** get ready

7

1 getting dark/to get dark
2 get started
3 have gone missing
4 to be getting anywhere/to have got anywhere
5 're going anywhere
6 getting a new TV, is getting a bit old
7 gone rusty
8 get involved

8

1 It is most commonly used to describe the activity
2 having the work done by a professional
3 to describe someone doing something for themselves
4 of having someone else do it for them

5 to get it promoted
6 getting things done yourself
7 the need to get specialists to do

6.3 Better by design

1

1 a public declaration of your aims and policies **2** political parties

2

1 he trained as an architect and interior designer, but ended up designing functional objects, e.g. record players. These things were linked through a focus on practical design in general.
2 'less, but better' philosophy

3

a 5   b 3   c 8   d 1   e 10   f 6   g 4   h 7

4

1 understandable   **2** impenetrable
3 thorough   **4** transient   **5** aesthetic
6 intuitive   **7** unobtrusive   **8** durable

5

1 ✓   **2** ?   **3** ✓   **4** ✓   **5** ✗   **6** ✓   **7** ✓
8 ?   **9** ?   **10** ✓

6

1 shoddily
2 scientifically
3 greatly, highly
4 widely
5 brightly
6 prohibitively, reasonably
7 beautifully, perfectly

7

2 Rams said that good design makes a product (easily) understandable.
3 Ibuku uses natural sustainable materials to create homes and other buildings.
4 Even though it is breakable, carbon fibre is one of the strongest known materials currently used in manufacturing.
5 His art is very hands-on and interactive with a number of exhibits with movable parts.
6 The detail and the intricacy of the painting are unimaginable until you get up close and see it with your own eyes.
7 The book is invaluable and irreplaceable.
8 The band is instantly recognizable as soon as you hear the first few bars of their songs.

8

1 g   **2** f   **3** a   **4** b (note that 'flammable' has the same meaning)   **5** d   **6** e   **7** c   **8** h

9

1 malleable   **2** inflammable   **3** inexplicable
4 illegible   **5** durable   **6** irreparable
7 pliable   **8** edible

6.4 Common sense

1

Extract 1: T   Extract 2: F
Extract 3: U   Extract 4: T

2

1 Do, find, that, depends
2 would, say, suppose, say, why, do, say, that
3 situation, where, would, do, first, instinct, is, would, go, about
4 Imagine, that, what, would, be, that, tricky, question, Let, me, have, think

3

1 In **a** situation ... what **would** you do?
I suppose **I'd** talk
2 **Do** you find
that depends
3 **Imagine** ... what **would** you do?
That's a tricky question.
4 How would you go about **appealing** to
Let me have **a** think
5 Would you say **you** are
My first instinct is **to** say yes
And why **do** you say that?

4

1 She's got a strong imagin**a**tion and has a lot of very good i**de**as.
2 He's got a lot of inter**na**tional experience.
3 She's got **ex**cellent communi**ca**tion skills.
4 He's a**ppa**rently got a photo**gra**phic memory.
5 He's got a **back**ground in eco**nom**ics and **po**litics. ('politics' is an exception to the 'penultimate stress in -ic words' rule)
6 What experience and qualifi**ca**tions spe**ci**fic to trans**la**tion do you have?
7 We need an e**ffec**tive and cre**a**tive **pu**blic speaker.
8 A lot of what we do re**quires** a strong **in**stinct and intu**i**tion.
9 The **sal**ary will de**pend** on **var**ious factors.
10 I think I'm quite ass**er**tive and enthusi**as**tic.

5

1 I did it before last summer and I managed to get some good sales figures.
2 How do you think the recent changes to EU data protection law will affect the way the company operates?
3 I'd be happy to look into it if you want me to.
4 If you are invited for a second interview, then we will probably need to talk about it.
5 Because you've just graduated in business and because you've got experience and have done the job last year, we thought/ think you might be suitable as our new marketing manager.

6

1 She asked me what I knew about the company.

2 They asked me what I thought the main challenges would be if I got the job.
3 They wanted to know what I thought my colleagues would consider as my best qualities.
4 He said (that) they would be in touch if they needed any further information.
5 They advised me to look at other options before I made a decision. / They advised (me) that I should look at other options before I made a decision.
6 He questioned why I wasn't applying for a more senior position.
7 They told me (that) they thought it would be a week or so before they knew/would know anything.
8 I asked (them) if they knew how many other candidates had been shortlisted.

7

2 asked me/wanted to know what I could offer them that other candidates couldn't. I said/told them (that) I was very experienced, (that) I'd got a lot of insight into the sector and (that) I knew the market.
3 They asked me/wanted to know where I saw myself in five years' time. I said/told them (that) I hoped to be heading up my own marketing team.
4 They asked me/wanted to know what I thought was the number one key to successful marketing, of any product. I said/told them (that) I thought the number one thing was to have a clear strategy, which was implemented consistently.
5 They asked me/wanted to know what I saw as my strengths. I said/told them (that) I'm a good organizer and I plan everything in detail. I'm creative, and as I mentioned, I know the market.
6 They asked me/wanted to know if I could think of any improvements to their products. I said/told them (that) I thought their products were second to none. But (that) I did think the marketing and advertising could be freshened up a little.

WRITING 3

1

the main features of the app
why the features are useful
anything the users should be aware of before they download the app
Points to include: student's own ideas

2

a 2   b 4   c 1   d 3

3

1 The user wants to increase the range of recipes they know.
2 It can be difficult for the user to find the information they want.
3 The app copies the ingredients automatically.

4 Recipe Record allows you to cross off ingredients so you don't forget what you've used.

5 It's simple for some websites, but not all.

6 The user thinks the price is fine because of the range of functions.

4

1 build my repertoire of dishes

2 When it comes to shopping

3 search in vain

4 A note of caution

5 It ... was well worth the £6 I paid for it.

6 anyone looking to

5 Suggested answer

Anyone looking to get fit could do worse than download VidFitPlus. You can use it to **build your repertoire of exercises** quickly and easily. No longer will you have to **search in vain** for videos showing you the safest way to stretch your quads or a new yoga breathing technique: they're all in one place within the app. **It's well worth** every minute you spend using VidFitPlus. **When it comes to** the price, it's a bargain at just 99p. **A note of caution** though: it's addictive. Once you start using it, you won't be able to stop! I'd recommend it to all you fitness fans out there.

6

1 What **is the** secret **to** its **success**?

2 Contrary **to what you** might think…

3 **It's** far **from easy** to do this.

4 **By and** large, the developer manages to….

5 The app **in** question…

6 The app **takes an unusual** approach.

7

1 exceptional, outstanding

2 riveting, gripping

3 dull, tedious

4 entertaining, hilarious

5 baffling, over-complicated

6 extremely, highly

7 undeniably, unquestionably

10 Sample answer

Matt Cutts' TED Talk 'Try something new for 30 days' is short and sweet. Despite being only three minutes long, it has the potential to change your life completely.

You could say I was meant to watch it. On the day in question I was feeling a bit depressed, stuck in a rut at work and uninspired at home. I had the TED app automatically generate an 'inspiration' playlist for me, and this talk was the first one that came up. After listening to the very entertaining Matt Cutts, I'd found the answer to my problems.

In his talk, he describes how he took an unusual approach to changing his lifestyle through a series of 30-day projects. So what is the secret of his success? By breaking down each goal into manageable chunks, he created new habits which fitted around his life. Another unexpected side effect he described was that life became much more memorable instead of passing by in a tedious haze. Who wouldn't want that?

After watching his talk, I was inspired to have a go at my own 30-day project. I've been learning English for years and had long intended to add a new language to my repertoire. Contrary to what you might expect, after studying Mandarin for just ten minutes a day for a month, I can already have simple conversations and recognize over 200 characters. Matt's 'little and often' approach really works!

As well as providing this kind of motivation and inspiration, TED Talks are wonderful tools for English learners. They cover a wide range of accents, and there are subtitles to help you understand them. Because they range in length from just 50 seconds to eighteen minutes, you can select one that fits the time you have available. So why not make your first 30-day project choosing a TED Talk a day to watch, and start with Matt Cutts' riveting talk to inspire you as he did me?

Workbook audioscript

Audioscript

TRACK 3

My name's Paul Dummett and I'm one of the authors of the *Keynote* series. I've seen this talk quite a few times and I still get really emotional watching it. I think it has something to do with the kind of overwhelming kindness – love even – that Rita F. Pierson shows her students. Her pupils seem vulnerable or they're from disadvantaged backgrounds ... and that sort of tugs at the heartstrings too. I think it also has to do with her power as an orator – a bit like Martin Luther King Jr. or something – she knows how to use words to make an emotional appeal. For example, when she says 'I've had kids so educationally deficient I could have cried'. Or the bit where she talks about all the former pupils coming spontaneously to her mother's funeral.

I'm a teacher and teacher trainer myself and I absolutely know what she says to be true. The best teachers are the ones who seem to befriend their pupils and win them over – being playful with them, but always showing deep down that they like them as people and want them to do well. I don't understand education systems that put a big emphasis on order and discipline. It seems to me that if you're having to demand respect and good behaviour from your students, then you've probably failed to keep them engaged in other ways. I love the example she gives of the boy who got only two questions right out of twenty and she put a smiley face on his paper and told him he was on a roll. Kids have to feel that you're on their side and rooting for them.

One of the most telling things she says is early on in the talk – that we all know why kids underperform at school: it's basically an accident of birth – being born into poverty or the wrong surroundings. I think that's so true. When you're not fed or clothed properly or your family life is a struggle, your chances of doing well at school are really affected.

Unfortunately, Rita F. Pierson died not long after this talk, but she certainly left a legacy – just as she said her mother did – of the power of human friendship and connection. The talk is called 'Every kid needs a champion'. I think it should be renamed 'Every teacher should see this'.

TRACK 6

A: I know you said you don't go to the cinema that often, but what sort of films do you like?

B: Well, yeah, I'm not that into films to be honest. It's not really my thing, I don't know why. I do like watching a good film, yeah, but I'm not very good at sticking with a film that's not doing it for me. It's sort of odd, I hardly ever watch a film, at home or at the cinema, but I do generally enjoy it when I do watch one, if that makes sense. I do like a good psychological thriller, though, something where you really get involved in trying to work out what's what or where you really start to feel for one of the people, one of the characters. But I'm not so keen on the more lightweight stuff, that there tends to be a lot of.

A: What sports are you into?

B: I'm a huge rugby fan. My favourite sport by a mile. I'm not really into football. It's OK, but I can take it or leave it. I like the big tournaments, like the World Cup, I get into those. And to be honest any big sporting event, I'll tend to watch if I can, tennis, golf, the Olympics. I'm really into live sport, whatever it is.

A: Do you have any favourite artists?

B: Well, I'm a big fan of Van Gogh. I don't really know why and I'm not an expert at all, but I just like him, his colours and just his feeling for things. Whenever I've seen his actual paintings in a gallery, I'm just sort of transfixed by them. There's something quite enchanting or mesmerizing about them. I can't really get excited about much contemporary art, to be honest. It just doesn't appeal to me at all. I much prefer the older painters and old masters. I quite like Turner as well, especially his seascapes.

TRACK 7

1   One thing I'm good at and one thing I'm not good at? OK, let me think. Well, I play the piano so I guess that's one thing I'm quite good at. But I'm not great at singing. In fact, I'm pretty terrible, actually.

2   Well, I think I'm quite a natural at teaching, to be honest. Well, that's what my students tell me and I do find it quite easy and enjoyable. A born teacher, maybe. But I'm most definitely not a natural when it comes to all the admin side of it, like report writing and record keeping and meetings and that sort of thing. I find that a real chore most of the time.

3   Mmm, let me think. Well, I can tell you one thing that I'm no good at, according to my friends that is, and that's making a cup of tea. Apparently, I can't make a cup of tea to save my life. But it always tastes fine to me, so anyway. But at the same time people say I do have a talent for cooking. I've never learned how to cook properly. I just sort of make it up as I go along, or maybe take a recipe and then do my own thing with it. But people are often saying what a good cook I am.

4   Something I'm good at and bad at? Er, well, I'm pretty good at spending money and I'm pretty hopeless at saving it. Is that OK? Will that do? But seriously, I'm a born spendaholic. Life's too short, you only live once. You can't take it with you and all that. What's money for if it's not for spending?

TRACK 10

My name's Mike Harrison and I'm a teacher trainer and materials writer. I've heard the expression that laughter is the best medicine, so I was interested to watch this TED Talk exploring how medicine intersects with another creative pursuit – music. The person who gives this talk, Robert Gupta, seems to embody this space in between medicine and music – as he was caught between a career as a doctor and as a violinist.

Certainly I know that music has a powerful impact on people and their emotions, but music therapy is still something of a mystery to me. Gupta talks about his medical training and at the same time pursuing his passion of playing the violin.

I think the key point that Gupta makes about music is about its potential to help people in really dire circumstances. Using the example of acting as a violin teacher to a homeless man in Skid Row, Gupta shows us how music can give society's most marginalized some sort of hope that they have not been forgotten.

I love the combination of the talk and the music in this TED Talk – I think it adds something more to the experience of listening to Gupta than if he were just delivering it as a lecture.

Finding out more about how music and sounds affect us is something that does really interest me, in particular how it can stimulate our imagination and creativity. It's something that I've experimented a little with in my own career as a language teacher.

I can't claim to be much of a musician myself – I learned the clarinet in my early teens, but never kept at it – but I really agree with the idea that music has this power to inspire people in many different ways. I think it's sad that most of the time we take music and other sounds for granted, without considering the impact, or potential impact, that it can have on our lives and the lives of people around us, particularly when it can be so effective at articulating our emotions.

I see the sun in your smile
Watching it rise in your eyes
See the dusty road ahead
Stretching out for miles and miles
Sick and tired of skipping the stones
Dodging the holes in the road
I need a helping hand
To help me shoulder this load
Do, do you, well, wouldn't you
Do the same in my shoes?
I wouldn't do, just couldn't do
Another mile without you
Another mile without you

TRACK 13

I've spent most of my life trying to make a career out of being a songwriter. I've had a few successes – a couple of songs that have made it onto albums – but no big hit and it's been really hard sticking at it. I've often had to take other jobs to make ends meet – waiting tables at restaurants, boring clerical jobs and so on. A few years ago I was about to give up, partly 'cos I have a young family now and I just thought it's unfair to expect my partner to shoulder the burden of earning enough to keep us all going. But then by chance I read an article in a magazine while I was waiting to have my hair cut about the author, J.K. Rowling. I'd heard that she hadn't had it easy, but reading the details of her life gave me new impetus. She got the idea for the Harry Potter books when she was coming back from London on the train. But, soon after she started writing it up, her whole life was thrown into turmoil. Her mum died of multiple sclerosis at the age of 45. Feeling kind of lost, she moved to Portugal to teach English, got married to a local and had a daughter. But the marriage failed and she moved back to the UK, where she lived on welfare and looked after her child, writing when she could find the time – mostly in local cafés. During this period she went through terrible bouts of depression, but all the time she kept focussed on bringing that good idea that she'd had to fruition and the rest … well, we all know what happened. And I thought, well, she got it right; she stuck at what she loved doing and what she believed in … and that's what I should do. And now, actually I'm on the brink of something that could be quite big. I've teamed up with a singer and we're writing songs together and we're getting a lot of interest.

TRACK 14

Plagiarism is when someone copies or paraphrases someone else's work or ideas without full acknowledgement. You need to be aware that the university routinely checks submitted work for evidence of plagiarism and that all essays, assignments and presentations must fully acknowledge other people's work, ideas or data. This is whether they are obtained from published texts, such as books and journals, from unpublished text, such as from lectures, or other students' work or from websites. And on that subject, we strongly advise against using open-source websites such as Wikipedia that have unverifiable content. In the event of plagiarism, you will be given a formal warning and have to rewrite your essay. The worst case scenario is that you risk being kicked off your course and thrown out of the university.

To avoid plagiarism, the best thing is to become familiar with the principles of good academic practice as soon as you start your university studies. That way, you'll more quickly develop an awareness of the requirements and the dos and don'ts of academic writing. Avoiding plagiarism is more than making sure your citations and references are all correct, although it is advisable to thoroughly check them through before you submit your work. Nor is it about changing enough words so your paraphrase will not be noticed. Avoid simply using a few synonyms and changing the word order. The chances are that you will be caught out. Take time and make the effort to make wholesale changes and express the ideas in your own words. It can be a fine line, so if you're not sure, ask your tutor. Following his or her advice will ensure that your work is plagiarism-free.

TRACK 16

My name's Lucy Constable and I'm a Regional Marketing Executive for National Geographic Learning. I couldn't really tell from the title what this talk was going to be about and I had to watch it a couple of times before I got 'the message'. But I didn't mind re-watching, because I found it really fascinating. Mira Calix is a composer and she talks about how she uses music to change people's perceptions of their environment. Actually, I put that badly. It's not her intention to *change* their perceptions, but to *add* to them.

TRACK 17

My name's Lucy Constable and I'm a Regional Marketing Executive for National Geographic Learning. I couldn't really tell from the title what this talk was going to be about and I had to watch it a couple of times before I got 'the message'. But I didn't mind re-watching, because I found it really fascinating. Mira Calix is a composer and she talks about how she uses music to change people's perceptions of their environment. Actually, I put that badly. It's not her intention to *change* their perceptions, but … to *add* to them.

She worked on a project to transform an old railway tunnel in the city of Bath in England into a commuter walkway and leisure space. It was a really dark and uninviting space, but – along with lighting and design specialists – she made walking through it a great experience. So, as people pass along the tunnel, they trigger light and music installations. She's very open about the fact that we don't really understand exactly how music (and colour and light) affect people's emotions. Instead, she just tries to coax a certain *kind* of emotion out of her audience, leaving the precise interpretation to them.

What I found really thought-provoking was the idea that there are things – sights, sounds, smells – that evoke certain emotions like happiness or sadness, but evoking them doesn't necessarily make us *feel* that way ourselves; it just makes us *think* of those feelings.

When I was in Lisbon about fifteen years ago I went to a bar where a woman was singing *Fado. Fado* is a deeply melancholic genre of music – it's about a yearning for things or people lost or things that have disappeared into the past. Her singing didn't make me feel a sense of yearning myself, but I really felt her emotion – in fact, I can still feel it to this day; it was so powerful.

So, … I think Mira Calix's message is that we mustn't try too hard to analyze or try to be too scientific about music and emotion, because sometimes feelings are beyond words and explanation. That's what I took from it anyhow …

TRACK 20

1   In the work place, the conventional wisdom is that your computer monitor should be about 50–60 cm away. In actual fact, the best distance is as far away as possible while you are still able to read what's on the screen. The 50–60 cm recommendation is probably too near and could be damaging to the eyes over time.

2   Supposedly, we should be drinking eight glasses of water a day. But in reality the amount we need depends on a number of factors, such as what food we eat, and varies from person to person. It seems that this figure was thought up basically as part of an awareness-raising campaign and eight glasses is a nice manageable and easy-to-remember number.

3   It has often been said that Albert Einstein failed mathematics at school. But this, however, is not the case. On the face of it, Einstein was actually very good at maths as a child. He did, however, apparently fail the entrance exam into polytechnic school in 1895. But, at 16, he was two years younger than the other students at the time and he allegedly scored highly in the mathematics and science sections.

4   The popular belief is that Sherlock Holmes used to use the phrase 'Elementary, my dear Watson' when explaining a crime he was solving to his partner Dr Watson. The truth is, however, that the character never actually said those words, not in the original books at least. The words 'my dear Watson' and 'elementary' did both appear a few lines apart in the Sherlock Holmes novel *The Crooked Man*, but they never in fact appeared together as in the famous misquote.

TRACK 24

I'm Nick Yeaton and I'm an Operations Analyst at the Boston office of National Geographic Learning. I watched Emily Balcetis's talk about how perception is ultimately subjective, and that, at times, our 'mind's eye' may actually work against us in life. She explains this by describing an experiment that she conducted with her team examining the connection between fitness, motivation and goals. In the experiment they asked participants to visualize their goal or finish line. The results of the experiment demonstrated that a person's motivation can affect their perception; for example: the finish line in the experiment seemed further away to the unmotivated participants than the motivated ones. The motivated participants also moved at a quicker pace during the experiment, implying that the exercise felt easier to them – the suggestion being that we ought to adopt what the speaker calls an 'eye on the prize' strategy in order to achieve better results in our exercise programmes. More than that the 'eye on the prize' strategy could be transferable to other areas of daily life, meaning that a similar strategy could potentially help people cultivate other healthy habits in their lives, such as stopping smoking or eating more healthily.

Personally, I found this research and these results very compelling, mainly because I am a person who sets great store by fitness and a healthy lifestyle. I found it interesting how the 'eye on the prize' strategy could be used by those who need help adhering to a fitness regimen – who lack the requisite willpower to see such a programme through. I have to say, I'm also kind of curious about what other similar strategies could be developed and deployed to alter a person's perception beneficially in other areas of their lives, such as their work or relationships.

In the past, when my motivation was lacking, I used my own variations of the 'eye on the prize' strategy to continue lifting weights. Appreciating my own progress kept me focussed on my ultimate goals in weightlifting: the 'prize' of personal records each month made the early morning, bleary eyes trips to the weight room possible. Incremental improvements to my levels of strength have been 'prizes' unto themselves, and they have allowed me to remain focussed on my ultimate goals in weightlifting.

TRACK 27

There are various parallels made between Edwardian postcards and modern social-media messaging. One interesting area is the reaction of the establishment at the time to the phenomenon. Some thought that such postcards were insulting in themselves because they showed that the writer could not be bothered to send a proper letter. Also, because the messages were written in informal language, people worried about its effects on literacy, particularly among the younger generation. That is quite a common theme among educators nowadays when they discuss text messaging. *The Times* newspaper and other commentators referred to the postcards as 'vulgar', and 'destructive of style' and 'a threat to standards'. Another concern, perhaps more legitimate, was that the authorities were unable to control the sending of messages which were defamatory or libellous. Effectively, you could say what you liked about someone in a postcard without any comeback or legal implications. This has an obvious parallel in the struggles of governments today to control content on the World Wide Web.

TRACK 28

Conversation 1

A: Bad news. There's a problem with the RBC deal. I think we need to discuss this as soon as possible. How about Friday?

B: I'm not available Friday. Thursday suits me though if that's any good for you. Or we can discuss it over the phone if you like.

A: No, I'd rather we meet in person. But, yeah, Thursday's good. Shall we say my office, two-ish?

B: Oh, by the way, I said I'd tell Julia when we were meeting. Shall I let her know?

A: Sure. Or I can give her a ring if you like.

Conversation 2

A: Can I give you a hand with that? It looks heavy.

B: That's very good of you. Thanks.

A: Not at all. Don't mention it.

Conversation 3

A: Can I have a quick word?

B: Sure. What is it?

A: My mum's gone into hospital. I'm going to have to go up and see her, which'll mean taking a day or two off, if that's OK.

B: Oh, sorry to hear that. And, of course. Just let me know.

A: Yeah, she's been ill for a while now, actually.

B: Oh, I didn't realize. Look, just take a couple of days off. We'll be fine here.

Conversation 4

A: I can give you a lift to the station if you like.

B: Are you sure? I don't want to put you out.

A: No, it's fine. I need to go that way anyway to the bike shop, so I can drop you off on my way.

Conversation 5

A: I'm going to grab a drink. Can I get you anything?

B: Yeah, a coffee thanks.

A: Latte, cappuccino ...?

B: I don't mind, either's fine. Thanks.

Conversation 6

A: This is to say thanks for helping me the other day.

B: Oh, really, you shouldn't have.

A: No, it was a big help. And much appreciated.

Conversation 7

A: I'm meeting Jenny in that new bar on Jackson Street this evening. Fancy joining us?

B: I'd love to, but I'm busy this evening. Shame, I haven't seen Jenny for ages.

A: OK, never mind. Another time.

B: Yeah, for sure. And say hi from me.

TRACK 30

The first thing I noticed about this talk, before I even clicked on the play button, was a picture of the TED speaker and how young he was. I've seen quite a few TED Talks, but I was immediately curious to learn what such a young speaker was going to talk about.

Richard Turere has essentially been given an opportunity to tell an audience how he managed to solve a problem. What I found impressive was that he, at such a young age, was given the responsibility of looking after his father's livestock. He was then faced with a major issue and set about trying to work out a way to resolve it.

TRACK 31

My name's Ruth Goodman and I'm a freelance editor. I've been working on two of the *Keynote* Workbooks.

The first thing I noticed about this talk, before I even clicked on the play button, was a picture of the TED speaker and how young he was. I've seen quite a few TED Talks, but I was immediately curious to learn what such a young speaker was going to talk about.

Richard Turere has essentially been given an opportunity to tell an audience how he managed to solve a problem. What I found impressive was that he, at such a young age, was given the responsibility of looking after his father's livestock. He was then faced with a major issue and set about trying to work out a way to resolve it.

What's nice about his talk is how he takes us through his process of trial and error. He tells us about the failures along the way and what he learned from them. We hear how he analyzes the problem, comes up with some ideas and then works towards a solution.

Whilst I can't really relate to the speaker's experience of being given such a huge responsibility at a young age, what I admire is his determination to learn and not to give up on a challenge. I often want to find a solution to things and always try to find a way through them rather than giving up and becoming down about a difficult situation.

I'd like to know a bit more about Richard Turere's background to get a better understanding of where he got his incredible confidence from. I'd find it really frightening to be in front of such a large audience. How did he get to be so mature? I'd also love to know what made him such a curious child. Was he motivated by not wanting to let his father and the rest of his family down or is he naturally good at working things out? Finally, I think he has an amazing ability to be resourceful. Is that a result of always having only limited resources to fall back on? What did his family teach him that meant he was able to come up with such a great invention?

The talk not only looks at the process of problem-solving, but the speaker inspires people to want to cultivate the same personal qualities of maturity, resourcefulness and curiosity.

TRACK 33

Conversation 1

A: I read something the other day that said that at least a third of an average landfill is made up of packaging material.

B: I can well believe that. I would've thought it was more, to be honest.

Conversation 2

A: Someone the other day was saying that Americans throw away about 50 million plastic bottles every hour.

B: I'd take that with a pinch of salt. That'd be about one in every six people using a plastic bottle at any one time. I'd be surprised if that was the case.

Conversation 3

A: Apparently, over 80% of all household waste can be recycled.

B: That doesn't surprise me at all.

Conversation 4

A: I read the other day that thousands of animal species are becoming extinct every day.

B: I very much doubt that. We were doing something on this at college the other day and no-one really knows. But it's more likely to be in the low hundreds at the absolute most, and more likely much less, and that's animals and plants.

Conversation 5
A: When I was little we used to say that if there are lots of holly berries on the trees and if trees lose their leaves late in the year, then it's going to be a bad winter.
B: That's just an old wives' tale. I don't think there's any truth in that.

Conversation 6
A: I read the other day that half the world's oxygen is produced by plankton in the oceans.
B: I suspect that's true. Especially when you think over 70% of the earth is water.

Conversation 7
A: We should all drink eight glasses of water a day, right?
B: That's a common misconception, actually. I was talking to my doctor friend about this only the other day. He was saying that each of us needs a different amount, some more and some less, and it depends on things like our size, what we eat, how much we exercise and what our metabolism is like. He thinks it's just a pretty random figure.
A: Well, it was in an ad I saw the other day for some new bottled water.
C: Well, that's what they'd have you believe, isn't it? But, yeah, I think we should all drink probably more than we do, though.

Conversation 8
A: They say the single biggest way we can help the environment is to change our habits when it comes to using energy and electricity. Walking or cycling instead of driving, turning off lights and sockets, putting more clothing on instead of turning the heating up and so on.
B: Yeah, I think they've got that spot on. But unfortunately it's a bit easier said than done, though.

TRACK 37

My name's Karen Richardson and I'm an ELT materials writer and business English trainer. My first reaction to this talk was not at all sceptical. I just thought – what a fantastic idea! But then I began to wonder about its impact on deforestation and about how safe a wooden skyscraper would be during an earthquake. So I was pleased when the speaker addressed and alleviated both these fears in his talk.

Personally, I wouldn't want to live in a wooden skyscraper – but that's not because of the wood – I love wood – it's because I wouldn't want to live in a skyscraper at all. However, if the need for new urban housing is really set to increase at the rate the speaker describes, then, for the sake of the planet, I really hope that new multi-storey homes will be made of wood.

I can completely relate to what he says about people hugging the wooden columns in his buildings. For me, wood is a warm, natural, welcoming material, and one that I need to have around me. I travel half an hour each week to go to a yoga class which is held in a completely wood-built studio, not because the teacher is better than the ones locally, but because the building itself provides me with a wonderful sense of well-being.

And after working for three years on 'temporary' IKEA plastic desks, I was so pleased to take delivery of new wooden desks made to measure for my office by a local carpenter. I can't begin to describe how much this has improved my work space – mentally and in a tactile way.

There are two questions that I'd like to ask the speaker: one is financial and concerns the length of time it takes even young trees to grow to the size needed to mass-produce the timber panels he talks about – he mentions ten to fifteen years. How would he convince foresters and potential new growers to wait that long before they see a return on their investment? The other question is more of a psychological one: I live in an old house that, although it has been renovated and adapted many times during its life, still cracks and creaks and makes other loud and sudden unsettling noises as the wood expands and contracts – especially during weather and temperature changes. Our loud house only has two floors and an attic. I wonder what these noises would sound like if they were multiplied by twenty storeys.

TRACK 40

A: Would you say Henry Hoover's innovative?
B: Well, yes – there's nothing else like it, is there?
A: That's not the point. It's supposed to achieve a harmony between form and function that didn't exist before.
B: Well, I'd say it did. Also, it's completely obvious what it is.
A: OK and is it aesthetic?
B: Definitely … and fun.
A: What about understandable and unobtrusive?
B: Yes, its functions are all really obvious, but actually by painting a face on it, they've kind of made it jump out at you haven't they?
A: Yes – I'm not sure I agree with Rams that a product shouldn't be showy.
B: So does that mean it isn't honest?
A: No, I don't think so. It's not like they're pretending it's anything else; they've just given it some character.
B: Are they long-lasting?
A: Too early to tell – I've only had mine a year.
B: But the design has been around for ages.
A: Yes, it has, so in that sense yes.
B: Is the design thorough down to the last detail?
A: Can't really comment on that – I wasn't the designer.

B: No … I see that. What about environmentally friendly?
A: Umm … I don't think it's any more efficient that other vacuum cleaners, is it?
B: Not as far as I know.
A: And lastly is the design pure and simple?
B: Definitely. There are no frills or gadgets in a Henry Hoover.

TRACK 41
Conversation 1
A: Do you find that working at home makes it easier or harder to be self-disciplined? I imagine there are a lot of potential distractions.
B: Well, that depends, I guess. When the work's flowing, it's easy to stay focussed. But sometimes, when things aren't progressing so well, for whatever reason, then yeah, it's a bit easier to get distracted or to go off and do something else. But, in a word, I think I'm pretty self-disciplined.

Conversation 2
A: In what environment do you work best, would you say?
B: Mmm, I suppose I'd say, like, a small office or workspace environment, say with two or three people.
A: And why do you say that?
B: Well, I've worked in open plan, and I don't find it so conducive. In my experience, they tend to be a bit unnaturally quiet, no-one wanting to disturb anyone else. But in a small office it's easy to get your head down but, as long as you all get on, can be quite interactive as well.

Conversation 3
A: In a situation where you, for some reason, think someone else in the company is making, or has made, a bad decision or is not performing as you think they should, what would you do?
B: My first instinct is to say that I'd keep quiet and see how things develop. It might not be my place to get involved. But if it directly affects me in some negative way, then I think I'd probably have to talk to someone about it. Someone above us.
A: And how would you go about doing this?
B: Well, I suppose it depends on the situation. But I guess I'd ask for a meeting and explain my concerns.

Conversation 4
A: And one final question. Imagine that you're on a deserted island and can take with you just one book, what would it be?
B: Mm, that's a tricky question. Let me have a think. Er, can I take a blank book, with empty pages, like an exercise book?
A: Er, yes. Why not.
B: OK, then a book with blank pages, so I could write in it. Assuming I could also have a pen, that is.

Keynote Proficient
Student's Book
Paul Dummett
Workbook
Jon Hird and Paul Dummett with Mike Harrison and
Sandy Millin

Publisher: Gavin McLean

Publishing Consultant: Karen Spiller

Project Manager: Karen White

Development Editors: Jess Rackham, Ruth Goodman

Editorial Manager: Scott Newport

Head of Strategic Marketing ELT: Charlotte Ellis

Senior Content Project Manager: Nick Ventullo

Manufacturing Manager: Eyvett Davis

Cover design: Brenda Carmichael

Text design: Keith Shaw, MPS North America LLC

Compositor: MPS North America LLC

National Geographic Liaison: Leila Hishmeh

Audio and DVD: Tom Dick and Debbie Productions Ltd

Cover Photo Caption: Mark Ronson speaks at TED2014,
Session One - Liftoff! - The Next Chapter, March 17–21,
2014, Vancouver Convention Center, Vancouver, Canada.
Photo: © Ryan Lash/TED.

For permission to use material from this text or product,
submit all requests online at **www.cengage.com/permissions**
Further permissions questions can be emailed to
permissionrequest@cengage.com

Student's Book and Workbook Split A ISBN: 978-1-337-56134-1

National Geographic Learning
Cheriton House, North Way, Andover, Hampshire, SP10 5BE
United Kingdom

Cengage Learning is a leading provider of customized learning solutions
with employees residing in nearly 40 different countries and sales in more
than 125 countries around the world. Find your local representative at
www.cengage.com.

Cengage Learning products are represented in Canada by Nelson Education Ltd.

Visit National Geographic Learning online at **ngl.cengage.com**

Visit our corporate website at **www.cengage.com**

Printed in China by RR Donnelley
Print Number: 01   Print Year: 2017